THE TRUTH IS

1. Leveling up your craft to write a story that lives long after you've left the planet is what some might call a ridiculous goal.

2. You know that you will not tell that story after reading just one how-to-write book.

3. You know that you will not tell that story as the result of taking one seminar.

4. You know that creating a timeless work of art will require the dedication of a world-class athlete. You will be training your mind with as much ferocity and single-minded purpose as an Olympic gold medal hopeful. That kind of cognitive regimen excites you, but you just haven't found a convincing storytelling dojo to do that work.

5. The path to leveling up your creative craft is a dark and treacherous course. You've been at it a long time, and it often feels like you're wearing three-dimensional horse blinders. More times than you'd wish to admit, you're not sure if you are moving north or south or east or west. And the worst part? You can't see anyone else, anywhere going through what you're going through. You're all alone.

WELCOME TO THE STORY GRID UNIVERSE

HERE'S HOW WE CONTEND WITH THOSE TRUTHS:

1. We believe we find meaning in the pursuit of creations that last longer than we do. This is *not* ridiculous. Seizing opportunities and overcoming obstacles as we stretch ourselves to reach for seemingly unreachable creations is transformational. We believe this pursuit is the most valuable and honorable way to spend our time here. Even if—especially if—we never reach our lofty creative goals.

2. Writing just one story isn't going to take us to the top. We're moving from point A to Point A^{5000}. We've got lots of mountains to climb, lots of rivers and oceans to cross, and many deep dark forests to traverse along the way. We need topographic guides, and if they're not available, we'll have to figure out how to write them ourselves.

3. We're drawn to seminars to consume the imparted wisdom of an icon in the arena, but we leave with something far more valuable than the curriculum. We get to meet the universe's other pilgrims and compare notes on the terrain.

4. The Story Grid Universe has a virtual Dojo, a university in which to work out and get stronger—a place to stumble, correct mistakes, and stumble again, until the moves become automatic and mesmerizing to outside observers.

5. The Story Grid Universe has a performance space, a publishing house dedicated to leveling up the craft with clear boundaries of progress, and the ancillary reference resources to pack for each project mission. There is an infinite number of paths to where you want to be, with a story that works. Seeing how others have made it down their own yellow-brick roads to release their creations into the timeless creative cosmos will help keep you on the straight and narrow path.

All are welcome—the more, the merrier. But please abide by the golden rule:

Put the work above all else, and trust the process.

THE THRESHING

A STORY GRID CONTENDER ANALYSIS GUIDE

TIM GRAHL

Edited by
SHAWN COYNE

STORY GRID

STORY GRID

Story Grid Publishing LLC
223 Egremont Plain Road
PMB 191
Egremont, MA 01230

First Story Grid Publishing
Paperback Edition April 2020

For Information about Special
Discounts for Bulk Purchases,

Please visit www.storygridpublishing.com

ISBN: 978-1-64501-009-8
Ebook: 978-1-64501-010-4

For

All Past, Present, and Future Story Nerds

HOW TO GET THE MOST OUT OF A STORY GRID CONTENDER

The process for mining information from this book is simple.

1. First, read the novel without worrying about any of *The Story Grid* stuff. Just skip it.

2. Then, re-read each chapter while thinking about *The Story Grid* principles. Here are the particulars:

a) The bolded words in each chapter correspond to a particular element that Story Gridders would include on their Story Grid Spreadsheet. To see the entire Story Grid Spreadsheet for *The Threshing* (it's far too long and detailed to include in this book), visit https://storygrid.com/contender/threshing/

Please note that some bolded sections may not be part of the Story Grid Spreadsheet. The reason we've highlighted them is to point out a particularly telling passage from the book that illustrates one of the Story Grid's wealth of analytical tools.

b) At the conclusion of each chapter, we've included an

additional section entitled *Analyzing the Scene*. By answering four simple questions, we'll walk you through how to determine the critical information for the Story Grid Spreadsheet – *Story Event* and *Value Shift*.

c) Another section we've included at the end of each chapter/scene is "How the Scene Abides by the Five Commandments of Storytelling."
That is, for each and every scene in *The Threshing*, we indicate the **Inciting Incident, Progressive Complication, Crisis, Climax,** and **Resolution.**

For those unfamiliar with the Five Commandments of Storytelling, you can read about them in the book *The Story Grid*: *What Good Editors Know* or you can read numerous articles about them for free at www.storygrid.com. Just access the "start here" or "resources" section of the website and read at your leisure.

d) In addition to The Story Grid Spreadsheet for *The Threshing*, you can view and download the Foolscap Global Story Grid and the Story Grid Infographic at https://storygrid.com/contender/threshing/.

INTRODUCTION

THE PRIMACY OF ACTION STORIES

A brush with death can change lives.

We can have one of two responses to such an event. We can come away from the trauma believing that we're not living up to our potential. Since childhood, we have had beautiful dreams of how we'd spend our lives working to create something that epitomizes who we are and what we stand for, something that no one but us could imagine or execute. After a near-death experience, we return to those dreams and put them at the top of our priorities to fulfill.

Alternatively, we can consider our death and conclude that we are not enjoying the everyday wonders of the world. We're so goal-oriented that we can't seem to even enjoy a moment hanging out at a coffee shop with a friend or watching an old movie on a rainy Sunday afternoon. We resolve to slow down, to take life as it comes, to live more in the moment.

Both of these responses are extraordinarily meaningful. Having a run-in with the unknowable experience of death (what philosophers refer to as 'the noumenal') centers us on these two fundamental truths of life:

1. We have limited time to create something that can

contribute to the greater collective unconscious of our species.

2. We need to lock into the phenomenal, moment-by-moment revelatory beauty inherent in the natural world.

Both mindsets are indispensable, if somewhat paradoxical.

This struggle to integrate the quest for contributing to something greater than ourselves with taking life as it comes is what is at the heart of action stories. While we often consider them a guilty pleasure (at least the ones that are heavy on spectacle and less concerned with the meaning of life and death), they are incredibly primal. Action stories are the great cross-cultural connector. Every person on the planet understands the power of a great action story, no matter the language, identity group, or gender of the creator/s.

So, as a thought experiment, let's look at action stories through one of Story Grid's favorite parlor games.

The game is to play with this thought: What if tomorrow you forgot everything you've ever known about storytelling, what would you do, where would you begin to relearn your craft?

Of course, barring some highly improbable blunt-force trauma to our noggin, we're not going to lose everything we know about story structure overnight. But it could be highly instructive to use our imaginations to consider what we would do if a storyteller's worst nightmare were to happen.

For anyone who has played competitive sports, having to start all over again is not unusual. And the longer you participate in athletics, the more likely you are to find yourself injured and having to reform your skills.

The soccer player who blows out one knee's anterior cruciate ligament on the field on a Friday faces unavoidable surgery on the Monday. And that unnerving experience is soon followed by one of the most painful words in the English language—rehab.

Rehab is a process of managing pain in the service of regaining fundamental skills. It doesn't just require an acceptance of intense discomfort. It involves the abandonment of a taken-for-granted reliance on previous, practically unconscious mastery.

In rehab, you have to relearn how to stand before you can walk. You have to relearn how to walk before you can jog. And it would be best if you jogged before you tried to run. Then you have to relearn what muscles must be rebuilt to best change direction.

That's when the real pain begins—when you are ninety percent back to form. The last ten percent is what separates your skills from everyone else's, and so they are the most difficult to regenerate. You have to learn how to be yourself again.

Relearning is a humbling process, but it's not baffling.

You do what you need to do to stand. You do what you need to do to walk. You do what you need to do to jog. You do what you need to do to run. You do what you need to do to change direction. Repeat. Those are the five stages of rebuilding a knee.

Which begs the question, what would be the equivalent series of intellectual steps necessary to learn or refresh our understanding of storytelling? What must we do to 'stand' as storytellers?

Good old Roman emperor and philosopher Marcus Aurelius recommended we peel back the onion layers of a skill, which is an excellent place to start. He suggests, "*Of each particular thing ask: What is it in itself? What is its nature?*"

Those who've read anything we Story Gridders have written about story structure in the past will not be surprised by our go-to starting point to figure out what 'story' is in itself.

We examine story through genres.

So, first, let's ask ourselves a simple question: Did all story genres come from some primal place?

We think they did.

WHERE STORIES CAME FROM

How did we *Homo sapiens* survive such a hostile environment all those thousands of years ago when we first began to thrive on Earth?

The emergence of story exponentially increased our adaptive advantage. Narrative was the critical metaphysical psycho-technology —something that came from our conscious minds—that allowed knowledge between individuals to spread.

Sometime back in the Stone Age, connection and communication between individuals enabled us to adapt far faster to our environment than any other species. Stories in the form of cave paintings, songs, sculptures, and eventually formal language were how we humans became much more formidable together than alone.

If I know something that will save your life and I share that knowledge with you, together we become a mini-force of two that can do far more than either of us could do alone. In this case, one plus one does not equal two. The potential of two people working together is exponentially greater than the sum of the two working alone.

And the way we work together is through storytelling.

Stories give us survival advantages, and they spread exponentially. They prepare us for the unexpected. The complex nature of reality ensures that random events will drop into our lives at any moment, challenging our adaptive abilities to process them. Stories give us the means to not panic when the unexpected happens.

When the unexpected does occur, we can search our internal story-memory facility and quickly find a way to model our behavior to our best advantage. Stories tell us how we might get what we want by mimicking how someone else (a life-like fictional figure or a real-life icon) got what they wanted. Alternatively, they teach us how to avoid the behavior of those who failed to obtain satisfaction. Stories are knowledge-storage tanks, and what's more, there is no limit to their size. Abundance is built into the system, and we all drink from and refill the same tank.

Stories give us quick possible options and profound existential answers to help us solve severe unexpected problems.

Just think of asking a friend for advice about how they learned a particular skill. Unconsciously, you ask because you're collecting possible options you could action to learn what they know. You're building a story-memory facility in your own mind for that particular want or need. What better way is there than to see if a related story has already been created before we plunge into the darkness?

Your friend may respond with: "When I first set out to learn how to _____, I _____" and off they'll go with a detailed description of how their ambition to learn a skill faced roadblocks but ultimately triumphed. The success story they may tell you will serve as a prescription for your behavior on your journey to achieve what they already possess.

On the other hand, when we hear stories of failure, they serve as cautionary tales for avoiding the behavior that led to dissatisfaction.

We use stories to model our behavior, as frames of reference to compare and contrast how we're doing in life's great journey.

So, if that's true, what was the first story ever shared?

What is the essential want and need combined that we all possess?

It's pretty simple. We all want and need to survive, to stay alive. Action stories give us myriad ways by which we can effectively survive the unexpected. That is why we find them so compelling.

Action stories were the first to be communicated because they offered very specific survival advantages. They concerned overcoming life-threatening external forces, such as avoiding a pack of hungry wolves or surviving a snowstorm.

The stakes for action stories are at the outer limits of experience— brushes with death. And because the line between life and death is tenuous in their telling, we can't help but pay attention to them. We lock into them as if we were facing the plot circumstances ourselves.

Ancient cave drawings prove how important these stories were to our loincloth-clad forebears. Securing water, food, and shelter were critical to our survival, and the behavioral prescriptions to get those survival needs met were the most important to communicate. A quick scan of a cave painting will give you an almost immediate understanding that those first communicated stories were about how to hunt or gather food.

That is a perfect illustration of our metaphysical toolbox serving our physical needs. Obviously, our bodies attune our minds to the natural world first with our five senses and the feelings they generate. Then our minds must 'make sense' of those feelings, figure out what they mean, and then prescribe a series of motor actions that attune our bodies to the reality of the natural world. It's a dynamic system.

Our bodies tell us we're cold, and our minds respond by activating our walking to the closet and putting on a sweater.

This coupling between our minds and bodies is why the Story Grid community works diligently to link our storytelling investigations to natural phenomena as cataloged and analyzed by science. We maintain that story can be investigated and thought of as a science. So, we assume that there is a clear link between story and other investigative scientific disciplines, primarily holistic cognitive science. Science is a big fancy word for categorizing phenomena, understanding what induces the phenomena to emerge, and then figuring out a way to cause it to occur on demand. We wish to cause effects.

Story Grid is about causing the future effect of a working and cathartic story.

Our genre content categories map onto Abraham Maslow's

schematic psychological representation of human needs. For a deeper dive into this relationship, visit **www.storygrid.com/beats/action.**

As stories are psycho-technologies (mind tools) that give human beings adaptation advantages to contend with unexpected environmental change, they are indispensable to us as we navigate the complex natural environment. They do this by helping us get what we need in the face of unexpected conflict. They warn us and teach us about how to handle an unexpected event before it happens to us or how to metabolize it after it's happened.

So, we believe it's reasonable to think that each genre content story category is associated with satisfying the different kinds of fundamental human needs.

And the primal need above all others is to **survive.** If we can't stay alive, then everything else we may need or want isn't going to matter.

This core survival focus is why action stories are so compelling and why they form the on-the-ground narrative for every story told. They address head-on the problem of staying alive when forces beyond our control threaten our very existence.

So, let's go back and directly apply Marcus Aurelius's questions to an action story: *"What is it in itself? What is its nature?"*

An action story is a tool to help us survive unexpected external changes in our environment. That is its essence. When we get stuck creating an action story, we need to go back to that core definition. Action stories are prescriptions for survival or cautions about behaviors that will lead to premature death.

THE CORE LIFE VALUE OF ACTION STORY

Action Story, which is how we will refer to the action genre from here on, is all about a character or characters' movement along the universal life–death value spectrum.

Each scene in the story takes the protagonist/s closer to, or further away from, staying alive. While the majority of scenes will also have unique micro values embedded within them, such as 'alone to together' or 'excited to despairing,' the result of every scene can be evaluated at the 'on-the-ground' life/death level too. Again, is the character closer to or further away from death at the end of the scene?

Let's clarify what we mean by 'value.'

A value is each person's rule of thumb about whether something is meaningful to them. Does the change condition make life meaningful and 'good,' or does it push into meaninglessness and 'bad?'

There are some universal values with which we all generally agree.

We inherently value life, safety, justice, love, truth, respect, and courage, etc. Our interpretations of these values fall along a spectrum and are context-driven. But generally, we would agree that our lives find meaning in their pursuit. When we move closer to a purer form of justice, for example, we find that experience pleasant and meaningful.

When we drift further away from our ideal definition, we see the experience as unpleasant and meaningless.

As Action Story's primal concern is life, every scene in the story should have a polarity shift within that moves the character/s back and forth between varying qualities of the life value.

So, the question to ask when evaluating an action story is: "Does the scene move the character closer to life or to death?" Tracking this global movement of value on a Story Grid graph will generate the arc of an action story. It is a way for you to see if the narrative is varied and compelling.

What exactly do we mean by value spectrum? Take a look at the Life/Death Value Spectrum graphic.

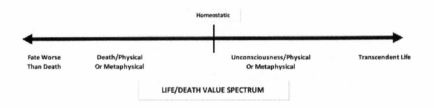

The line to the right of 'Homeostatic' represents life in all its existential nuances, while the line to the left represents approaching death. At the far end of the positive side, transcendent life would be akin to creating a legacy of behavior worthy of emulation, both in our lifetime and after our death. That's metaphorical immortality. And, yes, there is a 'fate worse than death,' the equal and opposite metaphorical damnation vs. transcendence. Here, life is so reprehensible that it serves as the iconography of how not to 'be.'

Consider a situation where death would be merciful, where someone is in such torment that to lose their life would be a relief. That torment could be physical (the body is incapable of sensing anything other than pain) or metaphysical (the mind is in a state of such distress that it's embodying and confronting the darkest components of the universe).

While the 'fate worse than death' or 'damnation' value is essential to establish in genres such as horror and thriller, it is not necessary to bring it into play in Action Story. The reader should be able to intuit this extreme negative value within the context of the story; it does not need to be 'on the stage' in Action Story's events. The characters don't have to experience it.

Life and death values have many different expressions, far more than just the five we've placed on this spectrum.

When we're not feeling 100%, say we have the flu, we're not living at the most positive end of the life value. We're close to our best physical selves, but not quite there. Similarly, if we accidentally veer off of the road while driving and approach a cliff that drops a thousand feet into the sea, we're perilously close to death, but not quite there yet. So, you can see that there are innumerable variations on being close to life or close to death. It is in the imaginative ways that storytellers play with these variations and nuances that make Action Story compelling.

We can represent this state of being through time in the form of a scene using a value spectrum, with the negative end on the left and the positive end on the right.

For example, a scene may concern whether or not the protagonist can convince the guardian of a building to let her inside. The entire scene will be about the tools the protagonist uses to convince the guardian to do what she wants. So, this particular scene will shift from the value of 'unconvincing to convincing' or 'outside to inside.' But it will also move on the global life–death value shift as the protagonist will need to gain admittance to the building or she will find herself closer to death. So, it's essential to understand that scenes can turn on multiple life values.

The trick is to make sure that you choose one value to focus on shifting in your scene and stick to it. Others will emerge from that concentrated effort, and your reader will intuit them naturally.

However, if you're writing an action story, you will need to check that the choice you've made also has the overarching life–death value shift embedded in it. Otherwise, even if it's terrific, it won't 'feel right' to the reader. It won't be one that's within the action story category, and thus, it will confuse the reader and ultimately disappoint them.

That is, to use the example of the character trying to gain admittance to a building, the successful movement from 'unconvincing to convincing' will also increase the probability that they will live to see another day. So, this scene has a micro value movement of 'unconvincing to convincing' and a macro value movement of 'closer to death to closer to life.'

Keep in mind that it's best not to overwhelm yourself with evaluating micro and macro values simultaneously. Go through your work, focusing on just one of these levels of analysis (one lens) at a time.

And it's worth stating the following clearly and consistently: Don't even think about these editorial tools while you are writing. Allow your inner storyteller to drive your drafts, not your outer editor.

When it's time to check your work to make sure you are delivering the action story, the best method for evaluating values at stake in scenes versus the global story is to concentrate on each of these qualities separately. We call this skill 'shifting levels of analysis,' from the overarching big-picture lens (the universal life–death value) to the microscopic view (the scene-specific value). In other words, top/down macro analysis vs. bottom/up micro analysis.

Commit to one level of analysis at a time.

Examine the scene as it relates to the global story. Or look at the global story in relation to the scene. Do the scene and the global story align? Do they work together? Or are they at odds? If the scene does not have a shift in the global value at stake—in the case of Action Story, life/death—then revise it so that it does. If the universal value at stake doesn't serve the indispensable scene, consider a global value shift and switch genres.

Value shifts are critical components of a story and must be present at every unit/level of its construction. Values are what 'change' from the beginning to the end of the scene and from the beginning of the story to the end of the story.

ACTION STORY'S CONTROLLING IDEA

Let's go back to Marcus Aurelius's first principles and ask, "What is the purpose of a story?" Writer Joan Didion's view is constructive:

> "We tell ourselves stories in order to live...We look for the sermon in the suicide, for the social or moral lesson in the murder of five. We interpret what we see, select the most workable of the multiple choices. We live entirely, especially if we are writers, by the imposition of a narrative line upon disparate images, by the 'ideas' with which we have learned to freeze the shifting phantasmagoria which is our actual experience."
> — Joan Didion, *The White Album*

"The imposition of a narrative line upon disparate images" is the storyteller's job, making sense of a documented real-life event (nonfiction) or creating a fictional event modeled on real-life experiences. So, stories are sense-making tools that help us metabolize and integrate unexpected changes in our lives (which, at Story Grid, we call 'pheres'). They make events meaningful.

When something makes sense to us, we're able to act accordingly.

For example, if we know that the object of a particular game is to get a ball into a goal without using our hands, we can make sense of playing a soccer match.

So, the controlling idea of the story of soccer is, 'within the defined arena, without players using their hands, the winning team will get more balls in the goal than their opponent' That statement is the controlling idea of every story about soccer ever written. The story of soccer can only happen under constraints (the rules of the game and the defined arena).

Controlling ideas are the boiled-down lessons of story, the embedded knowledge inside of the entertainment. Stories don't just rely on controlling ideas—they are their very purpose. They are the message we take away at the end, whether we realize it or not. And they stay inside of us too, directing our sense-making of what Didion calls our "shifting phantasmagoria" of real-life experience.

What else can we say about controlling ideas? If we were to divide them into just two categories, what would they be?

They would fall into two sides, to the same end:

1. Positive Prescriptions— "To win, kick the ball across the goal line more times than your opponent" or
2. Negative Cautions— "If you don't kick the ball across the goal line more times than your opponent, you lose."

It would seem that every story has just two possible abstract outcomes. The character either adapts to and integrates a change event into their life history and finds the meaning of that event positive or they fail to adapt to and integrate the change event and find the meaning of that event negative. And depending on the storyteller's choices, the reader, listener, or viewer will learn how to make sense of their own life experiences by using the creator's story as a frame of reference.

That is, in our minds, we map a new story onto our own life's phantasmagoria in such a way that it helps us make sense of our lives. And when we make sense, we can make meaning, and when we make meaning, we can make behavioral choices to enact as the means to adapt to change. This process, making sense of incoming perceptions (Didion's phantasmagoria), fires our meaning-making machinery, which condenses into a binary choice decision, which we can choose to enact. Our actions then cause effects in the environment.

As action stories are our most primal, they must have a global prescriptive or cautionary life lesson component embedded within. They provide direction about what to do or what not to do to survive.

This fundamental first principle is a cause and effect relationship that can be defined by a single sentence, what we call the controlling idea. Many storytellers use the word 'theme' instead of controlling idea, so when you read or hear writers talk about themes, they are usually referencing the takeaway message or messages within their stories.

Story Grid adopts the extremely clear and specific approach that story thinker Robert McKee uses to define controlling ideas. Our interpretation of McKee's definition comprises three components:

1. A controlling idea must be boiled down to the fewest possible words and cannot be longer than a one-sentence statement.
2. It must describe the climactic value charge of the entire story, either positively or negatively.
3. It must be as specific as possible about the cause of the change in value shift (the effect).

In other words, the story makes sense to us when its unexpected cause creates an effect that results in a behavioral prescription to model or a cautionary behavior to avoid.

Let's apply this to Action Story—what would be its two kinds of global controlling ideas?

A Prescription Action Story Controlling Idea

Survival requires the protagonist to insightfully outwit or overpower mortal threats from an unexpected environmental change, unexpected lethal threats from another person or group, or both.

A Cautionary Action Story Controlling Idea

Death results when the protagonist fails to induce the insight necessary to overpower or outwit mortal threats from the forces of antagonism (unexpected environmental change, unexpected threats from another person or group, or both).

After considering both of these possible controlling ideas, it's apparent why most Action Story that we find masterful or a guilty pleasure resides in the prescriptive category.

We have certain expectations of stories about life and death. We expect to feel better about facing our mortality after experiencing them. So, unconsciously, our desire to arm ourselves with new ideas about the indomitable human spirit is what motivates us to engage with Action Story. We want to be inspired by heroic deeds from extraordinary and even ordinary beings facing seemingly impossible-to-overcome circumstances.

To part with hours of our time concentrating on a storyteller's creation and then to walk away with the confirmation that we're fallible and incapable of holding back death does not equate with most people's definition of time well spent.

If the protagonist dies in the end, it's a bummer.

Does this mean that every action story has to end happily ever after?

Of course not.

But death at the end of an action story has to be meaningful for it to satisfy the audience. The protagonist has to die for a reason. They must sacrifice themselves for the benefit of those they leave behind, the survivors.

Why that is has to do with the necessity for all of us to be both self-reliant and capable of conforming and integrating into a larger group. This pull between 'self-first' and 'group-first' has evolved over millions of years. Optimal attunement to both necessities is evolution's recipe for the best chance to survive. So, taking care of one's personal primal needs first and then extending oneself into the cooperative synergistic properties of a trusted group is the path to a meaningful life.

So, if the story's protagonist perishes in the service of a 'greater good,' that action reinforces a core truth that we all inherently understand. To leave the earth as an example of a life well-lived and in the service of those who remain is meaningful.

If there is no sacrificial component to a protagonist's death, the audience despairs. They despair because the takeaway from the experience puts forward the idea that life is meaningless, that human beings have no purpose/role on the planet. That all that we've sensed, felt, thought, and enacted amounts to nothing.

Now you may believe some postmodern ideology that life is random, meaningless, and relative, and you may wish to represent that worldview in a story. And you may have wonderful reasons why that story with the takeaway that 'life is meaningless' is profound and vital, but what we at Story Grid would suggest is that that kind of story will not work.

That is, it will not work according to how we define 'work.'

We define 'working' as a story that satisfies readers to the degree that they share and recommend it to others at a rate that has the possibility of transcending time. A story that transcends time, for example *Pride and Prejudice*, spreads even when the creator is no longer living. That's the Story Grid pinnacle of story creation. The thing that we all hope to achieve one day.

It may genuinely be that there is no purpose on earth to human endeavor. Perhaps a random series of coincidences led to our time here, and eventually, we're all going to die because our behavior will inevitably lead to the destruction of our entire ecosystem. So, if that is true, whether or not your story 'works' according to our definition doesn't matter anyway.

Your story may work for you and an audience of like-minded nihilists, but we suggest it won't work through time.

Hmm. Let's leave it at that.

So, how does one write innovative Action Story using the Story Grid methodology?

If stories that put forward prescriptive models of behavior result in the same old ending (the protagonist's triumph), and cautionary tales without meaningful sacrifice result in meaningless death (the protagonist's choices fail to defeat overwhelming forces), what's an aspiring Action Story writer to do?

What some have done in the past is to focus on spectacle. To create innovative fight or chase sequences that readers/listeners/viewers have not experienced before. Sometimes, these volatile movements distract us enough to forget about deriving meaning from the story, and we fall in love with the motion blur. We've all experienced these kinds of stories. We even enjoy them to a degree.

But these stories are the equivalent of fast food. Our moment-to-moment experience inside of them is compelling, but there is no nutritional value to the meal.

Isn't there a way to create spectacular active movement in a story and also embed a meaningful message?

Yes.

There is a third variety of controlling idea for Action Story. It relates to Story Grid's conception of a cognitive science-based meta-myth above all of the more narrowly defined takeaway messages for each of our specific content genre definitions. Let's begin to figure this third option out in more detail by stating Story Grid's notion of the controlling idea behind all stories we find most meaningful.

The Transcendent Story Grid Controlling Idea

We gain meaning when we self-actualize and then actively pursue our individualized primary concern through exploratory being, growing, and creating over time.

Geez. That's pretty abstract and a lot to digest.

We simply need to figure out who we are and what we should be doing here, and then doing that thing as a means to serve the rest of our ecosystem. Story Grid people have a primary concern for exploring the wonder of storytelling. So that's what drives our growth and our creations.

This global controlling idea has to be super-abstract because we're attempting to boil down the essence of a vast pot of stories. Keep in mind, too, that this idea is a Story Grid conception based on our desire to align story theory with the exploratory findings of cognitive science. We will parse out this entire paradigm in future projects, but for now, let's look at what we mean by this controlling idea for Action Story only.

Let's translate that big abstract statement into the specific pursuit of survival in Action Story.

The Transcendent Story Grid Controlling Idea for Action Story

The meaning of life and death reveals itself when, in pursuit of their survival, the protagonist insightfully learns to self-sacrifice in the service of promoting their fellow human beings' continued survival and creative growth.

If the protagonist dies, they must do so sacrificially so that others gain the power to apply their agencies to transform their potential into creation. This third variety of controlling idea is the message underneath compelling Action Story that does not end with the protagonists' external triumph.

Can you see how negative-ending stories can have prescriptive messages embedded inside of seemingly cautionary-only tales? Integrating this dynamism is the stuff of the masterful storyteller.

ACTION STORY'S SELECTIVE CONVENTIONS

Conventions are essential concepts to understand and apply to all stories. They constrain them, give them boundaries.

Remember that stories are simulations of life and that life involves all sorts of domains. The total of these domains is the particular arena in which we agents (the people trying to get what we want and need) apply our agency to cause a changing effect.

Causes to create effects. That's what we do.

We're hungry (sustenance domain), so we cook something (cause) to effect a change (no longer hungry). We actualize our choice by eating what we cook and thus satisfy a sustenance domain need.

We live in extraordinarily complex environments. They're so complex that we may be incapable of even approaching an understanding of just how intricately structured they are. But we endeavor to do so anyway.

We do this by creating complicated systems. Complicated systems allow us to follow specific step-by-step procedures in such a way that we can cause an effect with certainty. If you want an apple, and it is being sold for a dollar, you can use a dollar that you have earned doing other things or borrow it from someone else to cause an effect. You hand over the dollar (cause), and you get the apple (effect).

We take that indispensable system for granted today. But thousands of years ago, trading with someone else was a very big problem. Until we figured out how to create currency (money), getting an apple from someone willing to part with one for a reasonable exchange of value was very difficult.

The mind tool (psycho-technology) that solved the trading problem was figuring out how to constrain all of the innumerable ways to approach it. By creating a brand-new metaphor for valuable things (money) and getting everyone to accept that constraint, we created a complicated system to make sense out of the complex, finding a way to work with each other to the best advantage.

There are two kinds of constraints.

We have **selective constraints that narrow a big problem into a solvable search space.** And we have **enabling constraints that give rise to possible eventful solutions to the big problem.** Selective constraints funnel the problem into a specific category, a need-based domain. And enabling constraints inside that particular domain give rise to the causes necessary to output event-specific effects.

Let's begin our exploration of Action Story's conventions by focusing on its selective constraints, the ones that narrow the problem domain. Remember that Action Story sets out to explore the 'life–death' problem. So, we'll need to identify the kinds of environments, the settings, that give rise to life and death conflict.

THE SETTING

The setting of Action Story is critical as it selects for the quality of the events that will come on stage. While there are limitless settings to choose from, the fictional world you are creating has to have some specific abstract qualities to serve as the ecosystem that will believably give rise to intense, primal life/death conflicts.

A disturbed, unbalanced physical and social environment that gives rise to conflict

The world you present at the beginning of your action story cannot be a perfectly attuned system. If everyone is precisely integrated into its social structure and has their primal needs provided for, you will have difficulty getting an audience to suspend their disbelief. No matter how satisfied any of us may be, we're very good at finding imbalances in other life domains. Very rarely do we feel 'at one' with our entire ecosystem.

So, what is required in Action Story is a 'beneath-the-surface' asymmetry. That is, there should be a bubbling sense among the characters on the page (and within the audience's mind) that something negative is about to happen, that conflicting worldviews are about to clash.

To take a traditional example, the 'realistic' action stories written during the Cold War all had a primal disturbance at the core of their setting. The fate of the planet rested on maintaining a very delicate balance of power between the United States and the Soviet Union. So, the action stories that came out of this era concerned a destabilization of that balance and the efforts necessary to restore it to equilibrium.

Similarly, in a story such as *127 Hours* (the movie adaptation of Aron Ralston's memoir *Between a Rock and a Hard Place*), the sense that the audience has is that there is a genuine danger beneath the surface of the environment. This story begins with the protagonist enjoying a beautiful day in the desert environment. But we, the audience, know that there are many asymmetries of power inherent in that ecosystem. People in that arena could make a small mistake and suffer severe consequences. They are at the mercy of the indifferent environment that, at any moment, could snuff out their lives. That is the primal environment we all inhabit, no matter how secure we may feel at any one time.

So, the setting you choose, be it a dystopian future such as Tim Grahl's *The Threshing* or a law firm's office (*Die Hard*), must have a complex set of asymmetries of power that give rise to unexpected events.

Dueling Hierarchies

A core tool of Story Grid is using our 'hierarchy lens' as a means to pinpoint conflict opportunities within your setting, where and how you might embed power asymmetry.

There are two kinds of hierarchies. The first is what we call the **Growth Hierarchy**. 'Growing up' is a series of progressive cognitive leaps we make from the moment we're born until the moment we die. It's how we 'become' more adaptive versions of ourselves, with ever-higher skills and capabilities.

Becoming requires agency, the ability to choose an action, and enact it.

The growth hierarchy ascension requires two additional components, the rise of an inspiring salience, where something becomes extraordinarily relevant and resonant to us, and help from other people. To become a 'classical-music appreciator' or a 'civil-war buff' requires a behavioral model to emulate. We seek iconic mentors and their works to guide us to the actualization of our aims.

If we wish to become masterful at a skill, we look for advice from those who have already mastered that skill. We then model our behavior on those masters, and step-by-step, we climb up the skills hierarchy in ways that make us better and better craftspeople. The growth hierarchy is a crucial human phenomenon that allows for our species to grow and survive in a way that serves the individual and, ideally, the greater society too. Unless, of course, the growth choice is to become the best destroyer of worlds versus the creator of worlds.

The growth hierarchy is the sense-making and meaning-making system that keeps us on the progressive path and is responsible for our ever-increasing ways of bettering our cognition. It is how we align ourselves with truth and embed ourselves in metaphysical reality.

This pursuit of climbing the creative growth hierarchy is, in Story Grid terms, the thematic and climactic 'way of the luminary agent.' More on the luminary agent shortly.

The second kind of hierarchy is the **Power/Dominance Hierarchy**. Power is what we usually think of when we hear the word 'hierarchy.'

This type has nothing to do with growth or becoming. It is merely a pyramid built on the status and domination of others. It is the structure by which people, through earned or unearned power, deprive others of agency. It is when the mentor dominates and belittles the apprentice to keep them from surpassing them. Or when the politician with few skills beyond coercion and manipulation dominates a particular institution.

The 'shadow agent,' the antagonist to the 'luminary agent' protagonist, is the brilliant intellectual force that wishes to strictly order the world according to their ideology, to reach the top of the power pyramid and to control those beneath. The way of the shadow agent is to claw to the top of the power/dominance hierarchy and rule the lesser beings beneath by robbing them of an agency or coercing them to give up their agencies.

These hierarchies are not necessarily horrific black or white conditions. We don't live in pure growth systems, nor do we live in pure power systems. There are elements of both in every social construct. Only in the extremes do we find malevolence. Isaiah Berlin famously considered the difficulties in managing democratic agency in his seminal 1958 lecture at Oxford, *Two Concepts of Liberty*, a paradoxical investigation that continues to provide context to world events.

Many power/dominance hierarchies work, and many people find comfort in their position. Plenty of heads of authorities (CEOs, political leaders, mothers, and fathers, etc.) hold their places with humility and do their best to encourage those in their system to grow. Likewise, those beneath the CEO recognize the skill sets above them as more comprehensive than their own and understand that decisions require the more experienced and knowledgeable having the final say.

Some enlightened leaders have risen to the top of hierarchies and used their power creatively to encourage growth in those less powerful. Marcus Aurelius was one such leader who endeavored to stress growth for the individual as well as the controlled order of the mass into his leadership.

So, like most things we do at Story Grid, we view the hierarchical framework not as either/or but as a spectrum of value. An extremely tyrannical power/dominance hierarchy is on one end of the spectrum, and a pure transcendent kind of growth hierarchy is on the other.

By using the hierarchy lens when creating your setting, you can position your fictional world along this spectrum and think through what changes might occur that would move the political disposition of the environment one way or the other.

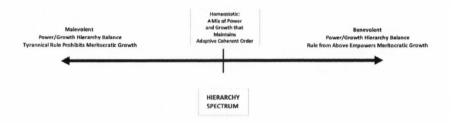

The two poles of this spectrum are the first consideration.

A pure power/dominance hierarchy is one where there is a central authority figure or star chamber of members. What they decide is the gospel; all those beneath them must abide by their dictates. All citizens of that world must turn over their agencies. And any who question the omnipotence of the authority figure/s are cast out, punished, incarcerated, or killed. Tyranny is a state that is maladaptive to changes in its environment and is on the verge of collapse into chaos. Once the power figure is gone, so is the order.

The pure growth hierarchy is a utopian vision and one likely to tumble into chaos too. If no person or group is at the controls of the order then all of the inwardly directed people leveling up their skills will struggle to have their primal physiological needs met. Without a power structure in place in which decisions are made to fortify the multi-domains of the society, including a just system for all to pursue their creative capacities without causing harm to others, the order will become unstable and soon collapse.

The choice that Tim Grahl made in his novel *The Threshing* skews to the left of homeostatic. The power/dominance hierarchy is practically a tyranny at the start of the novel, but by the end, the very structure of society becomes a question mark, and chaos is a definite possibility.

To recap, the unbalanced setting and dueling hierarchies within that setting are the selective conventions of an action story. These conventions give rise to internal conflicts within the protagonist and antagonist. The result of those internal conflicts is the emergence of external conflicts in which the protagonist and antagonist agents apply opposing agencies.

The constraints allow for life-like and believable internal conflict within the fictional character that gives rise to their external action.

Action Story's selective constraint settings are the substance of its sub-genres.

ACTION STORY'S FOUR SUB-GENRES

The selective constraints of Action Story's setting can be divided into four sub-categories, each with four different dispositional qualities to further constrain the story environment. Again, selective constraints narrow the story's boundaries to home in on primal life/death conflicts.

Sub-Genre One

Action Adventure/Human-Against-Nature Stories: These are stories that use unexpected events of the natural world or a specific setting/arena as the villain/force of conflict. They can be further delineated by four kinds of plot devices, or obvious hook attractors:

- Labyrinth Plot: The object of desire is to save victim/s (what we call the agency-deprived) and get out of a maze-like edifice. The movie *Die Hard* is a prime example.
- Monster Plot: The villain (the shadow agent) is an animal or other living thing. *Jaws* is a prime example.
- Environment Plot: The villain (the shadow agent) is the actual global setting/environment. *Gravity* is a prime example.

- Doomsday Plot: The victim (the agency-deprived) is the environment. The hero (the luminary agent) must save the environment from disaster. *Independence Day* is a prime example.

Sub-Genre Two

Action Epic/Human-Against-the State Stories: These are stories where the hero/luminary agent must confront group-derived interpersonal conflict, societal institutions or tyrants (the shadow agents).

- Rebellion Plot: The protagonist (the luminary agent) is pitted against a visible tyrant, such as Darth Vader (the shadow agent) from *Star Wars*.
- Conspiracy Plot: The hero/luminary agent is up against an invisible tyrant/shadow agent. For example, *Enemy of the State* and *The Bourne Identity*.
- Vigilante Plot: The hero/luminary agent is up against a criminal organization/shadow agent. For example, *Above the Law*.
- Savior Plot: The hero/luminary agent is up against someone/the shadow agent who wants to destroy society/return it back to pure chaos. For example, *The Dark Knight*.

Sub-Genre Three

Action Duel/Human-Against-Human Stories: These are stories where the hero/heroine/luminary agent must confront direct and tightly defined interpersonal conflict, one person against another person.

- Revenge Plot: Heroine/hero/luminary agent chases the villain/villainess/shadow agent. For example, *True Grit*.

- Hunted Plot: Villain/villainess/shadow agent chases the heroine/hero/luminary agent. For example, *The Fugitive.*
- Machiavellian Plot: Heroine/hero/luminary agent sets two villain/villainess/shadow agents against each other. For example, *A Fistful of Dollars.*
- Collision Plot: Villain/villainess/shadow agent sets two heroine/hero/luminary agents against each other. For example, *Troy.*

Sub-Genre Four

Action Clock/Human-Against-Time Stories: In these stories, time is the extra-personal force of conflict.

- Ransom Plot: A deadline imposed by the villain/villainess/shadow agent. For example, *All the Money in the World.*
- Countdown Plot: A deadline imposed by natural circumstance, which serves as the villain/villainess/shadow agent. For example, *Armageddon.*
- Hold-out Plot: Heroine/hero/luminary agent has to hold out until others can rally. For example, *The 300.*
- Fate Plot: Time is the villain/villainess/shadow agent. For example, *Back to the Future.*

ACTION STORY'S ENABLING
CONVENTIONS

Now that we have a handle on the selective constraining conventions that narrow the Action Story problem, let's turn our attention to the **enabling constraining conventions that give rise to possible eventful solutions to the problem.**

Remember that selective constraints funnel the problem into a specific category, a need-based domain. And enabling constraints inside that particular domain give rise to the causes necessary to output effects.

Enabling conventions allow for life-like and believable internal conflict within fictional characters to surface. And that inner conflict then results in choices for behavioral action.

So, enabling conventions are the means to set up eventual payoff actions that emerge unexpectedly later on.

These unexpected events will be the key ingredient in creating a responsive conflict. All of these conflicts then give rise to a change in value in the scene (micro) and across the entire life–death Action Story (macro).

Another way to look at this is that enabling conventions afford the causes that generate effects. The effects are the outcome events that answer the fundamental question posed by the genre. For Action Story, the fundamental question is: "Will the protagonist and the agency-deprived victim survive antagonism?" So, the following conventions of Action Story enable the obligatory events that will answer that question.

The starting point for Action Story is the necessity of clearly defining a trinity of character roles across all of the nested units of story. The audience needs to know which character is playing each of these three roles in every beat, scene, sequence, act, sub-plot, and in the global story, so we need to assign these roles with care.

The good news is that we writers intuitively understand these roles. And the majority of the time, we put them in our story units unconsciously. So, it's not necessary to overthink these roles once you've figured out their representations. But later on, in the editing stage, it's a good idea to double-check to make sure they are clearly defined.

So, what are these must-have roles?

Consider the world in which we live as our global arena. Inside that global arena are specific domains (home domain, work domain, education domain, etc.)—a bunch of circles inside a vast circle.

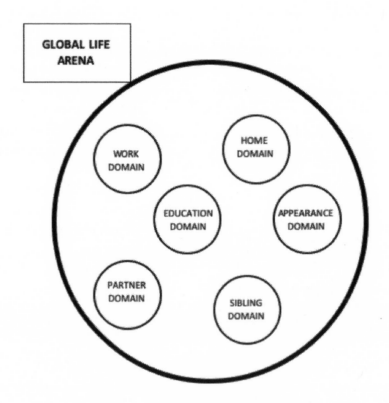

A human being's arena is the totality of their physical and metaphysical experience, explicitly represented by one of those domains. What they sense physically, how they process those senses metaphysically inside their unconscious and conscious minds, and how they act upon the fallout from the unconscious and conscious processing is a fancy way of describing how we live.

What can happen, though, is what we think is true/real can be severely misaligned. We misread signs and signals and have difficulty conforming to our life's greater truth. So, to align ourselves better, we have to change our processing of signs and signals. This isn't very easy to do, hence our need for stories on which to model our behavior.

The arena has a whole slew of specific domains embedded within it, and the above is just a small sampling. And as you'd expect, the genres themselves live inside each of our arenas as they concern the acquisition of wants and needs to keep us stable.

A single person inside of their arena is an **agent**.

And the processing-plus-action system they have to respond to the ever-changing physical and metaphysical environment of their particular arena (choices) is **their agency**.

So, **agents have agency** (the ability to choose and enact those choices) **that they apply inside their arena in response to unexpected events that change that arena.**

In Action Story (indeed in all stories), there are three must-have players inside the story's selectively constrained arena.

ACTION STORY'S CONVENTIONAL CAST OF CHARACTERS

Role Number One:
The Luminary Agent
Protagonist/Heroine/Hero

Traditionally, this role has been referred to as 'hero' or 'heroine.' In our quest to merge storytelling with the cognitive science realm, however, Story Grid proposes another term. It's a more abstract one that can rise above any particular gender associations from story grammars of the past, which we think unnecessarily emphasize people's differences rather than their similarities.

In our conception, the luminary agent is a figure who casts light into the darkness and is usually the protagonist of Action Story. This central figure of Action Story is an agent that responds to the threat of death by applying their agency in the service of illuminating a path to survive and thrive for the greatest common good.

The greatest common good is defined as the path for the highest number of agents freely applying their agency in the service of creating a meaningful future. Exploring and systemizing cause-and-effect technologies out of the complexities of the unknown for the benefit of the ecosystem is how we define meaning-making in Action Story.

Role Number Two:
The Shadow Agent
Antagonist/Villain/Villainess

The shadow agent is usually the antagonist of the action story. We Story Gridders like the affiliation with darkness metaphorically as we define dystopic existence as one in which people are deprived of agency. If human beings are deprived of their agency, they will not be able to create anything out of their embedded internal potential.

Not to get too philosophical about it, but one of philosopher Martin Heidegger's foundational ideas is that we human beings lack a clearly defined human universal 'essence.' What this means is that we can't be categorized into Platonic and Aristotelian ideas such as 'living things that fly' or 'living things that live in the water.'

And by extension, because we can't be put into one single box, we must continuously strive to explore our 'becoming.' Climbing the growth hierarchy is the only way for us individually to get closer to figuring out our particular essence, to 'self-actualize.' When we do, the answers to those big questions of who we are and why we are here crystalize.

So, if we are deprived of our ability to pursue that striving to become, we will be confined to never knowing who we are or why we are here. That, for us at Story Grid, is darkness incarnate.

We succumb to darkness when we are forced or coerced into, or even willingly, turn over our agency to a shadow agent. When we hand over our ability to 'become' to an external or internal force, we lose our ability to discover who we are and what we're supposed to be doing here.

The shadow agent is the role in a story that deprives other human beings of their agency, either through force, coercion, or charismatic persuasion. In contrast, the luminary agent opposes the deprivation of agency. So, naturally, these two forces conflict.

Role Number Three:
The Agency-Deprived/Victim

The agency-deprived is a character or group of characters in Action Story who have lost their ability to initiate, execute, and control their actions in the world. The domains in which they will lose their agency are reflected in the selecting constraints of the sub-genres.

In human-against-nature stories, the power of the natural world emerges to rob us of our ability to apply our agency. A hurricane, a drought, a fire, an avalanche, these can all cut us off from the rest of the world and deprive us of primal physiological needs. And as those needs remain unfulfilled, we slowly lose our agency, until someone, or a group of people, has the necessary insights to save us from death.

In human-against-the state stories, the power of social institutions can coerce or rob us of our ability to apply our agency. You'll see in Tim Grahl's *The Threshing* that his action sub-genres become progressively more complicated. The environment in his story initially constrains human beings in its ecosystem to adapt. They then must create artificial environments within the global environment to survive.

But to maintain control over the systems, these virtual environments have to level up their attraction. And soon the people in the story reach a place where they've turned over their agency to an addictive technology created by unseen human forces far away. Thus, the story shifts from one of human-against-nature to one of human-against-the-state. You'll discover many of these sorts of shifting sub-genre moves in a lot of action stories.

In human-against-human stories, the luminary identifies the single source of agency-deprivation and focuses on defeating that figure or force. You'll see this rise of the story within *The Threshing* too.

Lastly, in human-against-time stories, the luminary discovers that there is only a limited amount of time to release the agency-deprived from captivity. Thus, the urgency of action takes center stage. As you might expect, time also plays a role in *The Threshing*.

ACTION'S ENABLING CATALYSTS

The Speech in Praise of the Shadow Agent/Villain

How does a storyteller establish these destabilized environments and dueling hierarchies? How do they make clear to the audience these extraordinary abstract story structures at play?

This is where convention catalysts come in.

Thankfully, Action Story has just the thing to tell the audience what lies at the heart of the conflict. It's called the 'speech in praise of the villain,' or in Story Grid terms, the 'speech in praise of the shadow agent.'

We're all very familiar with this convention. There's the moment in all action stories when someone discusses just how powerful and brilliant the opposing force is. Either the shadow agent themselves lays out their philosophy and thinking process, or one of the players opposing the shadow force explains what the luminaries face. Either way, Action Story requires this convention so that the audience can understand just how difficult the task is for those trying to overcome antagonism.

The speech in praise of the shadow agent defines the large power gap between the protagonist and the antagonist.

The Clock

Another excellent tool to set up intensity of conflict is by using time as a means to accelerate the series of choices the players must make and enact. The 'deadline' is an enabling convention of Action Story. For example:

- There is only so much air left in the chamber where the 'victim/agency-deprived' is being held.
- A bomb will detonate if the luminary agent does not comply with the demands of the shadow agent.
- If the bus speed dips below 35 mph, it will explode.

Clocks pump up tension and stress in the players in the story and, by extension, they simulate a virtual excitation in the audience. This sets up the active payoffs later on with intensity.

Set-Piece Action Sequences

We are all very familiar with these conventions. There's the big chase scene where the luminary agent barely escapes the clutches of the shadow agent. There's the heist scene where a character must take a valuable resource from someone or something else to move forward in their mission to rescue the agency-deprived. These mini-action stories within the global action are essential to set up the payoffs later on.

Not only do these sequences entertain in the moment of experience, they also illustrate the worldview of the luminary agent in such a way that they reveal strengths and weaknesses. The skilled storyteller will show how the luminary agent births new skills in these set pieces. That is, they'll 'learn' a new skill/technique inadvertently in these sequences that they will insightfully activate to solve a more significant problem later on. Patricia Highsmith was a master at employing this technique in her Tom Ripley novels. Ripley, of course, is both a shadow agent and a luminary agent in one, one of the first postmodern anti-heroes.

Conventions for Action Story constrain a storyteller's choices, which in turn allows for the emergence of innovation inside a particular genre. Without constraints, storytelling would be incoherent. Embrace the conventions (selective and enabling) as the means to limit the search space of your imagination. Knowing what needs to be clearly in evidence for Action Story will laser focus your ability to try new solutions to solve age-old story problems insightfully.

ACTION STORY'S OBLIGATORY EVENTS

Conventions set up conflicts. And from conflict come changes in value from scene to scene and across the entire Action Story arc.

But where and when do these conflicts take place?

The answer comes in the form of obligatory events. When the conventions of Action Story are thoughtfully adhered to, the following events will emerge organically.

What follows is a list of twenty events in Action Story that we've determined align with the five commandments of storytelling. Five scenes represent the Inciting Incident, the Turning Point Progressive Complication, the Crisis, the Climax, and the Resolution for each of our Story Grid global components. Also, there are five scenes for the Beginning Hook, five for Middle Build One, five for Middle Build Two, and five for the Ending Payoff.

Keep in mind that after these events have been considered and created, they can be edited inside a global framework that is not linear. A story such as *Pulp Fiction* is a perfect example of a rejigging of events in nonlinear form. You'll also discover that many of these events can be whittled down to moments within other scenes, withheld entirely, or manipulated in unique and potent ways. What a writer must know, though, is precisely how each event is represented in their work.

Remember that these obligatory events in your story are the payoff moments that your genre's most dedicated fans are experts in picking out of the work. What they're looking for are innovations and exciting tweaks to their favorite deeply ingrained form. So, while it may be challenging to freshen these events in Action Story, you ignore them at your peril.

Beginning Hook (approximately 25% of the Story)

1. The Inciting Incident: Attack

The global and beginning hook inciting incident of Action Story must have an embedded agency-depriving and life-threatening attack by the forces of antagonism. This attack can be on a single character or a group of characters, but it must have a profound life-destabilizing effect on your protagonist.

The unexpected attack (phere) can be causal (a purposeful action by an antagonist) or coincidental (a non-human antagonistic force, such as a wild animal or a significant weather event).

At first, the protagonist fails to register the necessity for their action regarding this attack or chooses to avoid engagement because they are focused on a different goal. They assume the attack is someone else's problem and make the minimum effort necessary, skirting responsibility.

The protagonist begins the first metabolic stage of the fear response to the unexpected. They 'freeze' and behave as if everything is as it has always been and use the same goal-oriented behavior to evaluate their circumstances. The protagonist is inattentive to the reality that their ordered life has been disturbed by the phere event and that they are now living in a confusing and disordered system.

2. The Turning Point Progressive Complication of the Beginning Hook: Sensing Disorder

The protagonist's inattention to the antagonistic force builds until such time as their life value or the life value of others turns dangerously closer to or tips over and into death.

This turning point is the result of the antagonist attacking again. Or, more revelatory information reaches the protagonist about the earlier unexpected event or events such that they can begin to recognize and make sense of the disordered nature of the system. The protagonist realizes the forces of antagonism are life-threatening to themselves and to others.

3. The Crisis of the Beginning Hook: Running Away to Reluctant Engagement

The crisis question of the beginning hook is when the protagonist derives the meaning from their making sense of their disordered state. It's a best bad choice/irreconcilable good decision. They must decide whether to look out for #1 and evade the antagonistic force to continue pursuing their ego-derived goal or to engage with the antagonism and take up the mission to restore order for those deprived of their agency.

4. The Climax of the Beginning Hook: Agreeing to Fight

The climax of the beginning hook results in the reluctant protagonist agreeing to engage with the antagonistic force. The protagonist realizes their refusal to fight deprives not only their own agency but also that of others, and as such they are responsible for the others' suffering. The resulting internal torment is untenable for the protagonist. So, they agree to engage, deciding that the only real option is to deal with the threat.

The fear response to the unexpected attack at the beginning hook —freeze, flight, and then reluctantly fight—pushes the hero into engaging with the unknown.

5. The Resolution of the Beginning Hook: The Fix it and Forget it Mission

The beginning hook resolves with the protagonist agreeing to engage with a pre-programmed strategy to make the minimum effort necessary to restore order. Their ego misdirects them into thinking that they have the necessary capabilities already in hand to achieve this goal.

Middle Build One (approximately 25% of the Story)

6. The Inciting Incident of Middle Build One: A Whole New World

The inciting incident of the middle build is a clear 'before and after' liminal shift from the old, familiar environment introduced in the beginning hook to an unknown, new environment.

The protagonist must adapt and excel in this environment to cause the effect they desire, but they make the mistake of assuming their usual bag of tricks will suffice for this. The protagonist wants to 'get back to normal' as quickly as possible, so their confrontation with an entirely new environment (another big unexpected phere event) disorients.

Here, the protagonist meets the threshold guardian, an archetypical figure who indoctrinates them into this new world.

7. The Turning Point Progressive Complication of Middle Build One: The Protagonist Becomes the Target of the Antagonist

It is here that the protagonist comes 'into the sights' of the antagonist or forces of antagonism and is thus closer to death. The protagonist meets a challenge that requires them to outmaneuver the antagonist in some way and either successfully or unsuccessfully thwart the antagonist's agenda. Regardless of their success or failure in the event, the protagonist demonstrates extraordinary ability or a 'shining through' in the challenge.

The antagonist (or indifferent force of antagonism) recognizes a formidable agency when they see it and resolves to engage the protagonist. If the antagonist is human, they target the protagonist. If the antagonist is indifferent, the protagonist has made themselves 'environmentally vulnerable.' That is, they are now exposed to more significant effects from the forces of antagonism than before. They are on a cliff face.

Unlike the protagonist, the antagonist is not disoriented or confused about how to apply their agency in this environment. Antagonists have tremendous confidence in their abilities and power and have trained themselves to attack unexpected events as soon as they arise. It is for this reason that the middle build of a story is often described as 'owned by the villain.'

It may be helpful to think of the protagonist as the big unexpected event (the phere) that drops into the life of the antagonist. The antagonist must destroy or coerce the protagonist into following their commands or risk not attaining their goal.

Because of their powers, the protagonist finds themselves alienated from the rest of their social class and must contend with enemies within the group they've been tasked to aid, while they also cultivate allies. They are vulnerable to shape-shifters, covert agents loyal to the antagonist, or independent agents playing personal, hidden goal-oriented games.

The protagonist is destabilized at the turning point, but they think if they can hold out, their skills will see them through and get them back to normal.

8. The Crisis of Middle Build One: Should I Comply or Defy?

How the protagonist makes sense of the antagonist or vice versa raises a meaningful crisis question: "Do I 'work with' this agent, or do I 'oppose' this agent's plan?"

Considering the crisis of middle build one from the antagonist's point of view can be extremely helpful. The antagonist is always looking for powerful-agency figures to use as tools.

The response of the antagonist to the shining of the luminary agent protagonist could be to attack them or attempt to coerce them. This crisis event either gives the protagonist a false sense of security (closer to life if the antagonist is recruiting them) or sobers them up in such a way that they understand just how difficult their task is (closer to death if they are attacked again).

9. The Climax of Middle Build One: The Shadow Agent Asserts their Dominant Power

The climax event of middle build one is an active assertion of power by the antagonist in response to the protagonist's decision to oppose them, or even if they join them. It is such a monstrous execution of force that the protagonist's behavioral toolkit fails.

The protagonist is overwhelmed and responds in a way that the antagonist does not anticipate.

10. The Resolution of Middle Build One: No Way Out, The Point of No Return

The resolution of middle build one is the irreversible change event of the global story. The response of the protagonist to their fall into chaos results in the entire system becoming chaotic too. The antagonist and all those in the environment find themselves unhinged by the protagonist's reaction.

Chaos is the experience of not knowing what to do or even what is going on, with no knowledge of how to contend with random unexpected events. The world is unconstrained.

All the tools the protagonist has used before to give themselves a power asymmetry against the rest of society completely fail (or so they think). The antagonist doesn't know what's going on either, and neither do the rest of the figures in the story.

This moment in Action Story is often referred to as the mid-point climax, but it is structurally the resolution event of middle build one. The luminary figure protagonist discovers that they will never 'get back to normal.' That their 'fix it and forget it mission' is impossible and that their skills and plans are inadequate to deal with the reality of the challenges they face.

The trick to this event is to let it run without offering any solutions. The rest of the middle build (middle build two) is all about how to climb out of this chaotic situation. This is the moment when your audience will lock into the story and wonder how it is going to end.

Middle Build Two (approximately 25% of the Story)

11. The Inciting Incident of Middle Build Two: An Encounter with an Unexplained Event (the Noumenal)

The protagonist experiences a mysterious encounter with an unexplainable event. Something happens to the protagonist that is random and transformational, either positively or negatively.

This experience is symbolic of the noumenal realm, popularized by philosopher Immanuel Kant. The noumenal is all that we are incapable of explaining or of 'knowing.' It is counterbalanced by the phenomenal, which are knowable patterns (what we sense but have not fully defined or examined definitively) that can be converted into cause/effect procedures.

A very simple explanation of the encounter with the noumenal is the use of the glowing suitcase in *Pulp Fiction*.

How the protagonist and the antagonist contend with the unexplained event counterbalance each other. The protagonist makes an active choice to allow themselves to accept the disorientation of chaos, the lack of pattern, and constraints. This acceptance of 'not being capable of knowing everything' affords them the ability to learn how to respond to phere events accordingly. To take them moment-by-moment without predetermined strategies to exploit or destroy their emergence.

The antagonist reacts to unexplained events differently. They believe that their intellect and worldview are so perfectly conceived, rational, logical, and ordered that they can control anything, including the unexpected.

12. The Turning Point Progressive Complication of Middle Build Two: All is Lost

The protagonist comes out of their noumenal experience and begins to explore the world differently. Instead of pre-programed plans, they begin to pay attention to unexpected events as they arise. Still, as this is a new behavioral system, it emerges imperfectly. The protagonist then suffers a significant set-back, which turns the value to the inevitability of death.

Death is now a certainty. Someone is going to die (make sure someone does) because everyone dies. Death is the fundamental existential problem and the substance of Action Story. So, the value shifts at this turning point from life to death.

The protagonist despairs that all is lost. They don't know how to proceed with the now-certain death.

13. The Global and Middle Build Two Crisis: How can my death be meaningful?

Middle build two is when the global crisis of the story emerges— what is the best way to live if we're going to die?

The protagonist must decide, now that death is imminent, what they can do to make their life meaningful. How can they contribute to the collective knowledge of their entire species before they leave earth?

If the protagonist just saves themselves in this dark situation, others will suffer. This is what we at Story Grid call an 'irreconcilable goods' crisis. What's good for the protagonist is bad for everyone else. So, as the protagonist realizes that they are eventually going to die anyway, they must decide whether to selfishly put their wants and needs above all others or sacrifice themselves for the greater good.

Here, Action Story gets right to the heart of the life/death conundrum.

The antagonist, though, does not face these existential dilemmas. The antagonist sees themselves as 'above the crowd,' with a 'responsibility' to do what it takes to remain alive. They justify that selfishness as the means to 'serve the greater good.' They reason that the world needs leaders, not martyrs. And they make very compelling cases for their ideology.

So, the crisis event of middle build two is also the global crisis. Do I save myself, or do I sacrifice myself to serve the greater good?

14. The Middle Build Two Climax: Absolute Commitment

The protagonist decides to confront the antagonist and release the agency-deprived from their power. No matter what.

The critical element for this event is that the protagonist acts willingly and with the courage to engage with the antagonist's powerful algorithms (definitive tactics), using only their reasonable heuristics (rules of thumb) to defend themselves and their allies.

15. Resolution of Middle Build Two: Preparations to Enter the Ultimate Arena

Middle build two resolves such that the protagonist begins to prepare with great humility for their big fight with the super-powerful antagonist. They will fight to save the victim even though they are likely to die in the process. They commit to making meaningful choices and act with as little noise in their heads as they possibly can by getting in the arena of the antagonist and applying all their capacities.

They say goodbye to their loved ones. Last suppers are held.

The protagonist has now climbed up and out of chaos and is prepared for the complexity of the natural world and the showdown with the antagonist.

The Ending Payoff (approximately 25% of the Story)

16. The Inciting Incident of the Ending Payoff: No Holds Barred

The inciting incident of the ending payoff is where the protagonist enters the sanctum of the antagonist. This event requires a leveling up of the spectacle so that the stakes and balance of power are precise and asymmetrical.

With a definite home-field advantage, the antagonist hits the protagonist with serious firepower from the outset. A big life-threatening phere drops in to kick off the final push of the story. The phere should 'mirror' the beginning hook of the story, that is, the phere should be in the same category as the global inciting incident, but at a much higher level.

The point of this mirroring effect is to highlight the change in the protagonist from the beginning of the story to the end. They dealt with the initial phere from the beginning using their usual behavior, which was insufficient and which led to the reanimation of this same phere at the ending payoff with a much higher level of power.

The protagonist gains an understanding that it will take more than one mind to defeat such a powerful force. The entire ending payoff will be a demonstration of participatory knowledge cultivation. The protagonist listens to and relies upon others (like they never have before) in this final quadrant of the story.

17. The Turning Point Progressive Complication of the Ending Payoff: Someone the Audience Cares About Dies

The turning point progressive complication of the ending payoff of Action Story requires a literal shift into death.

To bring storytelling's cathartic effects embedded within Action Story into full play, an experience of loss is required. We need to see that the battle at stake is life and death. A character or characters that the audience cares about must die to escalate the stakes for the protagonist. They aren't just fighting to define the meaning of their own life anymore but for their allies' too.

18. The Ending Payoff Crisis: Do the Ends Justify the Means?

The protagonist must face a best bad choice/irreconcilable goods decision. Is their mission more important than the life or agency of a single person? Do the ends justify the means? Are they willing to let an individual die in order to save a whole group of the agency-deprived?

Can the protagonist generate an insight at this moment that does not betray the sanctity of the individual to save the group?

This crisis is a crucial choice for the protagonist. Of course, the antagonist has no problem sacrificing anyone to their mission. Hence, these moments can also turn on shape-shifter actions, the unexpected responses from figures the audience does not anticipate being on the same team as the protagonist.

19. The Ending Payoff Climax: The Protagonist at the Mercy of the Antagonist

This is the global climax of the story, as well as the climax of the ending payoff. This is the core event of Action Story, the moment audiences will come to judge the storyteller. It's the big moment that must be satisfying to your audience. You can do everything right throughout the story, but if you fail to make this event surprising, you will disappoint your audience.

The protagonist is plunged into a seemingly inescapable, unsolvable conundrum. The antagonist has them dead to rights and will undoubtedly enjoy their suffering and death. Remember that the antagonist has been irritated, challenged, and tormented by the protagonist since the point of no return. Now, at last, they can rid themselves of this menace.

The trick to figuring out how the protagonist will get out of this situation is that they will defeat the antagonist by either: 1) physically overpowering them, 2) outwitting them, or 3) a combination of these.

The protagonist will be successful because of the emergence of a new skill or the adapting of an old skill.

20. The Resolution of the Ending Payoff and Global Story: The Reward

The protagonist either defeats the antagonist or sacrifices themselves in such a way that the antagonist will be destroyed or face innumerable challenges from other adversaries in the future. The protagonist is rewarded for their efforts either externally (a big thank-you parade, etc.) or internally (martyrdom in the service of the greater good).

WRITING ACTION STORY

Our abstract representations of the obligatory events of Action Story represent the fundamental 'on-the-ground' form for all stories. Remember that form constrains your choices, and understanding the substance of form will free you from confusion. That is the indispensable heuristic for a storyteller.

Action Story is made up of a wonderfully compelling series of choices (intentional solutions to a set of story problems) that the creator must confront and resolve. The higher the resolution of knowledge you have about each component of the greater whole of the form, the better your ability to directly engage with every formal decision with serious intent. We at Story Grid remain committed to exploring story form so that you can bring your best storytelling self to the fore.

We submit that Action Story is the primal evolutionary genre, the first story form, and the one from which all others have branched. With the understanding of Action Story's value and the options available to you to embed a meaningful controlling idea, as well as the conventions and obligatory events that make for a compelling action narrative, you now have a much richer understanding of the global Action Story creation problem.

While we've been conditioned to believe that action stories aren't deep or meaningful, that they are 'just entertainment,' they have emerged as the most important stories ever told. They saved lives thousands of years ago, and continue to do so today.

We can't stress this enough: embracing the primacy of action is a storytelling necessity.

A brush with death changes lives, and Action Story gives us that encounter with the inevitable safely. At its best, Action Story prescribes a way for us to live meaningful lives while also cautioning us how to detect and defuse those among us who wish to tilt the world to their will.

We need great Action Story now more than ever.

STORY GRID TOOLS TO WORK THROUGH YOUR ACTION STORY

As you will have experienced reading through this guide, there are a number of elements for the aspiring Action Story writer to understand and integrate into their work. We at Story Grid have three global strategic tools to keep all of these concepts in mind and at hand throughout your writing process.

They are:

I. The Story Grid Global Foolscap Page:

This tool allows you to track the development of your entire story on one sheet of paper. Visit https://storygrid.com/contender/threshing/ to learn more and to see an example of just how this macro outline is put together.

II. The Story Grid Spreadsheet:

This tool allows you to track the scene-by-scene progression of your entire story. Visit https://storygrid.com/contender/threshing/ to learn more about how to use a spreadsheet to

track the micro movements of your work as well as the
continuity of your story.

III. The Story Grid Infographic:

This tool is the culmination of your final work. Visit https://
storygrid.com/contender/threshing/ to learn more. The
infographic uses both the macro overview of the Story Grid
Global Foolscap Page and the micro scene-by-scene progression
of your story to create a graphical representation of how well
your story 'moves.' That is, it allows you to see how your
potential readers/listeners/viewers will experience the work on
an emotional level.

THE THRESHING
BY TIM GRAHL

THE PREPARING

CHAPTER ONE

Jessie stopped. Turning, she swung her lantern behind her and peered into the dark, trying to see beyond its half-circle of yellow light. She waited, listening, as her left hand crept into her pocket, feeling for the small, painted domino.

A voice came over her left, pink earphone, the side completely covered with a cushioned speaker. The other side was pushed back off her dominant right ear so she could take in the noise of her surroundings.

"Why'd you stop moving?"

"I thought I heard something."

"It's probably **them**. You know, I hear they eat **kids** when they can't scavenge enough food."

"Shut up, **Mark**."

"I'm serious! **My cousin's friend** got caught down there once, and they never saw him again. The only thing they ever found was one of the bones from his arm. It had teeth marks on it."

Jessie shook her head in the dark as she began to move back down the tunnel. Every step required her to stretch her legs just beyond her typical gait to secure her feet on the track's braces as she kept clear of the rails.

Another voice crackled through the radio.

"You know that story is bull. Right, Mark?"

"No way, **Libby**. **Bobby** told me all about it," Mark said.

"Then how'd they know it was his?" Libby challenged.

"His what?"

"His arm. If all they found was a bone, how'd they know whose it was?"

There was a long silence.

"Oh," Mark said. "Well, it's true that they live down there."

"Whatever," Libby said.

Jessie smiled as she continued walking down the path.

She was small and undeveloped for a twelve-year-old—even for children born and raised after the fires—which was why she was sent out on scavenges more than any of the **other Rats**. Her long dark hair was pulled back into a messy bun, and she kept her heavy backpack slung over one shoulder while swinging the lantern a bit forward to stretch for each step.

"You're just about there," Mark said. "You see the ladder yet?"

Jessie walked a few more yards before she saw it. The metal rails ran up the wall and into a small hole punched into the rock overhead.

"Yeah, it's here."

"Up you go."

Jessie nodded and set the lantern at the base of the ladder. She pulled off her bag and unzipped the main pouch, rummaging through it to ensure that all the equipment was in the right place. She slowly zipped the pocket back up and looked above her, peering into the black hole that swallowed the ladder whole.

"Are you moving yet?" Mark said.

"I'm working on it."

"We'll be out of daylight if you don't hurry."

Jessie slung the bag back on and then knelt beside the light of the lantern. She took a deep breath, let it out slowly, and then clicked it off.

Darkness engulfed her.

Climbing the ladder was always the worst part because she never knew when it was going to end. In the past, she'd counted the ladder rungs, but that somehow made the climb drag on even longer. Now, she only focused on the next rung. The next step. All that mattered was climbing to the next one.

She slowed as she reached the top. She could always tell when she was getting close. The sounds bounced differently. She could hear better, and her pulse quieted.

Jessie wrapped her arm around an upper rung of the ladder and reached up with her other hand to feel for the ceiling. She reached as far as she could without touching anything, so she carefully went up two more rungs, wrapped her arm around again, and felt out above her in the darkness.

She'd hit her head before and almost knocked herself out.

Her fingers raked against the underside of the lid on the floor above. She dug her fingers into the breast pocket of her shirt and pulled out a small clip, which she pinched and then placed on her nose to plug her nostrils. Next, she reached up and felt around on the lid until her hand closed on the latch. She pulled it down and then pushed up on the cover.

It hinged open and fell on the opposite side with a loud clang as she carefully climbed out of the hole and onto the hard, cold tile floor.

She quickly pulled out her lantern and unfolded it again. She dug into her pocket for the small flint and lit the wick in two tries. She sighed as yellow light filled the hallway.

People were lined up on both sides of the hallway sitting shoulder to shoulder on battered and scavenged metal and plastic chairs. They stared straight ahead with open, empty eyes. Thick cords ran up from the base of their skulls to the ceiling, which connected them to the larger, main conduits that snaked up and into the building's grid subsystems on the roof. Tubes ran from inside each of their pants, out the bottom, and along the troughs cut into the floors by the walls.

Even with the clip on her nose, she had to fight against gagging on the stench.

"Get moving," Mark said. "You have a lot of stairs to climb."

Jessie nodded to herself, keeping her eyes forward and off the vacant, gaunt faces she passed on her way up.

"Okay, take your second right. You'll pass the elevators. The stairs will be just past them on the left."

Welded shut after the fourth category-five storm surge, elevators were mostly a thing of the past. She threw her shoulder against the self-locking horizontal metal bar, set a jam to hold it open and started up the stairs. After half a flight, she took a deep breath, cinched the straps on her pack tighter around her shoulders and then began jogging up the stairs.

Several minutes passed as Jessie's breath settled into a steady rhythm of shallow gasps, but she'd not quite hit her flow.

"Slow it down," Mark said. "You've got a ways to go still."

Jessie stopped and put her hands on her knees, taking deep breaths. She glanced up at the "33" sign above the door. It was directly below the same framed picture of the same old man plastered across the entire city.

"How long until log off?"

"One hour fifty-six minutes and, wait for it, twenty seconds."

Jessie closed her eyes. She took a deep breath in, held it for a couple of seconds, and slowly exhaled. Then she started up the stairs at a jog again.

The floors went by now at a steady pace after she focused on each step, keeping the rhythm.

"Where are you now?"

Jessie slowed to a walk, working to control her breath.

"Just coming up on eighty-five."

Jessie took the last few stairs and then pulled open the door to the hallway. She was always thrown off by the plush carpet on the upper levels. She'd been in several of the city's skyscrapers, but this was the first time the Rats had gained access to **432 Park Avenue**.

Jessie loosened and dropped her bag, unzipped the main pouch and pulled out a small handheld screen. She unwound a short wire, plugging one end to her handheld and the other to the underside of the lock mechanism on the door.

She tapped several commands onto the screen and then waited as numbers scrolled down.

"Is it taking too long?" she questioned.

"**Balaam** got them. He's never wrong."

Jessie nodded and chewed on her thumbnail as she waited.

At last, the number toggling stopped clicking, and the green light above the lock came on. The lanterns had automatically lit around the spacious apartment as soon as she entered, helping her to move through the marble foyer that felt like a crypt and into the living room.

Her mouth fell open a little when she saw the view. She stepped slowly up to the floor-to-ceiling windows until her nose almost touched the glass.

This was her favorite part of scavenging. To the southeast, she could see across the tops of all the skyscrapers to the point in the distance where the ocean met the horizon. Shadows were already starting to fall across the city. She moved to another window to see the sun sinking behind the Palisades and then cast her eyes downward to follow the Hudson River's movement south into the harbor that led to the sea.

Though the trees and vegetation had been cut and burned away to keep the Scavengers from hiding, the vast Central Park rectangle stood out strangely from the mass of surrounding buildings as the last gasps of the city's natural landscape.

Jessie walked to the next window where she could easily make out the remnants of the Queensboro Bridge. She looked south to see the two towers of Brooklyn's bridge still sticking up out of the dark water. Her father had explained that the city's regents destroyed the bridges and tunnels years before Jessie was born to hold back the tide of Scavengers and terrorists intent on robbing the city's residents of nourishment.

"What's taking so long?" Mark asked.

"Yeah, yeah, I'm on it," she grumbled.

She turned down the main hallway of the apartment and walked quickly to the back bedroom. She pushed the door open, and her face screwed up in disgust when her eyes landed on the **two obese people** in the enormous bed.

While sheets covered their bodies up to their armpits, they were at least three hundred pounds each. Their tubes ran out from their sheets and twisted underneath the bed. Jessie knew the large pillows under their heads had holes specially sewn in to allow for their plugs and wiring.

The room was ornate with thick, white curtains covering the windows. The lamps next to their bed were golden with large shades.

Against the far wall, on a large chest of drawers, sat the Altar of the Reaper. All the Elites had them. Though most didn't believe in the theology, if they made it to Elite status, they knew what kind of show they needed to put on.

The foot-tall statue of a hooded figure with a sickle in each hand had a dusting of bread crumbs spread around its base with two candles that had burned the end of their wicks.

While tempted to knock it over, Jessie walked directly to the headboard and leaned against the wall to see where the wires ran.

"We have a problem," she said. "The wiring runs directly into the wall. There's no panel."

"That's impossible. There has to be one."

"It's not here. I know what a panel looks like." Jessie paused, biting her lip. "Get him on the line."

Jessie pulled the nightstand away from the wall and checked the back of it.

"Just bail. We can try again tomorrow," Mark said.

"The codes could change by then. Elites always have the best security. It's now or never."

Jessie reached as far as her arms could extend behind the bed, feeling around. She went to the other side of the bed and checked the back of the second nightstand. Her pulse quickened, and her breathing became labored.

She went to her hands and knees, crawling around the room to check underneath all of the furniture. There was no panel. No access point.

"Yes?" a staticky, computerized voice came on the line along with a loud hiss from the headphones.

"Balaam—"

"Doth not useth mine own name ov'r the radio," he said.

"Right, so, the wiring from the two Elites runs straight into the wall. There's no panel. I've searched the entire bedroom and nothing. We've got—" Jessie glanced at the large watch on her wrist, "—less than thirty minutes before the field hands log off. I need to find it now."

There was no response. Jessie stood in the center of the bedroom, chewing on her thumbnail again. Had using Balaam's name cost them this target?

"Lavatory. Under the sink."

Jessie slammed the bathroom door open and dropped to her knees. She opened the cabinets under the sink and immediately saw the blinking LEDs at the back.

"Got it!" she said.

There was an immediate click on the line, and the hiss cut off.

Jessie had already unzipped her bag and pulled out the tablet, wiring, and small toolset.

"I'm on it," she said.

"You have to hurry, Jessie. How long will it take you to get back down the stairs?"

"Less than ten minutes."

"You're cutting it too close."

Jessie reached under the cabinet and scooped all of the bottles and baskets onto the floor, shoving them out of her way as she stuck her head and shoulders inside the cavity.

With practiced precision, she untwisted each screw at the corners of the panel and laid them carefully down. She slowly pulled back the processing board to expose the mess of wires behind it and reached out to her wiring, pulling it into the cabinet. Carefully, she snapped each end of her wires to the corresponding wires on the back of the panel and then backed out.

She picked up the plug at the end of the wire, pulled her hair up and out of the way with one hand, and then shoved the plug into the hole at the base of her skull.

Everything went white in her mind before a single blinking cursor appeared on the panel's black screen. She thought through her commands as the characters formed words that quickly spit out across her vision. After she'd blitzed the minimum viable code from memory, she read over it again on the panel and then thought "Enter."

She settled her pulse and breathing with a deep inhalation through her mouth and slowly let it out through her nose. Just as she began her second breath, the credit counter appeared on the screen.

"**We're pulling!**" she said.

"Alright!" Mark said. "Just over fifteen until logoff."

Jessie sat cross-legged, watching the counter quickly click up.

"Five thousand!" Mark said.

Jessie nodded.

Two more minutes passed.

"Eight thousand! Okay, that's good. You need to get going."

Jessie stayed put.

"Jessie! You're under twelve minutes. You need to go!"

"A little bit more."

"This is plenty! More than we've ever scored. Get out of there."

Jessie thought of the Elite husband and wife sprawled out on the enormous bed in the other room and of her parents' cramped room and emaciated faces.

"No, not yet. I want to wipe them out."

"It doesn't matter."

"What they eat today could feed **my mom and dad** for a week. It's disgusting."

"They'll just get all the credits back if you get caught."

Jessie waited. The number ticked past twelve thousand.

"Ten minutes! Jessie!"

The number stopped ticking. Twelve thousand eight hundred and seventy-two.

"Done! They're empty!" she said.

"Great, fine, whatever. Just get out of there."

Jessie issued the logout command and then reached back and unplugged the wire from her skull. She wedged herself back into the cabinet and pulled her wiring out. She pushed the panel closed and quickly maneuvered the screws in their holes, turning each one just a couple of times—enough to hold it in place.

She shoved all her equipment into her bag, zipped it closed and threw it over her shoulder. She quickly scooped up all the bottles and toiletries and threw them back under the sink, shutting the cabinet doors and stepping out of the bathroom.

"I'm packed up and leaving," she said. "Time?"

Nothing.

"Mark! How much time do I have?" Silence.

The connection to Mark was gone.

"Hello, Jessie," **a deep voice** came from the other side of the bedroom door.

CHAPTER ONE

Analyzing the Scene

A STORY EVENT is an active change of life value for one or more characters as a result of conflict (one character's desires clash with another's).

A WORKING SCENE contains at least one Story Event. To determine a Scene's Story Event, answer the following four questions:

1. What are the characters doing?

Jessie is breaking into an Elite's apartment and robbing it. Her conspirators (Mark, Libby, and Balaam) are helping her from a remote location.

2. What is the essential action of what the characters are doing in this scene?

They are stealing.

3. What life value has changed for one or more of the characters in the scene?

Jessie and the group's tension grows as she makes her way to the apartment. She must overcome various obstacles before she successfully finishes the goal of the mission.

4.Which life value should I highlight on my Story Grid Spreadsheet?

Unsatisfied to Satisfied.

HOW THE SCENE ABIDES BY THE FIVE COMMANDMENTS OF STORYTELLING

Inciting Incident: Jessie sets off to rob an apartment.

Progressive Complication: Jessie can't find the panel to log into the grid/safe where the loot is kept.

Crisis: Best bad choice. Jessie can bail on the job, and they will lose the opportunity to steal the credits *or* she can continue to search for the panel and risk detection.

Climax: Jessie connects with Balaam and gets the location of the panel.

Resolution: Jessie steals more credits than they have at any other previous job.

NOTES:

This first scene establishes the skillset of the protagonist. She's a determined force who has capabilities that others in her group do not have. The way she navigates the world is outside of the law, but she has the ability to do so successfully.

CHAPTER TWO

"You've got less than seven minutes until log off. You're not going to make it!" **Mark** screamed into the microphone.

Still nothing back from **Jessie.**

Jessie dropped to her knees and put her back against the bedroom door.

There was a long moment, but Jessie could only hear her gasping breath.

"Come on in, dear. No need to be afraid."

With no way out, Jessie fought to control her breathing. She'd have to talk her way out of it.

But the bedroom was almost completely dark now, and **the Elite slobs** would rise at any moment. How would she talk her way out of their fright and then rage to then deal with whoever was on the other side of the door?

"Don't worry about them, dear. They won't rise until we have a little chat."

Jessie cracked the door and looked into the living room. She could just make out the shape of **a man** sitting in an oversized lounge chair that looked out over Central Park. He seemed to have a large bowl over his head.

His back was toward her as if he knew she'd need time to collect herself before seeing his face. It reminded her of the way **her dad** would turn his back to her when she had to change in their little apartment.

As she crawled into the room and started for the entryway, she saw **the crows** guarding the doorway. These were special forces of the **Faction guards**, but she had only seen them a handful of times in her life. They saw her too but didn't change their expressions. She heard a flint scratch a couple times and the room filled with light.

"Come on over here, Jessie, and have a seat. I've got plenty more crows out in the hallway. If I wanted you hurt, well..."

Jessie slowly stood, her legs shaking. When her eyes adjusted to the brightness of the lamp, she knew her **Rat** days were over.

The man stood and turned to face her.

If the deeply wrinkled face and long crooked nose didn't give him away, everyone in the city knew **Mayor Charles** was never without his enormous, brimmed hat.

"I trust you recognize me," he drawled. The few times Jessie had seen Charles address the city his accent was unmistakable. Mark swore that was how people used to talk before the burning down in the southern Americas.

"Yes," she said.

"Good. That makes things a bit simpler."

Charles waved his hand at the large, cream chair across from him.

Jessie pulled her bag to her chest with one hand, and her other shook as she pulled out the chair. She sat sideways, but turned her torso to face Charles as he took a small box out of his pocket and pressed a button.

"You're not going to make it. Jessie!" At last, Mark's voice crackled through the headphone. "What's going on? Why haven't you left yet?"

"Please remove those silly things so we can have a proper conversation."

Jessie pulled the pink headphones off her head so they fell around her neck.

"What was that!" Mark whispered.

"You're welcome to listen, Mark, but I'll need you to hush..." Charles' voice trailed off and he now spoke directly to Jessie.

"Okay, so you know who I am, which means you know how much trouble you're in?"

Jessie nodded.

"Stealing from the Elite is a pretty big crime on its own. But stealing while they're connected?" Charles let out a whistle. "That there is a capital offense."

Jessie's eyes widened.

"But this isn't your first time round the block. Is it now? You wiped out the **Anderson Elites** last night. **The husband** will be back on the lines tomorrow. **The wife** though—"

Charles paused, and Jessie furrowed her brow at him.

"Let's just say the loss was more than she could handle. Either way, we both know this isn't a fluke that I found you here. Prob'ly wouldn't be hard to prove neither. So now I've got a choice to make."

Charles rubbed at the stubble on his jaw, considering the small girl in front of him.

"An execution seems harsh, but you know how everybody feels about being helpless when they're connected. If they knew you were taking advantage of **people**, even the Elites, while they were in the grid...they'd probably take care of the execution for me." He walked into the kitchen, opened a cabinet, and pulled out a box of dried apricots. He peeled the top and popped one into his mouth, chewing and swallowing before coming back.

"Here's the thing, though. As much as I can't let you and **your Rats** run amok, I have no interest in having a twelve-year-old girl's blood on my hands. I think I've got a way out of this for the both of us."

Jessie met his eyes but said nothing. She couldn't stop thinking about the apricots as her mouth watered.

"As I'm sure you know," he continued, "the Threshing is this year. The Preparing starts next week, and we've already sent **our recruits** to Aeta. You're a bit on the young side, but you obviously have some skills. I've enjoyed watching your little heists. In Aeta, you'll have plenty of food and a nice place to stay. Lots of apricots."

He winked at her as if they were friends now.

"It's an honorable thing. **Your parents** will be proud. Unfortunately, you'll need to leave right away. I have transport waiting."

Jessie's eyes went to the floor. She swallowed, took a deep breath, and looked back up again, directly into Charles' cloudy eyes.

"**No thank you.**"

"Excuse me?"

"No. I won't go."

"I don't think you understand the position you're in."

"I do understand. I know that if I go to Aeta I'll never come back."

The man sighed heavily and sat back in the chair. "Yes, it's dangerous, but what choice do you have? I can't just let you go. You understand execution is on the table?"

Jessie jutted out her chin, crossed her arms tightly across her bag, and burrowed down a bit more in the chair.

"You can't execute me. I'm a child. Still twelve. I know the precepts. You can't execute **a farm hand**, or **any member**, until they are of age. Thirteen."

The mayor stared at her for a moment and then slammed his fist on the coffee table between them. The wood cracked and caused Jessie to jump at the loud noise.

"You were caught stealing from the Elites! You've been doing this for months, not to mention the Rats that support your thieving. And what about your parents? I could bring them into this too."

Jessie's face remained hard.

"Fine," he said, almost a whisper. "Then go. Get out of here."

Jessie wasn't sure what to do when she heard screams come from the bedroom.

Everybody but Charles turned to look at the bedroom door. He kept his eyes on Jessie.

The door slammed open and **the obese man** stood naked in the doorway. His wild eyes scanned the room until he found Jessie.

He pointed at her.

"You!" he screamed and lunged for her.

CHAPTER TWO

Analyzing the Scene

A STORY EVENT is an active change of life value for one or more characters as a result of conflict (one character's desires clash with another's).

A WORKING SCENE contains at least one Story Event. To determine a Scene's Story Event, answer the following four questions:

1. What are the characters doing?

Jessie and Mayor Charles are having a conversation.

2. What is the essential action of what the characters are doing in this scene?

Mayor Charles is coercing Jessie to agree to be a recruit for something called the Threshing.

3. What life value has changed for one or more of the characters in the scene?

Jessie is threatened with execution.

4. Which life value should I highlight on my Story Grid Spreadsheet?

Life to Death.

HOW THE SCENE ABIDES BY THE FIVE COMMANDMENTS OF STORYTELLING

Inciting Incident: Jessie is caught by the most powerful force in the city who has an agenda all his own.

Progressive Complication: The Mayor threatens execution if Jessie does not agree to his demands.

Crisis: Best bad choice. Jessie can become a recruit, but then she must serve the "lawful society" *or* she can refuse to become a recruit, but then she could face death, no matter her reading of "the precepts."

Climax: Jessie refuses the offer.

Resolution: The Mayor tells her she's free to go.

NOTES:

This scene represents the global inciting incident scene for the beginning hook and the global story. For some reason, Jessie has been targeted as a prime candidate to train and compete in something called The Threshing. Her refusal to do so will have consequences we the readers do not quite understand.

CHAPTER THREE

Jessie heard the apartment door slam behind her as she crashed into the stairway door. **The crows** didn't stop her on the way out. **Charles** and his guards seemed to enjoy watching **the fat couple** chase her through the room.

She took the stairs two at a time jumping down as fast as she could. Twice she missed a stepped and tumbled, but she was back on her feet before she stopped moving.

As she ran, **Mark** came back online, ticking off the minutes to her as they passed.

She wasn't going to make it before **the field hands** on the first floor awoke and unplugged. She kept waiting for the breach alarm to sound since she escaped, but nothing happened.

"Hurry, Jessie! The logoff is in 5...4...3..."

The sun had set outside and she still had five more floors to descend. Thankfully, the fat couple upstairs were at least a dozen floors above her. They didn't have the wind to keep pace.

When she reached the ground level, she pressed her face against the stairwell door's small window, straining to see down the hallway.

The street lights coming through the hall windows allowed her just enough light to see that it was empty, but she could hear people stirring. She could still make it.

She gently pulled the door.

Locked.

Her door jam was gone. The crows must have taken it out. She had no time to unscrew the lock box and wire up a passthrough.

Then she heard the Elite couple finally making their way down the stairs as she pulled her small flashlight from her bag and cast it on the wall. There were six inches of clearance between the stairway's rail and the wall. She slid through, pressed her back to the wall, composed herself and waited for the Elites to descend.

She held her breath as they panted at the landing. One of them fumbled for the lockbox and began entering their code into the door's keypad as Jessie slowly slid behind them.

"Hurry up!" **the woman** said to **her husband.**

At last the lock clicked and the wife pulled the door open.

"Where are you!" Mark's voice broke the silence. Just as the couple turned back to the sound, Jessie slid between them and made it through the open door.

In the next hallway, most of the field hands were already standing from their chairs and stretching. The dim of the night wakeup lights had come on and plugs were dangling from the ceiling above them. The tubes leading to the troughs in the floor lay below the chairs, but most had yet to completely disconnect themselves.

Jessie stepped into the mass, softly squishing her way through the disoriented field hands and kept her eyes on the floor. A few gave her odd looks, but most ignored her, oblivious to her existence.

"Jessie, where are you?" Mark asked.

"Shh," she replied.

Jessie made it to the hatch in the floor and stopped to look around. The hallway was now packed with people making their way toward the exits for the night.

"Stop her!" the fat Elites screamed from behind her.

Jessie waited for the next person to come to a stop on the hatch—**a woman** with long, matted blonde hair, her eyes dark and sunken. She was just as pale and thin as the rest of them. Jessie put her hands on the woman's stomach and shoved as hard as she could.

The woman screamed and flailed her arms, knocking down two others as she hit the floor. Jessie clicked on her flashlight and swung it around shining it directly in the eyes of all the field hands around her. They all covered their eyes and stumbled back away from the blinding LEDs.

Once she had a little space, she dropped to her knees, grabbed the hand hold on the hatch, and yanked it open.

The circle around her quickly widened as everyone backed as far away from the opening as possible. **Several people** gasped.

Only **the Numbered** used the hatches.

Jessie looked around at the crowd and then stepped down into the hole, pulling the hatch closed behind her. **She locked the seal** and climbed down into the darkness.

CHAPTER THREE

Analyzing the Scene

A STORY EVENT is an active change of life value for one or more characters as a result of conflict (one character's desires clash with another's).

A WORKING SCENE contains at least one Story Event. To determine a Scene's Story Event, answer the following four questions:

1. What are the characters doing?

Jessie is escaping the apartment building. She runs down the stairwell and makes her way through the field hands until she goes down the escape hatch.

2. What is the essential action of what the characters are doing in this scene?

Jessie is running away.

3. What life value has changed for one or more of the characters in the scene?

Jessie moves from being cornered and likely to be assaulted to being safe.

4. Which life value should I highlight on my Story Grid Spreadsheet?

Trapped to Free.

HOW THE SCENE ABIDES BY THE FIVE COMMANDMENTS OF STORYTELLING

Inciting Incident: Mayor Charles lets Jessie go.

Progressive Complication: Jessie can't figure out a way to get the door hatch in the floor open with so many field hands around.

Crisis: Best bad choice. Jessie can try to escape another way *or* she can draw attention to herself by making space for the hatch and hurting someone else.

Climax: Jessie pushes a woman out of the way. This creates the space Jessie needs to open the hatch.

Resolution: Jessie escapes down the hatch.

NOTES:

This scene illustrates how Jessie solves her problems. She isn't concerned about her actions at this stage in her life. She's robbed people of valuable resources and now she pushes someone out of her way. Jessie, while bright and capable, is extraordinarily ego-centric. It's important to establish an action protagonist's "code 1.0" early on in a story; that is, the way they solve problems and the way they perceive the world. At the beginning of action stories, the protagonist is not concerned with anyone beyond an extremely small circle of people, but that circle reigns as the primary concern beyond all others.

CHAPTER FOUR

Jessie kept her hands shoved in her pockets and her head low as she wound her way across town. As soon as she surfaced, she stored her headphones in her bag and replaced them with the hood from **her father's** old volunteer fireman jacket.

Technically, it wasn't illegal for an under thirteen to be out unsupervised, but it was definitely something **people** noticed. And at most she looked ten.

A wave of **field hands** crowded the streets, pushing their way to the evening food stations. Only five hours were available in the summer months for everyone to take care of their offline necessities before the sun chased them back inside to report to the grid. So no one paid much attention to a girl wearing her father's old jacket. They really couldn't even tell she was a girl.

She glanced at the people who wound around the ration queues and then looked away, shaking her head. Each one had to stop and scan the tag on their wrist before getting a pale bit of food slid under the glass to them.

Jessie wasn't sure why they scanned the wrists. Nobody ever fought over the food or tried to steal extra. It was gross. The hands didn't care about food—only credits. And the more time plugged in and harvesting, the more credits they could tally. Credits bought minimum viable food to survive, but you couldn't get actual good-tasting food and other luxuries on the street. They were delivered by **the Numbered** while everyone else was online.

How things got this way had been deeply drilled into her mind, just like it had for everyone else. Every day, the people learned about The Burning in the first minutes just after login for credit harvest. The session always began with the "why we're here" history lesson. You couldn't skip it no matter what.

Years ago, it began, before any of us were born, the global warming thing finally tipped and the world got hot. So hot that all the important resources like food and water became harder and harder to come by. Blah. Blah. Blah.

That's when the wars had started. Those with the biggest armies seized power as quickly as possible, and soon **the Factions** were born. It came down to **the last super powers** fighting over the waning resources.

And the only place left that had a great supply of resources was in the north, what had once been called Scandinavia. It's northern placement on the globe along with the shifting weather patterns made this the last temperate place where crops could easily be grown and animals wouldn't die from the extreme heat.

Finally, after a decade of war with **hundreds of millions of people** all over the world dead from starvation or as collateral damage from the firefights, the truce was created. Representatives from all of the Factions, now called **the Reapers**, emerged as the only ones who could be trusted with the last few resources. They took over the duties of agriculture and worked with each of the Factions to integrate the grid and global economy.

Now all the wars for the resources were fought digitally.

But even with the Reapers in charge, there still wasn't enough to keep everyone thriving. Electricity went off line in all the rural areas. Lakes dried up. Rivers stopped flowing. Everyone had to migrate north and south and congregate in a few major Faction cities.

The Factions jumped on this opportunity and quickly began

manipulating the grid to seize power and game the system so they could get more resources out of the Reapers. At last the Reapers came up with the Threshing and the credit system to keep the Factions in check. The people mining on the grid competed amongst themselves for their share of the Faction's allocation. The Faction at the bottom of the hierarchy, as determined by the results of the previous Threshing, got only minimal resources to split. A percentage of those in the bottom Faction didn't make it to the next Threshing, so desperation for credits among its citizens grew fierce.

A reboot took place every four years, and the winning Faction from the Threshing got the greatest allocation of food and resources from the Reapers for the next four years. Winning the Threshing saved lives. Losing took lives.

The **two obese slobs** Jessie had just relieved of their credits had spent a lot of time harvesting to make it to their swanky apartment. They also had to partake in their own sort of underhandedness to get there. Many burned out and dead field hands were left in their wake in order for them to make it that high.

Escaping that building was too close a call, but Jessie put it out of her mind as best she could. Right now, all she wanted to do was eat something, chill, and crash for an hour or two before heading back home.

She'd climbed out of the tunnel beneath 42nd Street and Madison and hurried up the avenue three blocks. She was now heading west on 45th Street. She slowed her pace again, forcing herself to take her time. A small girl might go unnoticed, but one in a hurry definitely would not. After everything that just happened, the last thing she needed was to draw attention to herself.

Once she hit Broadway, she glanced up at the LED billboards casting their rainbow of constantly shifting colors on the crowds of field hands hanging out in Times Square, the only place in the city fully lit at night.

The same picture of **President Marcus** showed momentarily before switching to the next bit of Faction propaganda. She wasn't sure what the point of the old white man with the top hat pointing out from the screen was, but the message was clear. Recruiting for the Threshing had begun. The old white man would shout, "Your Faction Wants You!" every thirty seconds making it inescapable.

Every parent in the city would be submitting their teen to the meat grinder they called training in Aeta. If your child was training, you got extra credits. And the longer they made it through the severing stages, the more credits you got. Jessie shook her head at the thought. She knew **her parents** would never give her up just to get a tin of apricots.

She pushed her way across Times Square to the other side of 45th and Seventh Avenue. She checked behind her to make sure nobody had followed her and then pulled out and lit her small lamp. She kept the damper mostly closed so she was letting out as little light as possible when she began moving into the darkness of 45th Street. She stayed close to the south walls, walking slowly in the darkness until she came to a closed-off old alleyway. She looked down, found and pulled on an old subway grate and hurried into the hole. Then she slid through a passageway chipped out of the alley's concrete wall to reach the other side. She pulled herself back up out of the hole and began to step deeper into the alley. There she found the door. It still had "Booth" etched into its gnarled old wood.

She put her hand on a metal box, waited for a click, and then yanked the door open to step through.

Jessie slowly closed the door behind her, careful to not let it slam. Once the latch had clicked into place, she turned and started walking down the hall. She climbed a short set of stairs and then opened the door to the spotlight room.

She still didn't fully understand why the oldest theaters were left empty throughout the city. All of the apartments and office buildings had been retrofitted for the masses of people connecting to the grid. The local Faction leadership had set up shop in the most modern theaters on Broadway. Maybe that was why. Maybe all the field hands were scared to go into any of the theaters now, especially a theater as old and haunted as The Booth.

Either way, this was where Jessie and **her friends** had found a home. They called themselves **the Rats** because of the old joke that the last living creatures on Earth would be rats.

Several lamps were flickering when she walked in, but **three of the five kids** were already asleep in the corner in the piles of old movers' blankets. Only **Libby** and **Mark** were still up.

Even though they were the only people in the theater, they had crammed everything in this little room. It felt safer than spreading out through the building. Desks lined the right side, and Mark and Libby were sitting there with their backs turned to her.

Mark was seated at one of the two terminals they had pieced together. The rest of the tables were overflowing with random circuitry, hardware, and wires. Boxes were shoved under the tables and everything was filled to overflowing.

They slept in the back of the room, but the rest of the room was filled with salvaged couches and chairs.

This was their den. They slept and worked here when they weren't mounting their attacks on the Faction and their **Elites**.

"You should be offline," Libby said, looking over Mark's shoulder as he tapped at the keyboard. "It's not safe."

"I know. I know," he said.

He finished a few more commands, powered down the terminal and then sat back in his chair. They turned back and saw Jessie looking at them.

"What are you doing here?" Libby asked.

Jessie shrugged and dropped her bag by the door. "Whaddya mean? I live here." Jessie grabbed and ripped open a stolen food pack from a shelf as she plopped in an office chair and spun herself back and forth, biting off chewy mouthfuls.

"You were caught and now you've led them back here!" Mark said.

"Don't worry. I got away clean. They couldn't have followed me."

"Are you crazy? I heard everything. If you don't go to the Threshing, **Charles** is going to Shame you. And what about us? He knows what we're doing now. Everything's over. It's a mess. **Balaam** won't respond to any of my 911s. You ruined it!"

Jessie shrugged. "What? Charles doesn't know about this place. He doesn't know who you are or Libby or anyone else. He wants me, not you! We've got tons of credits, and this will all blow over. I got away."

The silence hung for a minute and then Mark stood to loom over Jessie.

"No!" he shouted. "You have no idea what you've done. You need to leave now!"

Jessie shrank under the bigger boy's presence. Libby put a hand on his shoulder and he turned away. Libby knelt down in front of Jessie.

"They're gone," Libby said.

"Gone?"

"All of them. Every last credit we've stocked away is gone," Mark said.

"That's not possible." Jessie booted up a terminal to check. Her face went white when she saw the rows of zeros that had once been in the hundreds of thousands.

Just beneath the zeros was a message.

YOUR ACCOUNT IS LOCKED. TO RESTORE REPORT TO 1515 BROADWAY FROM THE BOOTH THEATER BY 00:01.

Mark and Libby cut their eyes at each other and then back at Jessie. But she was already running out the door.

CHAPTER FOUR

Analyzing the Scene

A STORY EVENT is an active change of life value for one or more characters as a result of conflict (one character's desires clash with another's).

A WORKING SCENE contains at least one Story Event. To determine a Scene's Story Event, answer the following four questions:

1. What are the characters doing?

Jessie makes her way through the streets of New York City to the rat's hideout. Offstage, Libby and Max assess and minimize the fallout from the earlier events.

2. What is the essential action of what the characters are doing in this scene?

All are in search of safety.

3. What life value has changed for one or more of the characters in the scene?

All of the characters move from Safe to Threatened.

4. Which life value should I highlight on my Story Grid Spreadsheet?

Safe to Threatened.

HOW THE SCENE ABIDES BY THE FIVE COMMANDMENTS OF STORYTELLING

Inciting Incident: Jessie emerges onto New York City's streets after escaping the apartment building.

Progressive Complication: All of their credits were removed from the account and their location was exposed.

Crisis: Best bad choice. Jessie can stay and try to avoid the punishment *or* she can leave and try to fix it.

Climax: Jessie leaves the hideout to turn herself in.

Resolution: (Comes after the scene) Jessie is arrested.

NOTES:

This scene is an example of a cliffhanger ending. We're not sure what Jessie is going to do after she leaves the hideout, but our gut reaction is that she'll probably do whatever she has to do to save herself. Her prior behavior was self-centered, so we assume she'll behave the same way. This is a setup to hint at Jessie's potential/authentic character early on so that later, when she makes very seriously sacrificial choices, the reader will believe her capable of such action.

CHAPTER FIVE

The din of **the crowd** filtered through the front of **1515 Broadway**'s Play Station Theater. The rows of seats were still in pristine condition as it was **the Faction**'s direct line to the people and home to its grid-wide streamed ceremonies and legal proceedings. Here the electricity worked fine and lit up the entire room. The acoustics were perfect, and the high-resolution cameras embedded into the walls, floor and ceiling were maintained and controlled by the "Estonia 4545," an artificially intelligent system that put on complex but highly cathartic and simple productions that even the most cognitively challenged **field hands** could understand.

Faction guards, dressed head to toe in grey, stood around the edges of the large room. Their body armor stood out as an even duller grey and their faces were unseen behind their expressionless masks.

Jessie sat on the edge of the stage, her feet dangling above the floor and idly swinging back and forth. She had been waiting here most of the day for the sun to go back down.

"Please, honey. Just end this. Go. Me and **your mother** will be fine."

Jessie just shook her head.

"Why? Why are you doing this?" Jessie lifted her head and stared at **her father** who was squatted down next to her.

"You know," she said.

"It was an accident. It wasn't their fault."

"Won't you miss me? What if I never come back?"

"Of course I'll miss you. I mean, we both will, of course. But it's better than this."

Jessie shook her head again and locked her eyes back on the ground. She'd turned herself in to keep **her Rats** safe. **Charles** wouldn't agree to release their credits since they were stolen, but he promised to not raid The Booth. However, even with his ongoing prodding, she still refused to be shipped off for the training in Aeta.

Her father glanced over his shoulder at his wife, who stood back from them, shifting her feet back and forth with her eyes darting around the room. She was always like this whenever she wasn't in the apartment. Being on the Faction's mainstage only made it worse.

Sound momentarily amplified from outside as one of the doors to the street opened and closed. Jessie looked up and saw **Mayor Charles** step into the theater. His deep wrinkles could be seen in the bright lights of the theater and made him look older than he really was. He was gaunt like the rest of the men in town, but his sinewy muscle still showed through the battered skin.

"It's time," he said.

Jessie's father stood.

"Is there nothing we can do?"

"Nope. She was caught stealing from **the Elite** while they were logged in. You know that makes everyone crazy. We have to feel safe while we're connected or everything falls apart. But," he continued, "if she requests right now, she can be transferred directly to the transport that will take her to Aeta for the Preparing."

"That's what we'll do then," her father said. "Let's do that. You have my permission."

The mayor shook his head.

"Has to come from her."

They both looked at Jessie, but she remained still. "Okay, Jessie," Charles said, "let's get this over with." Jessie stood, her arms still wrapped around herself, and kept her eyes down.

Her father hugged her and whispered, "I love you, honey."

The mayor began to lead Jessie toward the front and turned to see Jessie's father taking his wife toward the back of the stage.

"Aren't you staying to observe?" Charles called.

Her dad looked back at the mayor and then at Jessie. "Uh, no," he said, "it would be too much for her mother. And I can't bear to watch it."

"So you're leaving her on her own for this?" But her dad had already turned, leading her mother into the shadows and pretending not to hear.

The mayor's face hardened and shaded red. He waited for several long seconds before turning and kneeling down in front of Jessie.

"Listen to me, girl. You don't want to do this. Just take the offer and go to Aeta. Many people out there would kill for this chance and you're turning it down. This will not end well for you."

Jessie shook her head, tears pooling in her eyes.

Charles stood, took a deep breath, and then pushed the door open and led her out into the street. The crowd immediately erupted in angry shouts and jeers as Jessie squinted against the light. The Faction was obviously trying to make an example out of her. All of the lights and billboards in Times Square were lit up. She couldn't imagine the credits that was costing the city. And her crimes had been broadcast to all of the field hands when they logged in today to ensure the biggest crowd possible.

The guards formed a barricade directly through the crowd so the mayor could lead her to the center of the square. Jessie glanced up, just for a moment, so she could see the lights flashing and blinking throughout the square.

She'd never seen this much light in one place. It really was beautiful. And then Charles walked away from her, and the pelting began.

The rest passed in a blur. She stumbled to the center of the square and dropped to her knees on the stone circle that served as a platform. Charles flipped open the long razor he had pulled from his pocket. She already felt the bruises welling up where the stones had hit, but she held perfectly still—part from defiance and part from the fear of more nicks and cuts from Charles' rough shaving of her head.

The jeers and shouts pressed in around her like a stifling heat. She opened her eyes and saw the growing pile of dark hair lying below her. Her eyes focused on the drop of blood pooling at the end of her nose. It quivered there for a moment and then dropped down into the pile.

She winced again as the dry razor scraped against her scalp.

Finally, the pressure against her scalp released and she heard the razor snap shut.

Mayor Charles signaled the end. He walked over to her, squatted down in the dust and leaned in close.

"All done, hon."

He glanced up at the crowd that was getting louder with his inaction.

"All that's left—"

"I know," she said.

Their shouts were coalescing into a single chant.

"Plug her! Plug her! Plug her!" they yelled.

Charles let out a deep sigh.

"You know, this isn't what I pictured last night when we talked," he said. "This is why I..."

"Just do it," she said through gritted teeth.

He shook his head and stood, reaching into his pocket and pulling out the small black piece of metal. The bottom had the same form as the plug that all Faction members used to plug in, but the top was a smooth rounded cap, like the top of a mushroom. He fiddled with the bottom of the plug until a green light on the top began to blink.

"This is going to hurt," he said.

Jessie nodded. She'd seen this done before. She craned her neck down to give him as much room to work as possible.

She felt the pressure against the implant at the base of her skull as the mayor set the cap in place. He raised the hammer a foot above the cap.

"Ready?"

"Yes."

He brought the hammer down, and the cap slammed in place. Pain swept across Jessie's head. She released a short, high-pitched wail and then clenched her teeth to stifle it. The scream became a guttural moan in the back of her throat as she dropped to her hands.

It felt like roaches were fighting to chew their way out of her skull.

She gasped as her tears mingled with the sweat and blood rolling off of her face. Still, unlike all of those she'd seen Shamed before her, she remained conscious. She didn't pass out.

The crowd around her cheered.

Mayor Charles stood back, the hammer still in his hand, and looked down at her.

The crowd pushed in closer, and some got close enough to spit on her. She felt another rock bounce across her back.

"Alright!" Charles yelled, and the crowd quieted.

"It's done," he said. "Time to move on."

There were yells of protest.

"She has her punishment. She can't steal anymore. She's cut off."

Another stone sailed through the air and Charles stepped in front of it, letting it bounce off his sunken chest. He winced but stood his ground.

"That's an assault on a Faction mayor. Someone else want to risk that? She's a little girl," he yelled. "She's gotten her punishment, so go on. Don't you all have work to do? The sun'll be up soon."

The crowd jeered back, but Charles stood firm. Soon, the noise began to die out as people realized the show was over. Then they began to make their way back out of the square.

When the people had cleared out, the mayor knelt down next to Jessie. He let a full minute pass.

"Wait here," he said. "**They'll** come collect you."

She pressed her hands against her head and nodded.

Charles looked down at her as if torn on what to do next but then turned and walked away, out of the square.

Jessie knelt on the brick, still holding her head in her hands, alone.

The lights around the square blinked off and darkness fell in around her. She waited as the light slowly began to drift into the square. Sweat started running down her body as the heat quickly began rising with the sun.

A man and a woman appeared from around one of the buildings. They walked slowly toward Jessie, keeping an eye out for anyone who might still be milling around. They were dressed in baggy white clothes that were cinched around heavy boots and covered by gloves. They had large white helmets on with white masks that cover their faces.

The man knelt beside Jessie and picked her up in his arms. Her head lolled back as he squeezed her close.

"We've got you," the woman whispered.

She checked Jessie's pulse and felt around the cap at the base of her skull. Satisfied all was well, she nodded to the man, and they turned to walk out of the square.

The slanted light from the sun reflected off the white of their uniforms, and blinking green lights were barely visible from the base of each of their skulls before they slipped back behind the darkened lights of Broadway.

CHAPTER FIVE

Analyzing the Scene

A STORY EVENT is an active change of life value for one or more characters as a result of conflict (one character's desires clash with another's).

A WORKING SCENE contains at least one Story Event. To determine a Scene's Story Event, answer the following four questions:

1. What are the characters doing?

Jessie waits for the Shaming and discusses it with her father, who tries to talk her out of it. Mayor Charles leads her to the center of Times Square, where he shaves her head and plugs up the implant in her skull so she can't log into the grid anymore.

2. What is the essential action of what the characters are doing in this scene?

Jessie's father and Mayor Charles are trying to convince her to go to Aeta for the Preparing.

Jessie is refusing because she wants to stay home and is afraid of what will happen if she goes.

3. What life value has changed for one or more of the characters in the scene?

Jessie has moved from being embedded in the primary social structure (life in the city), as well as in her tribe (the Rats), to being cast out of both groups.

4. Which life value should I highlight on my Story Grid Spreadsheet?

Embedded to Exiled.

HOW THE SCENE ABIDES BY THE FIVE COMMANDMENTS OF STORYTELLING

Inciting Incident: Jessie will be punished in a way she isn't prepared for.

Progressive Complication: Mayor Charles gives Jessie one last chance to avoid the exile of Shaming.

Crisis: Best bad choice. Jessie must accept the Shaming *or* go to Aeta for the Preparing.

Climax: Jessie chooses to go through with the Shaming and stay in New York City.

Resolution: Jessie endures the Shaming and is picked up by two people right at sunrise.

NOTES:

This scene establishes Jessie's deeply held fear/repulsion of Aeta and participation in the Threshing. She's been called to adventure, but, at great personal cost, she refuses.

CHAPTER SIX

Jessie felt **someone** gently shaking her. She moaned and pushed her face deeper into the thin pillow.

"It's time to wake up. We have to go," **the woman** whispered.

Jessie squeezed her eyes shut and pressed her palms hard against her temples. Tears streamed out from the corners of her eyes.

The woman moved beside her and gently rubbed her back.

"I know it hurts, honey," she said, "but the best thing you can do is start moving. The pain will fade by tonight."

Jessie rolled to her side and squinted up at the woman. The first thing she noticed was the woman's bald head. It had been shaved so close that the dim light in the room reflected off it.

She put her hand to her own head where her hair used to be.

Then she registered the other shuffling noises in the room and opened both her eyes as she pushed up to her elbow to take in what was happening.

She was in a large room completely enclosed in concrete with no windows marring the walls. **Several other bald people** were making their way toward a single door.

The room's floor was completely covered in old cots with only rows in between for people to move.

The room was already half empty, but those still there were dressing.

"Come on. Let's get you sitting up," the woman said. She gently pulled on Jessie's arm and helped her into a sitting position. She wrapped her arm around Jessie's shoulders and pulled her close. Jessie let her head fall against the woman's shoulder as she rocked her slowly side to side.

After a few minutes, the woman stood and pulled on Jessie's sleeve, trying to get her to stand.

Jessie shook her off and stayed sitting.

"We have to go."

"Who are you?" Jessie asked. "Where am I?"

"You don't know?"

Jessie, her face still in her hands, just shook her head. The woman let out a frustrated sigh and sat down on the cot across from her.

"**The mayor** didn't explain?"

Again Jessie shook her head.

"What did you think was going to happen after your Shaming?"

Jessie shrugged, still pressing her palms into her forehead.

"Look at me."

Jessie raised her head just enough to look up at the woman. Now that she was no longer shocked by the lack of hair, she could see the woman was beautiful, even though lines were starting to surround her eyes and mouth.

"I'll explain everything, I promise, but we have to go now."

"Can you at least tell me your name?"

The woman stopped and looked back at Jessie.

She sensed the last few remaining people in the room pause as well.

"We're not much for names here. After our Shaming, we become **a Numbered**."

Fear and shock shot through Jessie.

"I'm a Numbered? No..."

"We don't have time for this. You can call me **Eighty-three**. Now it's time to go."

Eighty-three turned and started walking to the door.

Jessie stood slowly, one hand still against her head, and stumbled a bit as she began following the woman out of the room.

As they moved between the cots, Jessie finally noticed the odd way the woman dressed.

She wore a long-sleeved shirt and long pants that were completely white. And they didn't seem to be regular material. There were made of some kind of plastic. The cuffs of the pants were cinched tightly around the top of heavy-duty work boots.

They entered what looked like the kitchen and living area. Old and tattered chests of drawers lined the wall and had been pushed together for counter space. A stack of dishes stood next to two large buckets of water. A coffee maker was on the counter with a cracked carafe and sat next to dented toaster oven.

The living area was a series of mismatched armchairs and couches, most with bare spots and rips where stuffing was pushing its way out.

Eighty-three walked to the back of the room and opened an old stand-up metal cabinet, rummaging through the contents.

"We don't have anything your size but we'll have to make do with these."

She pulled out a shirt and pair of pants identical to her own that were much too large for Jessie.

"Put these on," she said, handing them to Jessie.

Jessie held them in her hand hesitating. Eighty-three had moved to a chest on the ground and opened it to reveal dozens of boots. She looked over her shoulder at Jessie.

"What are you waiting for?"

This seemed to snap Jessie into action, and she started pulling on the pants and shirt.

A minute later Eighty-three turned back to Jessie with a pair of mismatched boots.

"At least they're the same size. The smallest we have."

The next few minutes were filled with pushing and pulling and stuffing as the woman hurried to get Jessie dressed. In the end, Jessie stood with her sleeves bunched up and her pants gathered at the top of her too-large boots. They had ended up stuffing rags in the toes of the boots to get them to fit.

"Okay, that will have to do."

Eighty-three turned and started walking to the door with a red exit sign above it.

"Wait," Jessie said.

Eighty-three turned back to Jessie, obviously annoyed at another delay.

"Where are we going? What are we doing?"

"**You're a Numbered now.** We have to do our lines."

Jessie stared blankly at her.

Eighty-three pushed up her sleeve and checked a watch.

"I don't have time to explain. It's already almost eight and we haven't even started yet. It's only getting hotter out."

"Hotter? At eight?"

"Of course."

"But I..."

The woman waved her hand, cutting Jessie off.

"Let's go."

Jessie followed her to the door.

Eighty-three stopped at a bookshelf by the door. Instead of books, the shelves were covered with equipment.

Eighty-three reached to the top shelf and pulled down a white mask with a large rubber band attached to it. She put the rubber band over Jessie's head and the mask over her nose and mouth, pulling the band tight. Next she put thick goggles on Jessie, but the lenses weren't clear like the ones Jessie had seen before. They were tinted almost black.

Lastly, the woman put a large white helmet on Jessie's head and handed her a pair of gloves. They were made from the same plastic material as her pants and shirt with rubber pads on the palms and fingers.

"Put them on and tuck them into your sleeves."

Jessie did this and then looked up through the dark lenses at Eighty-three.

"Ready?" Eighty-three asked.

Before Jessie could answer, she lifted the latch on the door and shoved it open. The two of them stepped out onto a platform. Jessie instantly recognized the rails running along the ground about six feet down.

"You live down here?"

Eighty-three cut her eyes at Jessie.

"Come on. They're waiting for us."

Jessie hurried after her.

CHAPTER SIX

Analyzing the Scene

A STORY EVENT is an active change of life value for one or more characters as a result of conflict (one character's desires clash with another's).

A WORKING SCENE contains at least one Story Event. To determine a Scene's Story Event, answer the following four questions:

1. What are the characters doing?

Jessie wakes up among the Numbered. Eighty-three walks her through getting ready to leave for the day.

2. What is the essential action of what the characters are doing in this scene?

Eighty-three is indoctrinating Jessie.

3. What life value has changed for one or more of the characters in the scene?

Jessie is ignorant of her environment and begins to learn how it is organized and its workings, through the intervention of a mentor-like figure.

4. Which life value should I highlight on my Story Grid Spreadsheet?

Ignorant to Enlightenment

HOW THE SCENE ABIDES BY THE FIVE COMMANDMENTS OF STORYTELLING

Inciting Incident: Jessie wakes up in an alien environment.

Progressive Complication: Eighty-three will not allow Jessie to stay in bed.

Crisis: Best bad choice. Jessie can refuse to comply and stay by herself in this strange place *or* she can follow Eighty-three.

Climax: Jessie follows Eighty-three.

Resolution: Jessie leaves the Numbered's den.

CHAPTER SEVEN

Jessie saw the cart at the end of the platform. It sat on the rails packed with **the Numbered**, all sitting shoulder to shoulder in their white suits with their legs hanging over the side. One long bar ran the length of the cart, connecting in the middle to a triangular box, and had handles on each end.

Eighty-three crouched down and jumped off the platform. Then she turned and helped Jessie down. The Numbered scooted over a bit to make room for Jessie as she climbed up next to them. She turned and sat with her legs dangling as well.

"All right," Eighty-three said. "Does everyone have their assignments?"

Everybody muttered their assents.

"Okay, I'll be with the newb, training on her lines today, so I'll be out and about. You have any problems, radio on the open line and help each other out."

Everyone nodded.

"**One-o-three, Seventy-seven,** let's get going."

Two of the larger men were still standing down on the ground, and as Eighty-three took her seat next to Jessie, they climbed up on either end of the cart and grabbed their designated handles. As the first

Numbered pulled up on the bar, the other pushed down on the other side. Jessie could see the veins on his neck bulge.

Slowly, with loud creaks and scrapes, the cart began to move down the tracks. As it picked up speed, the two men, still pumping up and down, relaxed into a rhythm.

Within seconds the cart plunged into darkness.

Instinctively, Jessie reached out into the darkness for Eighty-three. The woman took Jessie's hand in hers and wrapped her other arm around Jessie's small shoulders. Jessie relaxed a bit at this but still tensed up every time she felt a sway or bump along the way. She tried to look around in the dark, but the only light came from the small green dots at the base of the Numbered's skulls.

After what seemed like a long time, Jessie heard the men relax their pumping. She could hear them breathing hard above the noise of the cart against the rails.

Jessie turned to look ahead and could make out another platform coming into view out of the darkness. A single lamp flickered in the dark and bounced off the old tiled walls and floors.

"23rd!" one of the men shouted out.

Jessie could feel shifting as two of the Numbered stood and made their way to the front end of the cart.

It had slowed considerably but was still moving at a good clip. As they approached the platform, Jessie could make out the two standing and holding the shoulders of those still sitting. They were squatted low, and as they came by the platform, both jumped up. One of them landed on their feet and stumbled a bit. The other fell and slid a few feet before regaining their feet.

As soon as the two were off, the two engine men were back on the handles pumping up and down. Within a few seconds those still on the cart were back in the dark.

Jessie leaned over to Eighty-three and whispered, "23rd?"

"That's right," Eighty-three answered. **"We're the sixline Numbered.** We've got from Washington Square Park up to the top of Spanish Harlem."

"What do you mean? What have you got?"

Jessie felt Eighty-three shake her head as if she'd explain later. "28th!"

A couple more of the Numbered stood and approached the left side of the cart. Again the men stopped pumping and the two jumped to the platform as they passed.

As darkness set in again, Eighty-three leaned over to Jessie.

"We're the next stop," she said. "33rd. Get ready."

Terror fell over Jessie. Get ready? Get ready to jump?

"33rd!" the voice called out. The pumping stopped. Eighty-three pulled Jessie up by the back of her suit as she stood. She kept her hand clenched on Jessie as they neared the platform. It still seemed like they were going much too fast and Jessie wasn't even sure she could clear the gap.

Eighty-three leaned down close to Jessie's ear.

"I'm going to count to three. Then we jump. Okay?" Jessie nodded. Her mouth was much too dry to speak. "1... 2... 3!"

Eighty-three and Jessie both jumped, but Jessie didn't entirely make it. She landed on her stomach on the platform, but her legs were dangling off. Eighty-three had held onto her suit, but when Jessie didn't make it, she had slipped on the floor with the change in weight and crashed hard onto her side. The impact jarred her grip loose.

Jessie frantically kicked, trying to find a foothold, but her body slipped a little bit. She screamed as she started sliding into the rail pit.

Eighty-three army crawled over to her, grabbed her hands, and pulled her up onto the platform.

Jessie rolled onto her back, breathing hard.

"Let's go." Eighty-three was already standing.

She turned and walked toward the gates. Jessie could make them out in the soft, flickering light.

She scrambled to her feet and hurried to catch up. Eighty-three quickly jumped the crumbling turnstiles. Jessie had to crouch down and squeeze underneath them, and her white suit somehow remained clean.

Eighty-three kept walking, and as Jessie followed, she could feel the temperature changing. As they approached the stairs, she could see the light filtering down from above.

Eighty-three stopped a few yards from the stairs and turned to Jessie.

"Goggles on," she said as she pulled hers up from around her neck and positioned them over her eyes.

"Wait," Jessie said, "where are we going?"

"Up the stairs."

"Outside?"

"Of course. How else are we getting to **the field hands** and **Elites**?"

"Field hands? Why are we getting to them?"

Eighty-three sighed and pulled back her sleeve to check her watch.

"Look, I don't have time to answer all your questions. Put on your goggles, cinch your hat down, and stay close to me."

Jessie did what she was told and finished cinching her hat around her chin as she followed Eighty-three up the stairs.

By the time they were halfway up, the heat was already suffocating. With every instinct telling her to hold her breath, in her mind, Jessie had to command herself to inhale the air.

As the two of them stepped to the top of the stairs, the sun was so bright that even with the thick dark lenses, Jessie had to squint. The heat seemed to bear down on her as if it were pushing her to the ground, easily piercing through her white suit. The wind came up in furnace blasts of gusts that pelted sand and dirt against her.

Eighty-three walked to a gathering of half a dozen carts scattered along the sidewalk. She grabbed one and pushed it over to Jessie.

She bent low and spoke loudly to Jessie over the wind.

"Stay close to me. Don't wander off."

She turned and started pushing another cart down the sidewalk.

Jessie recognized the buildings and the direction they were heading, but everything was in such a harsh brightness that she could barely focus her attention. It was like a snowstorm she'd read about in her history of Antarctica, only the opposite. She noticed Eighty-three was keeping her head down with occasional glances up in the direction they were heading.

She hurried to stay close, keeping her head down too.

The wind finally died down, and Eighty-three motioned to Jessie to come up beside her.

They picked up their pace and Eighty-three leaned down.

"You're going to be in charge of just two buildings for a while, but know that you'll be getting more and more as you get stronger. We've had some losses, which means everyone's workload is too high right now, and the rest of the group isn't going to have much pity for you for too long."

They walked a little further.

Eighty-three motioned to the wall. There was a large black box, about three feet square, painted on the wall with a white arrow pointing back the way they had come.

"Keep an eye on those," Eighty-three said. "That's how you find your way home if you get lost up here."

Jessie nodded as if she understood and then Eighty-three came to a stop.

"This will be your first one."

Jessie looked up. It was on the smaller side as far as apartment buildings in Manhattan went, probably only a couple dozen stories. She had to look away quickly as the light reflecting off the windows was too much for her eyes.

Eighty-three reached into her pocket and pulled out a keyring with a large rectangular metal piece attached to it.

"This will get you into your buildings and your apartments, nowhere else. It also tracks where you are at all times while above ground. So don't think **the bureaucrats** aren't watching."

She pushed the cart up to the doors of the building and swiped the card against the lock. It blinked green. She pushed the cart inside, let Jessie enter with her carriage, and then closed the door behind them.

Jessie plunged into darkness.

"Take off your goggles."

Jessie pulled them down to hang around her neck and looked around.

The lobby was still very dark. The windows were all covered in tinted film, but Jessie could see the rows and rows of **jacked-in field hands** sitting packed in their chairs. Like everywhere else, cables ran from the ceiling to the base of their skulls, with the evacuatory tubes poking out of their clothes and running to the edge of the room into the drainage troughs.

Jessie squeezed her nose shut with her fingers.

Eighty-three cracked a smile at her.

"We'll get to them last," she said and then turned her cart to the stair access. She left her cart outside the door and then pushed open the door to the stairwell. Jessie followed as they ascended the stairs. Once they reached the second floor, Eighty-three pulled open the stairwell door and approached the apartment. She swiped the key again and stepped into the apartment, Jessie close on her heels.

"Let's start in the kitchen," Eighty-three said, pointing. "The trash can is under the sink."

She opened the cabinet, pulled out the trash can, and set it on the counter. She began rifling through the contents.

"Here we go!" she said excitedly.

She pulled out a chunk of bread. It looked to be about a third of a baguette. Eighty-three set it on the counter and kept going through the trash.

"Okay, that's it on this one."

She handed the trashcan to Jessie.

"Go dump this in the shoot in the hallway."

"What's that for?" Jessie asked, pointing at the chunk of bread.

"That's for the cart. That goes back with us."

Jessie opened her mouth to speak, but Eighty-three raised her hand to cut her off and then pointed to the door.

Jessie hurried down the hall to the trash shoot and dumped the can before heading back to the apartment. She replaced the can and then walked down the short hallway looking for Eighty-three.

She stepped tentatively into the bedroom.

An elderly man and woman lay in the bed entirely still except for rapid movements under their eyelids. The man was in a pair of boxers and shirtless, the woman in a tattered nightgown.

"Trash done?" Jessie nodded.

"Okay, let's get the bedpans next."

Jessie squinched her eyes and pursed her lips. "Come on! We're on the clock!" Eighty-three said. She knelt at the foot of the bed and lifted the linen out of the way to slide out two metal basins. She blocked the tubes running into them and stood.

"Take these and dump them in the toilet."

"I'm not doing that," Jessie said, taking a step back.

"Excuse me?"

"I'm not doing any of this. That's disgusting."

A bitter laugh escaped Eighty-three.

"Hello? This, pointing to the bedpan in her hand, is what it means to be Numbered. You do your lines. Who do you think cleans up after the field hands and Elites? We're the bottom of the bottom, the cautionary class to keep everyone else in line!"

"I don't care, and I'm not doing this!"

Eighty-three took a deep breath, controlling the urge to smack the attitude right out of this girl, and walked over to kneel in front of Jessie so she could see into her eyes.

"I know this is a lot to take in, but it's best to stop thinking about how you're too good for it and do the work. It will keep you busy and your mind off of—" she paused. "Other things."

"I can't do this," Jessie pleaded.

"I know, dear. It feels like that, but you'll do fine. Like I said, just keep working, moving forward from one pee pan to the next."

She smiled, stood and pressed her hand against Jessie's back, pushing her toward the bed.

"Now grab that bedpan and dump it in the toilet. I'm going to wipe down the kitchen."

Eighty-three left Jessie to stare at the old couple in the bed. They were on the lower end of the Elites. Just enough credits to keep them out of the field, but they definitely would have never been a target for her and **the Rats**.

After a moment, she walked to the bed, knelt, and picked up the bedpan. She began walking toward the bathroom but kept cutting her eyes back to the bed. It was bizarre to see human beings so out of it that they didn't notice a girl walking around their bedroom. Just as she was about to enter the bedroom, out of habit, she found the panel and cable running into it.

She looked away at the wrong time and her elbow caught on the door frame. The pan tipped at the impact and Jessie overcorrected, sloshing some of contents down the front of her suit.

She tried to take a step back to regain her balance but caught her foot against a thick cord running along the floor. She fell back, crashing into the nightstand. The bedpan flew out of her hands and slammed against the floor, splashing the urine across the wall and floor.

Jessie scrambled to her feet and began looking around for something to clean up the mess.

A low moan came from the bed, and Jessie turned to see the older woman struggling to sit up. Her eyes were open wide, and her pupils darted around wildly. The large plug was still protruding from the back of her head with the thick wire running behind the headboard.

She finally reached a sitting position and turned toward Jessie.

The woman cocked her head to the side slowly, as if trying to figure out what was going on.

She slung her legs over the side of the bed and stood slowly.

"Are—are you okay?" Jessie stammered.

The woman stared at Jessie for several seconds.

Jessie took a step back from her, but she was too late. The woman let out a piercing scream and lunged for Jessie.

CHAPTER SEVEN

Analyzing the Scene

A STORY EVENT is an active change of life value for one or more characters as a result of conflict (one character's desires clash with another's).

A WORKING SCENE contains at least one Story Event. To determine a Scene's Story Event, answer the following four questions:

1. What are the characters doing?

All of the Numbered are making their way to their assigned places. Jessie follows Eighty-three to an apartment building and starts helping her clean up after the Elites.

2. What is the essential action of what the characters are doing in this scene?

Eighty-three is indoctrinating Jessie.

3. What life value has changed for one or more of the characters in the scene?

Jessie's old worldview is coming under assault. It's not attuned to this environment.

4. Which life value should I highlight on my Story Grid Spreadsheet?

Refusal to Surrender

HOW THE SCENE ABIDES BY THE FIVE COMMANDMENTS OF STORYTELLING

Inciting Incident: Jessie and Eighty-three board the train car.

Progressive Complication: Jessie comes to understand the procedures and that her job as a Numbered is to clean up after the field hands and Elites.

Crisis: Best bad choice. Jessie can refuse to do her chores and alienate the one person who seems to care about her *or* she can do the chores.

Climax: Jessie reluctantly starts the chores.

Resolution: She spills a bedpan and unplugs one of the Elites.

NOTES:

Jessie's self-sufficient and ego-centric worldview from her time with the Rats is undergoing serious challenges. In order for her to integrate into this new reality, she's going to have to put her ego aside.

CHAPTER EIGHT

Jessie threw out her arms to stop **the old woman**'s advance, but she was already upon her and much stronger than she looked. Jessie fell back against the wall. The woman swung her arms wildly, clawing and scratching at Jessie's face.

Jessie screamed and strained to push the old woman off her, but the attack was relentless. Jessie slid down against the wall and put her head down between her knees with her hands over her head. The old woman hit and scratched at Jessie's hands and head, all the while moaning and screaming.

Suddenly, the blows stopped, and Jessie heard something hit the bed. She looked up to find **Eighty-three** on top of the old woman fighting to gain control of her. Jessie sat frozen watching.

Eighty-three finally got ahold of the woman's wrists and was able to pin them down, but the old woman bucked and fought to regain control.

Eighty-three looked back at Jessie.

"What are you doing? Don't just sit there! Plug her back in!"

Jessie looked around wildly and saw that when she had tripped over the cord, she had pulled the end loose from the panel. She jumped forward and grabbed the plug, crawling over to the wall. She tried to plug it in, but her hands were shaking so severely she couldn't get it into the outlet.

She glanced back to see the old woman still struggling against Eighty-three.

Jessie turned back, took a deep breath, and slowly put the plug back into place.

She turned back as it connected to see the old woman go limp beneath Eighty-three.

Eighty-three sat back, looked at Jessie and then took in the mess from the spilled bedpan.

"I'm so sorry," Jessie said. "I bumped the wall and dropped the bedpan then tripped—"

"Stop," Eighty-three was already up from the bed. "It doesn't matter. We need to get everything cleaned up and get out of here."

She disappeared into the hallway and came back a few seconds later carrying several towels. She tossed them to Jessie.

"Make sure you get it all."

Jessie began wiping down the walls. Eighty-three went back to the old woman and examined her. She straightened the nightgown that had ridden up to her waist. She fixed her hair and put her arms straight by her side. She bent down low over the woman's hands and cleaned the flesh from under her fingernails.

After she finished, she knelt beside Jessie and helped her with the remainder of the spill. She took the bedpan and slid it back under the bed, securing the tubes back in place. She emptied the other one and put that one back too as Jessie watched.

Eighty-three came close to Jessie and gently inspected her face. Jessie winced and pulled back.

"She got you pretty good."

"Is it bad?"

"You'll be fine, but you've got some good scratches. They're not bleeding all that much. Luckily she doesn't have a scratch on her," Eighty-three said.

"Her? She came after me!"

"You need to hope she doesn't remember when she logs off tonight."

Eighty-three turned to leave the room.

"Come on. Let 's go. We still have a lot of apartments to hit. We have to be done and off the streets by dusk."

Eighty-three headed for the front door, but Jessie had stopped following her.

"Let's go!"

Jessie stood in place, her eyes staring but unfocused.

"What do you mean that I have my lines? You mean I have to clean these apartments every day?"

"Yes, that's part of it."

"By myself?" Eighty-three nodded.

"For how long?" Eighty-three cocked her head to the side, a questioning look her face.

"What do you mean?"

"When do I get to go home?"

"We can talk about that later. Let's keep moving." Eighty-three reached for the door handle.

"No! I want to talk about it now. I want to know when I'm going home. **My parents** live just a few blocks from here. They're in one of **the Elite** apartments too. I want to go see them. They're going to be worried about me."

Eighty-three sighed and let go of the handle.

"Yeah, I know where they live and what you lost, but you're not going home anytime soon. You were caught stealing credits while a member was plugged in. That alone carries ten years of service for a minor. And you must have been robbing the wrong people because when I got the work orders for you—"

Eighty-three paused and looked away from Jessie.

"What?" Jessie asked.

"Look, it doesn't matter—"

"Tell me!"

Eighty-three ran a hand over her face and sighed again.

"Your work order—you got the maximum time. You're Numbered

for twenty-five years. Home is not something you should be thinking about. This is your home now." She pointed at the urine-stained walls.

CHAPTER EIGHT

Analyzing the Scene

A STORY EVENT is an active change of life value for one or more characters as a result of conflict (one character's desires clash with another's).

A WORKING SCENE contains at least one Story Event. To determine a Scene's Story Event, answer the following four questions:

1. What are the characters doing?

The unplugged Elite attacks Jessie. Eighty-three saves her. They get the woman plugged back in and clean up the mess.

2. What is the essential action of what the characters are doing in this scene?

They are doing their jobs.

3. What life value has changed for one or more of the characters in the scene?

Jessie was under attack and saved, but then Eighty-three reveals Jessie's sentencing.

4. Which life value should I highlight on my Story Grid Spreadsheet?

Rescued to Imprisoned

HOW THE SCENE ABIDES BY THE FIVE COMMANDMENTS OF STORYTELLING

Inciting Incident: The unplugged woman attacks Jessie.

Progressive Complication: Eighty-three will not be straight with Jessie about what Jessie's full punishment will be.

Crisis: Best bad choice. Jessie can go along with Eighty-three *or* she can refuse to move until she has answers.

Climax: Jessie refuses to move until she has answers.

Resolution: Eighty-three tells Jessie the full punishment Jessie has been sentenced to.

NOTES:

This is another critical stage in Jessie's previous ego-centric worldview coming under assault. She's being sentenced to serving others for twenty-five years. This scene represents 'sensing disorder,' the turning point progressive complication for the beginning hook of the story.

CHAPTER NINE

Jessie slid up to the edge of the building, sweat running down her face. She dropped to her knees and slowly peeked around the corner. She was careful to stay in the shadows. The sun had already dipped below the horizon and, while it still wasn't technically nighttime, a few people were already emerging from the buildings. They were definitely **Elites** since **the field hands** didn't have the clearance level to log themselves off.

Since that first pee-splattered day with **the Numbered**, she'd been planning her escape, but it had taken her almost two weeks to get everything in place. **Eighty-three** watched her pretty closely for the first week before she let her guard down enough for Jessie to start sneaking out.

It had taken another week for her to find the passageway to the surface close enough to where she needed to be. She'd been operating on only a few hours of sleep a night but **the rush she got from outsmarting everyone kept her energy up.** (*A resurgence of Jessie's ego-centric worldview*)

She could see **two men** walking directly across the square, talking and gesticulating wildly with their hands. It was hard to tell if they were arguing or agreeing.

Jessie hated coming back to Times Square. It was impossible for her not to think about being pelted during the Shaming, but she had no other choice. Her eyes fell on the circle of bricks in the middle of the street. She ran a hand over her head and shuddered.

In only a few minutes, the streets would be packed with field hands as they poured out from the buildings and started making their way to the ration posts.

The two men continued moving across the square and then disappeared down a side street.

Jessie pulled her scarf up over her bald head and checked to make sure it was still covering the green light at the base of her skull. She cast her eyes around one last time before standing and walking directly into Times Square to the brick circle that held the stocks. She stopped, glanced around again, pulled a loose brick out of the ground, placed a small, folded scrap of paper underneath, and replaced the block.

She stood and hurried the rest of the way across the square while keeping her eyes roaming back and forth.

She was almost to the other side of the square when she heard a loud beep. Jessie froze and looked around wildly. Her eyes cut back across the square.

Still empty.

She couldn't locate the source of the noise, so she continued moving forward, now fighting the urge to break into a sprint.

As she turned east off Broadway and onto 39th Street, she broke into an efficient run as she moved through the street blocks, confident of her direction.

Jessie stopped beside the lobby of a skyscraper and flattened herself against the wall while she surveyed the street. By now the sun's last beams were dying out. The heat of daylight was dissipating too, and it wouldn't be long until the streets filled up.

She stepped out and moved at a fast walk across the street. She circled behind the small apartment building and found the service access point. She dragged the door open and took a step in.

Beep.

Jessie fell back out of the doorway, looking around again for the source of the sound.

She still couldn't make out any movement or determine where the source of the sound was.

After counting a full minute, she stepped back into the doorway and pulled the door closed behind her.

She moved through the pitch-black confidently, feeling along the wall as she went. When she reached the stairs, she quickly entered and started climbing them two at a time. She reached the third floor and stepped into the hallway.

She walked to the end of the hall to the door marked 301, pulled out the grey keycard she'd lifted from Eighty-three's area and swiped the door.

The light turned green and unlatched.

Jessie opened the door just enough to slide in and then gently shut the door behind her.

The apartment was small but homey. A "friend of the Faction" one bedroom, one bathroom about five hundred square feet. Jessie cracked open the door to the closet off the hallway. She dug into her pocket and pulled out a small lighter she'd nabbed before heading out for the night and flicked it on.

An empty sleeping bag lay on the floor alongside several cardboard boxes arranged upside down as makeshift desk and chest of drawers—a handful of small clothes folded in the corner.

She clicked the lighter off and then stepped back into the hallway.

Beep.

Jessie froze. She shook her head and headed down the hallway. A clang came from the next room, and a hushed voice muttered to itself. Jessie hurried toward the sound.

The hallway opened into a larger room. To one side was a living area with a matching sofa and chair. There was also a small, round dining table with four mismatched chairs pushed underneath. Everything was neat and tidy.

Across the room was a small open kitchen. The counters were white and spotless. The sink was empty, and dishes were stacked neatly on the shelves above. A man in a loosely tied robe was busy scooping a measure of coffee into a small pot over a propane stove.

"Daddy," she whispered.

The man turned quickly, almost knocking the pot off the stove. He let out a yelp when he saw Jessie.

"It's me!" Jessie said.

"Jessie! What are you doing?"

"Coming home. I missed you!"

Jessie's father quickly moved into the living room, looking to the left and right of her, and then down the hallway as if he expected to find other people in his house.

"You can't be here!" he said in a strained whisper.

"What do you mean?" she said.

"You're a Numbered now. We're not supposed to even talk to you, not to mention have you in the home with us."

"But, Daddy—"

"No! You have to go. We could be put back with the field hands. You know **your mother** would never survive that! She's been through enough. This apartment can be taken away at any time! Don't you see what you've done!"

"I want to come home."

"Well there's not much I can do about that now. Is there? *You* decided to start sneaking around stealing credits. *You* decided to go through the Shaming. Never a thought for anyone else."

"What choice did I have?"

"Go to the Preparing! Go to Aeta!"

"I'm not doing that! Is that really what you want for me? You want me never to come back either?" Silence fell between them.

"Daddy, don't you miss me?" Her father's face softened, and he pulled her into a tight hug. Tears leaked from Jessie's eyes.

"Of course I do."

"I'll just hide here. I'm good at hiding. They won't even know."

"It doesn't work that way."

Beep.

Jessie reflexively looked behind her, searching for the source of the noise.

"What is it?" her father asked.

"You didn't hear that?" she said.

"Hear what?"

"That beep. I keep hearing it. It's like it's following me. I don't know —" Beep.

"Ah!" she said. "Did you hear it that time?" Jessie's father screwed up his face and took a step back from her as if she was crazy.

"Jessie?" he said. "Are you okay?"

Beep.

Jessie clapped her hands over her ears and squeezed her eyes shut.

"What is that?" she said. "They're coming quicker now."

"Shhhh! Keep your voice down!" her father said.

Then a loud bang sounded on the door. Jessie and her father both jumped. They looked at the door and then each other.

There was another loud bang and then a voice yelled from outside. "Open the door!"

"It's the Faction guards," her father whispered harshly. "You brought them here!"

From down the hall came the noise of a door opening.

"What is going on? What's all the—" Jessie and her father turned to see her mother standing in the hall outside of the bedroom, her nightgown disheveled and hanging off one shoulder.

Her mother looked at her father, and then at Jessie. She opened her mouth as if to scream, but no sound escaped.

"What is she doing here?" she moaned.

Now the front door flew open with a crack as the deadbolt broke through the thin door frame. Jessie's mother whipped around to see the intruders and then dropped down to the floor, hugging her knees and burying her head deep into herself.

She began to rock and sing that awful song she had been singing for the last four years:

Rock-a-bye Randy on the tree top,

When the wind blows, his cradle will rock.
When the bow breaks, his cradle will fall,
And down will come Randy, broken like a doll.

Flanked by two bald men Jessie recognized as **Sixty-one** and **Thirty-three, Eighty-three** stepped into the apartment.

"Time to go."

CHAPTER NINE

Analyzing the Scene

A STORY EVENT is an active change of life value for one or more characters as a result of conflict (one character's desires clash with another's).

A WORKING SCENE contains at least one Story Event. To determine a Scene's Story Event, answer the following four questions:

1. What are the characters doing?

Jessie is creeping through the city so she can go home and be with her father and mother.

2. What is the essential action of what the characters are doing in this scene?

Jessie is running away.

3. What life value has changed for one or more of the characters in the scene?

Jessie assumes that she'll find protection with her family, but she discovers that is not a real possibility.

4. Which life value should I highlight on my Story Grid Spreadsheet?

Escaped to Caught

HOW THE SCENE ABIDES BY THE FIVE COMMANDMENTS OF STORYTELLING

Inciting Incident: Jessie leaves the Numbered's den to escape to her family home.

Progressive Complication: Her father tells her to go to the Preparing.

Crisis: Best bad choice. Jessie can keep pushing her father to let her stay and risk him turning her in *or* she can go back to the Numbered.

Climax: Jessie refuses to do as her father says.

Resolution: Eighty-three and two other Numbered show up at the apartment to bring Jessie back.

NOTES:

This scene represents the first in a sequence of scenes called 'Running Away to Reluctant Engagement.' It will culminate in scene twelve as the crisis of the beginning hook of the story.

CHAPTER TEN

"I'm not going back," **Jessie** said.

Jessie looked at **her dad. Her mom** sang her lullaby to herself as she continued to rock back and forth, balled up in the cramped hallway, her eyes averting Jessie.

"You don't have a choice," **Eighty-three** said.

Jessie's father put up his hand to stop her. He stepped forward and knelt in front of Jessie as he put his hands on her shoulders.

"You're my daughter—the only child I have left—of course I want you home."

Jessie jumped forward and wrapped her arms around his neck. He hugged her close and Jessie sniffled as her tears soaked into his shirt.

"But there's nothing I can do."

He put his hands on her shoulders and pushed her back.

"Do something!" she wailed, holding tightly to his neck. "Talk to **Charles**! Plead to **our Faction**! I'll pay back what I stole. I'll apologize. I'll do whatever. I want to come home now!"

Jessie's father pried her loose and put her back at arm's length.

"No! You know I can't do that. We are already on thin ice with the Faction with your mother and all of her **Randy** talk. I can't risk it."

"Daddy..."

He stood, his hands still on her shoulders and gently prodded her toward the front door.

Eighty-three stepped through the door and reached out toward Jessie. Jessie screamed and wrenched herself from her dad's grip, dropping to her knees and scurrying away from them. When she was out of arm's reach, she leapt to her feet and ran to the back of the living room. Her dad and Eighty-three both yelled after her, but she ignored them.

Her mother screamed as **a Numbered** ran by her going after Jessie, but the girl had already torn open the window and dived out onto the fire escape.

Beep.

She scrambled up to her feet and started running down the stairs. Below on the street, the handful of **field hands** that were milling about stopped and looked up at the noise.

"Jessie, stop!" a voice cried out behind her, but she kept pumping her legs. She heard more voices yelling at each other behind her. A set of feet hit the fire escape above her. They were coming after her.

"Jessie!" Eighty-three called. "You have to stop!"

Jessie didn't slow down. She got to the bottom of the fire escape and grabbed the final ladder, riding it to the ground. As soon as her feet hit the pavement, she was running again. **The few people in the street** jumped out of her way as she cut around the back of the building before darting down a narrow alleyway.

About halfway down the alley, she dropped to her knees next to a metal grate. She grabbed the slats with both hands and pulled it loose.

Beep.

She turned around and backed into the small space, pulling the grate closed behind her. She felt around behind her and found the small foldable lantern and flint set she kept stashed here and shoved them in her pocket.

Jessie stayed on her knees and fought to keep her breath quiet. She took deep, slow breaths, her small chest heaving as she fought for calm and listened hard into the night.

Beep.

"I think she went back here," a man's voice called out from the direction of the street.

Another minute passed.

"Jessie, it's me. Eighty-three. You have to come back with us. Please come out" she pleaded.

Jessie pressed her face against the wall trying to see. She could just make out the three Numbered standing at the end of the alley in the middle of the street. She fought to keep her breathing calm.

The two men stayed with Eighty-three, their eyes roaming back and forth. The woman waited, standing very still. A crowd was starting to form. They were shifting uncomfortably, staring at Eighty-three and the two men.

Beep.

"Hear that?" Eighty-three called. "I hear it too. It's a warning."

"We have to go now! Leave her," one of the Numbered men said. "She's not our responsibility!"

Eighty-three waved him off.

"Then go. I'll find her myself."

The man let out an exasperated sigh but stayed with her.

"Get to where you can see me. I'm going to turn around slowly. Look at my light."

Eighty-three spun slowly around. When her back was to Jessie, she could see the small light in the plug at the base of her skull. It was now glowing a bright yellow instead of green.

"We hear the beeping too. It means we're out of bounds. The beeps and the yellow light are warnings. That's how the Faction tracks us. You don't want your light to turn red."

More time passed.

Beep.

"That's it," the man said. "I'm going back."

He turned and ran off into the night. The other man with Eighty-three shifted his feet nervously but stayed by her side.

"We only have a few minutes left before our lights turn red."

Again, Eighty-three went silent and waited. Jessie put her fingers to the back of her head and felt the stubble of hair that was starting to grow back. She worked her fingers to the base of her skull and felt along the plug.

Beep.

Jessie heard voices float through the door. She peeked out again. Eighty-three and the Numbered man were whispering furiously. The murmur from the crowd was getting louder as **more people** joined them.

One of them shouted something Jessie couldn't make out, but several other people yelled their angry assent.

Eighty-three ignored them. She stood, waiting.

"I'm not going anywhere without you. You're a Numbered now, and you're my responsibility."

Beep.

"We probably have less than five minutes."

Jessie shifted anxiously inside the small space. She grabbed the grate, let go, and then grabbed it again.

She looked out at Eighty-three again. She was still standing, waiting.

Jessie took a deep breath, grabbed the grate with both hands, and then pushed it open. As soon as the sound of the grate scratching on the ground reached her, Eighty-three started sprinting down the alley with the other Numbered close behind.

Jessie froze and backed further into the space as Eighty-three approached. The woman dropped to her knees next to the grate, reached in and dragged Jessie out of the hole. She lifted Jessie onto her feet and spun her around to see her plug.

Eighty-three muttered a curse, turned Jessie around, grabbed her face and looked directly into her eyes.

"We have to run, okay? You have to keep up with me. I'm not going to stop. There's no time. Ignore everything and stay close to me. Got it?"

She looked over her shoulder at the other man.

"**Sixty-one**, we have to hurry."

He nodded.

The woman grabbed Jessie's arm, turned down the alley, and began running.

CHAPTER TEN

Analyzing the Scene

A STORY EVENT is an active change of life value for one or more characters as a result of conflict (one character's desires clash with another's).

A WORKING SCENE contains at least one Story Event. To determine a Scene's Story Event, answer the following four questions:

1. What are the characters doing?

Jessie tries to get her father to let her stay at their home, but she then escapes and runs when she realizes that's not an option. Eighty-three and her Numbered friends try to collect Jessie to take her back.

2. What is the essential action of what the characters are doing in this scene?

Jessie is running away from reality.

3. What life value has changed for one or more of the characters in the scene?

Jessie moves from belief in belonging to her family to understanding that she's all alone.

4. Which life value should I highlight on my Story Grid Spreadsheet?

In it Together to Alone

HOW THE SCENE ABIDES BY THE FIVE COMMANDMENTS OF STORYTELLING

Inciting Incident: Eighty-three demands that Jessie come with them.

Progressive Complication: If Jessie stays hidden, then their lights will turn red and something very bad will happen.

Crisis: Best bad choice. Jessie can stay hidden and she won't be stuck with the Numbered, but something clearly bad will happen, *or* she can come out of hiding and be stuck with the Numbered again.

Climax: Jessie comes out of hiding.

Resolution: Jessie, Eighty-three, and Sixty-one start running toward safety.

NOTES:

- This scene builds the cognitive capacity of Jessie. Facing the knowledge that she's endangering not only herself but the other Numbered, she decides to return with them.
- This scene also represents the second in a sequence of scenes called 'Running Away to Reluctant Engagement.' It will culminate in scene twelve as the crisis of the beginning hook of the story.

CHAPTER ELEVEN

When **they** hit the street, they paused for a moment as **Eighty-three** looked around to get her bearings.

Eighty-three cursed again.

"49th and 6th," she muttered.

She looked at **Sixty-one.**

"51st Street entrance?"

"That means we'll have to go through—" he answered.

"I know."

"That's a lot of people."

"We don't have time for anything else."

He shrugged.

"Let's do it."

Eighty-three took off, leading the way. **Jessie** pumped her legs as hard as she could to keep up, and Sixty-one brought up the rear. Eighty-three kept shouting at **groups of people** to move as they cut down the middle of the streets.

Jessie kept her eyes on the back of Eighty-three's head. The yellow light at the base of her skull was now blinking.

Suddenly Eighty-three stopped, and Jessie almost ran into her. She looked up ahead and saw why.

A massive crowd waited ahead of her. Jessie looked around and then up.

"Rock Center?"

Eighty-three cut her off with a wave of her hand.

Besides having the largest food station, this was the one place **the field hands** could buy and sell things. Scavenging was technically illegal, especially for the crazies that lived off island and shuttled back and forth across the rivers with flimsy boats, but here in the marketplace you could spend credits to get a few luxuries. There were appliances like dented toasters and cracked coffee makers. These were almost useless since the electricity they used cost more credits than most field hands made in a week. But it was also where you could buy additional blankets or extra food or clothes that were less ragged than your own—all of it was heavily taxed by **the Faction**, of course.

Several people at the edges of the crowd had already seen them. It was hard to miss **the Numbered's** bald heads.

Eighty-three reached back and grabbed Jessie's hand. She cut her eyes at Sixty-one and then started pushing her way into the crowd, cutting straight across the center square.

The first few people she shoved turned around with shocked expressions on their faces. When they caught sight of her bald head, they backed away to give her room—repulsed, as if being touched infected them.

But the silence and repulsion soon turned to anger. The Numbered were criminals, after all, and many of them were credit thieves, the most heinous crime of all.

The first person to shove Eighty-three was **a gaunt old man** missing most of his teeth.

"Filthy hackers," another yelled behind them. When Jessie turned to look back, she saw Sixty-one covering his head as **a woman** lunged at him, swinging her fists into the back of his neck.

With the first blow landing and no **Faction guards** nearby to stop them, the crowd pressed in on them. Jessie got the same feeling from them as she did during her Shaming. She gripped Eighty-three's hand tighter and grabbed her wrist with her other hand too. It was as if Eighty-three was her plow.

She felt a fist land on her back and then another on her head. She tried to keep her head down but didn't dare let go of Eighty-three's hand.

They kept pushing through the crowd as the yelling and cursing continued to rise.

Jessie chanced a glance up and saw they were almost across the square. She dropped her gaze again, but then she was stopped by a hand on her arm.

Before she could react, she stumbled, lost her grip on Eighty-three's hand, and fell to the filthy pavement. **A tall lanky man** towered above her. His lips were pulled back revealing bright red, empty gums. His eyes were bloodshot and dilated wide.

He pulled back his fist, and Jessie threw her hands up, but instead of a blow to the face, she felt nothing. She rolled over to see Sixty-one on top of the man. He slammed the man's head into the pavement hard enough to hear a sharp crack. The crowd gasped at Sixty-one's attack and backed up to give them room.

Eighty-three came back out of the crowd and grabbed Sixty-one by the back of the shirt.

"We have to go!" she yelled at them.

Eighty-three grabbed Jessie's hand, and they hurried through the rest of the crowd, now giving them a wide berth to avoid Sixty-one's wrath. Jessie kept her eyes on the pavement to avoid the disgust and ire of the field hands.

As they emerged from the other side of the square, Eighty-three dropped Jessie's hand and broke into a run again.

"Move!"

Jessie and Sixty-one took off after her.

They continued until they made it one hundred feet from Park and 51st. One more block and they'd make it to Lexington and the entrance to the Six Subway line. Jessie's legs felt like they weighed a hundred pounds as she struggled to keep up. She watched Eighty-three jump over something and then disappear around the corner onto 51st Street. As Jessie made the turn, she tripped over something in the road and hit the ground hard.

She tried to stand quickly, but her feet tangled in some wire. Prongs were sticking out from it, snagging her pants and cutting into her legs.

Just then, Sixty-one barreled around the corner. Jessie called out to him to jump, but he didn't hear in time. He tripped over her and entangled himself in the razor wire too.

Instead of unwrapping himself, Sixty-one started tearing at the wire around Jessie's legs. Jessie gritted her teeth against the pain as the barbs stabbed and scratched her legs. Eighty-three came running back, dropped to the ground, and helped. Finally, she grabbed Jessie under the armpits and pulled her up. At the same time, Sixty-one pulled at the wire, and Jessie's feet popped loose.

"Go, go," he said.

Eighty-three put Jessie on her feet. But instead she dropped down again to help Sixty-one. He batted her hands away.

"You have to go," he said. "I'll be right behind you."

Eighty-three held his eyes for a moment. He nodded, and she grabbed Jessie's hand and started pulling her again to run.

Jessie looked back once as she was running away and could make out Sixty-one still struggling with the wire around his feet.

They ran half the block but then Jessie skidded to a stop. Up ahead at the subway station entrance she could see a crowd of Numbered gathered at the top of the stairs. Packed in tightly, none of them stood on the sidewalk.

Eighty-three looked back as she kept running.

"Damn it, Jessie, come on! We're almost there!"

Jessie broke into a run again. She crossed Lexington and fell into **the crowd on the top step**, gasping. Eighty-three grabbed her shoulders and turned her around. She let out a sigh of relief.

"What?"

"You're back to green."

"What about Sixty-one?" Jessie said.

Eighty-three and Jessie pushed their way back to the front of the crowd.

He wasn't in sight.

"He's got to get back to us," she said.

Jessie looked up at her and bit her lip nervously.

"Come on, come on, come on, come on," Eighty-three chanted.

"How far behind you was he?" someone asked.

Eighty-three just shook her head and kept watching. All of the Numbered stared across 51st Street, tense and waiting.

A figure finally appeared around the corner of the building across Lexington Avenue.

The crowd let out a muffled cheer.

Sixty-one was struggling to move quickly. Something was seriously wrong with his foot.

Jessie shuffled her feet nervously.

He was about fifty yards off. He waved a bit and smiled.

Eighty-three let out a relieved sigh.

Sixty-one hobbled another few steps but then suddenly grasped his head and screamed. He stumbled and fell to the ground writhing on the sidewalk.

Jessie saw the light at the back of his head had turned red.

"No!" Eighty-three screamed and sprinted away from everyone toward him. After the first two steps, her light had already started blinking yellow again.

Another of the Numbered took off running after her. His light switched to yellow too.

Jessie stepped forward too, starting to run, but someone grabbed her from behind. She kicked and screamed to be let go, but her arms were held like a vise and she was lifted off the ground.

Eighty-three made it to Sixty-one first, and the other Numbered joined her right after. They grabbed Sixty-one under the arms and started dragging him back to the group. His screaming had died down, but he was still moaning and whipping his head around.

As they got closer, the person holding onto her let her go. Jessie dropped down but stayed put.

The Numbered opened up to let them drag Sixty-one down onto the stairs. They laid him down gently. He wasn't moving, and Jessie pushed through the mass of people for a better look.

"Light!" Eighty-three yelled.

Jessie pulled the small lantern out of her pocket and snapped it open. She tried to light it with the flint, but her hands were shaking too much.

Eighty-three snatched the lantern out of her hand and lit it with one flick. The flame jumped to life and she put it close to Sixty-one.

Jessie cringed.

His face from his nose down was covered in blood. It had poured across his mouth and down the front of his shirt. There were smears of it across his head to where he had been pressing his hands against his skull.

Eighty-three checked his pulse and then pulled each eyelid open, putting the lantern close.

Eighty-three sat back on her legs and sighed.

"Okay, let's get him into bed. You two, carry him down to the cart."

The two men she pointed at started gently picking up Sixty-one.

"And you," Eighty-three said, pointing at Jessie. "You sit up with him all night and make sure he doesn't die."

She looked down at the blood on her hands, wiped it off on her trousers, and then stood and pushed her way down the stairs leaving Jessie alone in the Numbered crowd. Not a soul looked at her as they followed Eighty-three back down into the darkness.

CHAPTER ELEVEN

Analyzing the Scene

A STORY EVENT is an active change of life value for one or more characters as a result of conflict (one character's desires clash with another's).

A WORKING SCENE contains at least one Story Event. To determine a Scene's Story Event, answer the following four questions:

1. What are the characters doing?

Jessie, Eighty-three, and Sixty-one are running through the city to get back to the safety of the subways.

2. What is the essential action of what the characters are doing in this scene?

They are trying to avoid pain.

3. What life value has changed for one or more of the characters in the scene?

They face imminent pain.

4. Which life value should I highlight on my Story Grid Spreadsheet?

Danger to Safety/Punishment

HOW THE SCENE ABIDES BY THE FIVE COMMANDMENTS OF STORYTELLING

Inciting Incident: Eighty-three tells them where to go.

Progressive Complication: Jessie gets free of the razor wire but Sixty-one is still stuck.

Crisis: Best bad choice. Jessie and Eighty-three can leave Sixty-one behind and they'll make it safely, but he might not *or* they stay and help him and then none of them might make it.

Climax: Jessie decides to go with Eighty-three and leave Sixty-one behind.

Resolution: Sixty-one almost dies.

NOTES:

This scene represents the third in a sequence of scenes called 'Running Away to Reluctant Engagement.' It will culminate in scene twelve as the crisis of the beginning hook of the story.

CHAPTER TWELVE

Light filtered in from the common room as **the Numbered** shuffled around getting ready for their lines. They were pulling on their protective pants and shirts, lacing up their boots, and drinking the last dregs of coffee before facing the day.

Jessie sat on the floor, her head resting on the side of **Sixty-one**'s cot. His chest rose and fell slowly. The bowl of water on the floor had long since chilled, a copper-colored rag lying next to it.

She'd cleaned up the blood from his face, and with the help of **Forty-seven**, replaced his bloody shirt with his cleanest spare they could find.

It was almost like the previous night hadn't happened.

The room emptied except for the two of them. As the hum of the motion from the common room filtered in, the single light bulb hanging from the ceiling cast cot-sized shadows across the floor, like headstones in the cemetery across the river.

Jessie and Sixty-one's chests rose and fell.

Minutes passed.

Sixty-one's eyes popped open and darted around the room. His hands came out from underneath his thin sheet, felt around his head and then moved to the back of his skull. He let out a long sigh.

He looked down at Jessie and nudged her.

She jerked awake and sat up.

"Hey, kid," he said, "get me some water?"

Jessie nodded and jumped to her feet, scurrying to the bucket at the back of the room. She ladled water into a small, crinkled plastic cup and brought it back to him.

Sixty-one sat up and swung his legs over the side of the cot. He took the cup from Jessie and drained it. He held it out to her, and she hurried back to the bucket.

He drained it again.

They sat in silence.

"I'm sorry," Jessie muttered.

He shook his head. "Not me you should be apologizing to."

"You're the one who got hurt."

"I did, yeah, but it ain't the first time. Probably won't be the last neither."

He sighed and rubbed his face with his calloused, cracked hand. "I was kind of hoping it would be, though."

"Why would you want that?" she asked.

He laughed. "There's not a lot of Numbered my age, dear."

"Were you **a field hand?**"

He shook his head. "I've been just about everything. But my last stop before the Numbered was Aeta."

"You were there? At the Capital?"

"Mmhmm," he said nodding.

"What was it like?" Sixty-one's eyes glazed over a bit as he stared off at the wall. "It was wonderful. Cool and sunny."

"What'd you do for them?"

"Nothing glamorous. Had a knack for wiring, so they brought me in to help with the early days of the Preparings. They kept me on to knock sense into the players."

"What do you mean?"

"Well, the young field hands they bring in think because they were decent in the city and scored high on some test that they'll come right in and soar to the top. That they'll win the next Threshing for **the**

Faction all by themselves. Well it was my job to disabuse them of that idea."

"You'd hurt them?"

"Sure, but it was for their own good. I'd plug in with them and knock 'em on their asses, show them the dark arenas outside the safety of the grid. Field hand stuff is hard work, but it's just that. Work. Like digging ditches. You can be really good at it, but it's still just digging ditches. When you're going for the Threshing, though, it's a whole new ballgame. The firewalls are gone. Things can go south pretty quick. You wire up the wrong thing at the wrong time and," Sixty-one snapped his fingers, "you're out."

"Out?"

He cocked his head at Jessie and took a deep breath.

"What do you think happened to me last night? When my light turned red."

Jessie shrugged.

"Know what happens if you get zapped on the grid?"

"Well yeah, everyone does."

"Right, you wander where you're not supposed to be, and you get a little zap."

"But that's the grid. And it doesn't kill you. It's just supposed to scare you."

"It's different for **the Coders** at the Preparing. They're running at the edges of the grid. You get zapped there, and it's lights out. Game over. No coming back from it. Nothing compares to it on the city grid. Sure, every once in a while, someone tries to wander to areas they're not supposed to be, and they get zapped, but for the most part city folk stay where city folk belong. They do their field work for their credits and keep at it. It's coded up real well that way. The more field work you do, the more credits you find, the more your brain gets juiced with pleasure, and the more you want to work. Works real well. Keeps everybody docile and doing their work. Sure some people's brains get a little fried on it, but that don't affect the Faction too much.

"It's even more of a rush as a Coder. Now, mind you, I never got past the grunt stage, but wiring against other Factions," Sixty-one licked his lips and wiped a few beads of sweat off his forehead, "well, it felt good. Anytime you fried another Coder; it's hard to describe just how good it felt. Makes any pleasure in this world seem dull and flat."

He paused.

"Still miss it from time to time. Nothing like it in this world," he gestured around him.

"So you trained recruits at the Preparing?" she said.

"Mmhmm," he said nodding, "got them up to speed on wiring. Smacked their heads a bit when they got it wrong."

"What do you mean?"

"Well, last night I just about made it back. Right? Then my light turned red? Well what happened to me was a minor smack on the head. Pretty much the same code they use for the Preparing."

"But you almost died."

"Yep, and if I'd laid out there a few seconds longer probably would have."

"And you did that to other people?"

"Sure. It's how our Faction wins the Threshing. Trust me. You don't want to live in a losing Faction. Believe you me. So the city folk does the field work. And the sum total of credits from all of those field hands are tallied up. Depending on how many, **the Reapers** award coding time at the Preparing. Now the Coders at the Preparing gotta learn how to wire up against the other Factions, or we all suffer. The more time they have to get ready, the better they get. It ain't a pretty game. We always lose Coders in the run-up to the Threshing and then we got to build back up quick with newbies. Find new talent to replace the washouts and get them up to speed. Fast. It might not seem like it at your age, but four years goes by like that." Sixty-one snapped his fingers.

"And you killed Coders that didn't learn fast enough?"

"Nah, never killed nobody. Just, you know, scrambled their brains a bit." He laughed again.

"So you were there for the last Preparing?" Jessie asked.

Sixty-one nodded, his eyes still unfocused.

"Yep."

"Do you remember any of the recruits you worked with?"

"Sure," he said.

"Do you remember one named **Randy**?"

Sixty-one's eyes sharpened, and he looked at Jessie as if it was the first time he noticed she was there. He waited for a moment staring at her and then shrugged.

"What time is it?" he said, looking around. "Where is everybody?"

Jessie pulled on his arm.

"Please tell me. Do you remember him?"

Sixty-one shook her off his arm and stood.

"Nuff war stories for today. Don't matter anyway. I'm Numbered now and don't see me ever going back. Come on," he said walking away, "let's get going. We got chores to do. Only getting hotter out there."

CHAPTER TWELVE

Analyzing the Scene

A STORY EVENT is an active change of life value for one or more characters as a result of conflict (one character's desires clash with another's).

A WORKING SCENE contains at least one Story Event. To determine a Scene's Story Event, answer the following four questions:

1. What are the characters doing?

Jessie is sitting with Sixty-one while he wakes up. They discuss Sixty-one's past in Aeta.

2. What is the essential action of what the characters are doing in this scene?

Jessie wants to find out if Sixty-one knows anything about Randy.

3. What life value has changed for one or more of the characters in the scene?

Jessie is worried that she was responsible for permanent damage to Sixty-one and gains relief.

4. Which life value should I highlight on my Story Grid Spreadsheet?

Despair to Hope.

HOW THE SCENE ABIDES BY THE FIVE COMMANDMENTS OF STORYTELLING

Inciting Incident: Sixty-one wakes up.

Progressive Complication: Sixty-one says that he was in Aeta for the last Preparing.

Crisis: Irreconcilable goods. Jessie can keep letting Sixty-one ramble *or* she can try to get him to tell her about Randy.

Climax: Jessie tries to get him to tell her about Randy.

Resolution: Sixty-one refuses to talk about Randy and gets up to start the chores for the day.

NOTES:

This scene represents the last in a sequence of scenes called 'Running Away to Reluctant Engagement.' Jessie is now reconsidering the best bad choice crisis choice she made about not going to Aeta earlier on in the story.

CHAPTER THIRTEEN

Jessie pulled up on the latch and put all her weight on the door, shoving it open. She stumbled through and quickly shut the door behind her.

Immediately, she started stripping off her suit. First, the goggles came off. She tossed them into the bin on the bookshelf. Next she stripped off her gloves and boots and then pulled off the long sleeve plastic shirt.

Her shirt underneath was drenched in sweat and stuck to her body. Sweat was pouring off her head and into her eyes. She wiped them hard with the palms of her hands.

She had taken too long on her chores and missed the cart ride back home. She'd had a long walk through the tunnels on her own as the reward. Already sweating from the heat while walking through the tunnel by herself in the dark with nothing but her lantern left her mentally drained.

Jessie turned into the common room. She stopped in her tracks when she saw everyone. **All of the Numbered** stared at her with disbelief and contempt. She could see **Eighty-three** on one of the beaten-up couches. Her spoon hovered over her bowl as she stared at Jessie.

The awkward waiting extended.

Finally, **Sixty-one** came out of the kitchen, saw Jessie, and smiled.

"Hey, kid! Hot one today, huh?"

He stepped forward and put a battered bottle in her hand filled with lukewarm water.

"Have a drink before you pass out."

Jessie looked at him and then back to the other Numbered who still sat in silence.

Sixty-one turned around.

"What are all you staring at? I'm the one that got scrambled. And it ain't like it was the first time."

Everyone seemed to relax at this. If Sixty-one could forgive the kid, maybe they should too.

"Come on, hon. **Let's get you something to eat.**"

He led Jessie into the kitchen where a big metal pot sat on a gas burner. Sixty-one lifted the lid and steam rolled out. He pushed a ladle in and poured the pale contents into a big tin mug. He grabbed a large crust of bread from a bowl on the counter and pushed both into Jessie's hands.

He ladled himself a large portion into a similar mug and then walked out of the kitchen. Jessie followed closely behind him.

They went toward the couch to sit with Eighty-three, and she scooted over to make room for them.

Jessie sucked back her water and then dug into her food. The Numbered's work was outrageously draining, but when it was over, the pleasure of the rest was ridiculously satisfying.

"So you okay?" someone asked Sixty-one.

"Course," he knocked on his head, "all the pieces are there. They've just been rattled around a bit."

"That was a close one, though," **a woman** said, cutting her eyes at Jessie. "I didn't think you were gonna make it."

Jessie put her eyes back on her food.

"Yeah, who'd we get to play the part of the crazy old coot around here if you got fried?" someone said.

The tension released, and the group laughed.

"Yeah, well you keep that in mind next time I'm running late on my chores," Sixty-one said.

"You got the easiest route of all of us!"

Sixty-one scoffed.

"Yeah, yeah. You like to say that, but no one seems to be in a hurry to switch with me."

The awkwardness had left the room as conversation picked up again. They shared stories of what they found in **the Elite's** apartments and trash throughout the day. Several pulled out small metal bottles and passed them around. They winced as they took sips.

The longer it went on, and the more they drank from the little bottles, the louder and rowdier everyone got.

One of the Numbered went over to the large cabinet in the corner and fiddled with some knobs. It crackled but then a bunch but tinny music began whining from speakers resting at the top of two shelves. Jessie didn't recognize any of it, but the other Numbered obviously did as several of them had already hopped up and started dancing.

Jessie kept quiet but let her eyes rove over the room as she ate. A few times when a group of the Numbered burst out laughing, or someone made a particular fool of themselves while dancing, she even smiled.

After a few hours, Sixty-one stumbled out of the dancing crowd giggling to himself over some joke no one else had heard and announced, "Time for bed!"

He leaned down and kissed Jessie on the top of her head twice. Then he turned, promptly tripped on his own feet and sprawled on the floor.

Everyone roared with laughter.

He laughed at himself as he got back to his feet, steadied himself, and started walking and weaving back to the cot room.

Eighty-three scooted closer to Jessie.

"You doing okay?" she said.

Jessie nodded, keeping her eyes down. She wiped a tear away.

Eighty-three wrapped her arm around Jessie and pulled her close.

A few of the other Numbered started making their way back to bed.

Several came over and patted Jessie on the back before heading to their beds.

Before long, it was down to Eighty-three, Jessie, and just a few other stragglers in the common room.

Jessie cried harder.

"What is it?" Eighty-three asked.

Jessie sniffed and wiped her nose against her shirt.

"Why are they being so nice to me?"

Eighty-three didn't answer for a minute but then sighed.

"I suppose they all remember what it was like their first few weeks as a Numbered. Even if they didn't run away—most of them don't have any place to go anyway—they know that feeling. It's hard to forget."

Eighty-three continued, "What else can we do? We're all stuck here together. None of us want to be here, but we can't leave. We might as well take care of each other.

"Plus, you're a pretty cute little girl, and it's been a long time since any of them have been around kids. It makes us feel a little more human to have you here, I think. Maybe even like a family."

Jessie cried for a few more minutes before quieting down. She wiped the last of the tears away and rubbed her eyes. Jessie nodded and said, "When I was sitting with Sixty-one this morning after he woke up, he was telling me about his time in Aeta."

Eighty-three rolled her eyes at this.

"What?" Jessie said.

"Look, he's a sweetheart. We all love him. But, honey, he's crazy. He's not joking when he says last night wasn't the first time he's been scrambled."

"So he never helped with the Preparing?"

Eighty-three shrugged. "Hard to say. I mean, sometimes it seems like his stories could be true, but most of what he says is nonsense. I don't think he even realizes he's lying half the time, but the stories he's told range from him fighting off **a dozen Faction guards** with a screwdriver and his love affairs with the most beautiful **Prefects** of the Faction to losing his arm in a mining accident and getting it reattached. Sometimes when you get scrambled the way he has, and you've spent so long plugged in..." Eighty-three paused, "it's just hard to tease apart reality from everything else that's been fed into your brain."

"Oh," Jessie said, unable to hide her disappointment.

"Don't put too much stock in anything he's said."

"Okay."

"Now, it's time for me to get some sleep."

"Okay," Jessie stood and went to follow after her.

"What are you doing?" Eighty-three said, a smile playing at the corner of her mouth.

"What?"

"Oh, I must have forgotten to mention the rule." Her smile grew bigger.

Jessie's eyes narrowed.

"Whoever's last with their chores has to do the dishes." Jessie looked around at the cups, mugs, and bowls strewn across the common room.

. Eighty-three laughed and then headed back to her cot.

"Have fun with that!"

CHAPTER THIRTEEN

Analyzing the Scene

A STORY EVENT is an active change of life value for one or more characters as a result of conflict (one character's desires clash with another's).

A WORKING SCENE contains at least one Story Event. To determine a Scene's Story Event, answer the following four questions:

1. What are the characters doing?

Jessie and the other Numbered are finishing out the day together after doing their chores. They are eating and enjoying music and each other's company.

2. What is the essential action of what the characters are doing in this scene?

Bonding together as a family.

3. What life value has changed for one or more of the characters in the scene?

Jessie moves from being an outcast to being accepted.

4. Which life value should I highlight on my Story Grid Spreadsheet?

Outcast to Accepted.

HOW THE SCENE ABIDES BY THE FIVE COMMANDMENTS OF STORYTELLING

Inciting Incident: Jessie is ostracized when she returns home late.

Progressive Complication: Everyone stares at her, waiting to see if they should still be upset.

Crisis: Two irreconcilable goods. Does Sixty-one accept her or reject her?

Climax: Sixty-one accepts her back into the family.

Resolution: They all enjoy the evening together as a family.

CHAPTER FOURTEEN

Jessie woke up but kept her eyes closed. She lay listening to the rustle of the white suits being pulled on around her. She listened to the banter floating in from the common room as they drank their coffee and readied for the lines of the day.

Jessie took a deep breath through her nose and slowly let it out as a smile played at the corner of her mouth.

She sat up on her cot and rubbed the sleep out of her eyes before bending over and pulling her suit and boots out from underneath her cot. She stood, pulled on her pants and shirt, rolled up the cuffs and shoved her feet into the mismatched boots.

When she entered the common room, **several of the Numbered** greeted her, and **Sixty-one** put a mug in her hands. She sat and sipped, waiting for everyone to start heading out for the cart ride to their drop-off points.

Jessie heard two light taps and looked around for the source of the noise. Several others did as well.

Quiet settled over the Numbered.

The taps came through again, this time clearly from the door.

They looked around at each other, unsure of what to do. Finally,

Eighty-three moved toward the door, but before she could get there, a heavy thud hit the exterior. A sharp crack came from the door frame.

Everyone froze.

A few seconds later, another heavy thud hit the door, and this time it flew open, splinters bursting as the wall blew out.

Immediately **three figures** stepped quickly into the common room. They were in the full matte grey body armor of the crows.

They spread out around the room with their weapons pointed at the Numbered. Everyone backed up in the room leaving as much space as possible between them and the guns.

A few seconds passed before **Mayor Charles** came through the door. His hat was pushed down low over his eyes, and his hands clutched a tablet in front of him. **Two more guards** followed him in.

Jessie shrank down, trying to avoid his gaze.

Charles looked briefly at them and then back down at the tablet. He opened his mouth to speak, but his voice cracked on the first word. He cleared his throat and spoke again.

"I need to speak with Numbered Eighty-three. Are you here?"

Eighty-three stood from the couch across from Jessie and pushed her way to the front. He held her eyes for a long moment before looking back down at the tablet in his hands.

"Are you Eighty-three?"

She nodded, her eyes on the ground.

"Okay, I have been sent here to discuss recent breaches in the Numbered code of conduct. We can do it here, or—" he glanced around him.

"Here is fine," Eighty-three said.

"Okay, yes. We can just do it here."

Charles cleared his throat again and tapped the tablet screen with his middle finger.

"Now, recite your role as head Numbered of Batch 244, please."

"To manage the Numbered, distribute chores and work lines, and, maintain the order of my batch."

As she spoke, Charles ran his finger down the display.

"Yes, okay. Almost word-for-word. And for this extra responsibility, what is it that you get in return from **the Faction?**"

"A shorter sentence."

"Yes. For each year of head of batch service, you get a year off your days as a Numbered. Is that correct?"

Eighty-three nodded.

"I need audible answers."

"Yes, sir."

"Yes, sir, to the years off your sentence?"

"Yes."

Charles nodded and looked back down at the tablet. He tapped it a few more times and then began reading.

"The Faction enforcement has received multiple reports of Numbered infractions. Charges include the following. Trespassing outside of prescribed hours. Trespassing outside of allowed boundaries. Trespassing in Elite living quarters. Assault on various Faction members. Theft. Destruction of Faction property. Reports have been filed by dozens of **field hands** and **Elites** including close **relatives of a Numbered.**"

Charles looked up at Eighty-three and then back down at his tablet.

"As a Numbered batch manager, you are solely responsible for the conduct of your assigned array. What say you to these charges?"

Eighty-three stayed silent.

"I'm going to need an answer."

"It's true."

"And who among your batch was responsible for this breach of conduct?"

Jessie sat forward and started to stand, but the Numbered beside her grabbed her arm and held her down. Jessie shot him a look, but he just shook his head at her.

Charles had noticed the movement, though. He locked eyes briefly with Jessie before looking back to Eighty-three.

He moved close to her and whispered something softly. She shook her head, no. Charles's jaw tightened. Two of the guards turned toward Charles, but he ignored them.

Again, Charles whispered something. Eighty-three shook her head no again.

Charles stepped back from her.

"It was me," Jessie pulled away from her protector. "I was working the lines with a couple of others, and I lost track of time. Before we knew it, it was dusk, and our lights had turned yellow. We were in a hurry to get back before we turned red and had to cut straight across town."

"That seems odd," Charles said, looking again at Jessie. "I'm no expert on this, but from what I've been led to understand, you get warning alerts as the dusk is setting that would have let you know you were getting close to time. Are you saying your plugs are malfunctioning?"

"No, sir."

"Then how did this happen?"

"I was careless, sir."

"Hmm," he said as he turned away from Jessie and gave his attention back to Eighty-three. He tapped a few more times on the tablet. When he looked back up, it seemed the lines in his face had deepened. He cleared his throat again.

"The Faction enforcement cannot let such an egregious breach of Numbered regulations stand without discipline. And as the batch head and perpetrator of said breach, you will be held personally responsible."

"I understand time will be added to my sentence. I accept that."

Jessie cringed at this.

Charles's face hardened. He met Eighty-three's eyes.

"Unfortunately, that is not what the Faction Enforcement has decided."

Eighty-three looked up at him for the first time. "That's the standard punishment."

"Yes, it is. Good on you for being so attuned to the structure of our society. However, **I've decided to override the standards of punishment.** I will not add any time to your sentence."

Eighty-three looked up, confused.

"Rather, your punishment is to do your normal line of chores at your normal time. Only, you are not to wear any protective clothing other than your goggles. Seeing is the indispensable sense, after all."

Several of the Numbered gasped as shock rippled through them all. A few even shouted at Charles.

At this Jessie ripped her arm out the Numbered's grasp and stood.

"No!" she yelled. "It was my fault!"

Mayor Charles gave her a sad look. Eighty-three turned and shook her head to quiet her, but Jessie ignored it.

"I ran out! She had to—"

Jessie was cut off as Sixty-one's hand clamped over her mouth and an arm wrapped around her chest. Jessie struggled against Sixty-one, kicking out at his shins and squirming violently.

Charles looked back at Eighty-three. "The sentence will be carried out today. These guards here will accompany you to make sure you are not aided in any way by your fellow Numbered here. I will return this evening to ensure that the punishment was enforced."

With this, Charles clutched the tablet to his chest, pulled his hat down again, and turned toward the door. Two of the guards followed him out, but the other three stayed behind.

Eighty-three waited a moment, chewing on her lip, and then stripped off her protective pants and shirt. She walked to the door and retrieved her goggles, but she didn't look back as she went out. The Faction guards followed her.

CHAPTER FOURTEEN

Analyzing the Scene

A STORY EVENT is an active change of life value for one or more characters as a result of conflict (one character's desires clash with another's).

A WORKING SCENE contains at least one Story Event. To determine a Scene's Story Event, answer the following four questions:

1. What are the characters doing?

Mayor Charles and the faction guards interrupt the morning preparations of the Numbered. They punish Eighty-three for all the trouble Jessie caused by running away.

2. What is the essential action of what the characters are doing in this scene?

Mayor Charles wishes to coerce Jessie to comply with his wishes.

3. What life value has changed for one or more of the characters in the scene?

Jessie moves from being safely past her mistake of running away to punishment that severely hurts another person.

4. Which life value should I highlight on my Story Grid Spreadsheet?

Relieved to Guilty

HOW THE SCENE ABIDES BY THE FIVE COMMANDMENTS OF STORYTELLING

Inciting Incident: The door is caved in by Mayor Charles and the faction guards.

Progressive Complication: The punishment is revealed to be Eighty-three doing her chores without protective gear.

Crisis: Best bad choice. Eighty-three can let Jessie take the punishment *or* Eighty-three can accept it herself.

Climax: Eighty-three accepts the punishment.

Resolution: Eighty-three strips off her protective gear and leaves with the guards.

CHAPTER FIFTEEN

Every exposed part of her body was bright red. The worst was her head, where blisters were already pushing up under the skin. All of it glistened under the ointment **Jessie** and **Sixty-one** gingerly applied on top of **Eighty-three**'s sizzling flesh.

She moaned and squirmed and twisted as they eased it on.

Now Jessie sat by her cot, gently holding her hand as Eighty-three slept fitfully. She could hear the others talking quietly in the common room over dinner. Gone was the boisterous conversation and laughing.

None of **the Numbered** had ever seen this kind of punishment before, and if any of them had any doubts about the power of the climate before, there were none now.

"Why are you crying, hon?" Sixty-one asked.

"This is my fault. All of it. If I hadn't run away—"

"Stop that," Sixty-one said, anger creeping into his voice. "This ain't your fault. It ain't her fault. It's **the Faction**. They did this to her."

"But—"

"Sure, if you hadn't run off maybe this wouldn't have happened. But these are the same people who Shamed a little girl. Same people who shoved these damn plugs into our skulls. Who keep us from the grid and living like all the others. Locked down underground like rats. There's nothing you could have done. You didn't know."

Jessie squeezed her eyes shut, forcing more tears down her cheeks. Regret roiled over her.

"It's them. You keep that fire in your belly for **them**. Not at yourself. Keep stoking that fire till it's burning white-hot. Maybe one day you'll get a chance to unleash hell on them. You'll need that fire to give them no mercy. Hide it in your heart, but never forget they are the evil—"

"Evil?"

Jessie and Sixty-one looked up quickly at the door to the common room. **Mayor Charles** stood in the doorway.

"Who's evil?"

Sixty-one looked at the ground, but Jessie held her eyes on the mayor as he stepped through the doorway. He sat down on a cot just a few feet away.

"I'd like an answer, please."

Sixty-one said nothing.

"Let's see," he consulted his tablet. "Sixty-one in the Six Line batch, is it? Who do we think is evil today? Is it the monsters you claim attack you throughout the city? Or the grid that tries to eat babies' brains at night?"

"You know who I was talking about."

"Surely not the Faction. Because we at the Faction believe only in protecting our citizens and—"

"Cruelty to children?" Sixty-one said.

Jessie shot him a look.

"Cruelty? How so?"

"You take a little girl," he said gesturing to Jessie, "Shame her, plug her up, send her down her to work the lines with us. That's not cruel?" Charles looked around the room as if he couldn't find someone.

"Who are we talking about here?" Sixty-one looked at Charles as if he were crazy and then looked over at Jessie.

"Her?" Charles asked. "Surely you're not talking about her."

"Course I am. She's a Numbered. She's down here with us. The only child. And—"

Charles barked out a laugh. Sixty-one looked at him, confused.

"She's nothing like you, Sixty-one. Sure, she's a Numbered. For now. But she most assuredly is nothing...nothing...like you!" Charles' contempt was palpable.

Silence hung in the air as Sixty-one looked directly at the mayor, his cautiousness gone as he seemed to wonder if he wasn't the crazy one after all.

"She's here with us, ain't she? Working the lines. She's been Shamed and plugged and sentenced."

"Well, that is factually correct. Sure. But Jessie is in no way a Numbered. That's absolutely, unequivocally untrue."

"How you figure?"

The room had now filled with the curious. To have the mayor come down into their depths one time was remarkable. To have him venture below twice made no sense at all.

Charles paused and looked at Jessie, his head cocked to the side.

"They don't know? You didn't tell them," he smiled, asking a question he already knew the answer to.

Jessie shook her head.

"What's he getting on about?" Sixty-one asked her.

Charles stood and called out.

"All of you, come on in here. The more the merrier. Don't be shy. And cart over the delightful Eighty-three too. She especially needs to hear this!"

The last few standing near the doorway pushed themselves inside the cot room.

"That's right. Come on in. All of you. I've got something you need to hear."

Charles waited patiently as all of the Numbered filed in. They took their places along the wall staying as far from the mayor as possible.

"Everyone cozy? Marvelous...now this girl," he said pointing at Jessie, "is not like the rest of you. No indeed. Not in any way, shape, or form. She has willfully chosen to be here."

The crowd didn't understand how that was possible.

"You see she was caught hacking into and stealing from **the Elites** while they were connected. Quite ingeniously too. So when I caught her, and we always do catch them, I offered her a place in Aeta for the Preparing. You know what that means. Right? She'd be living among the highest of **the Prefects** in Aeta while serving her Faction and providing a better life for **her own family.** And working for a better life for all of you too."

"Why's she here then?" Sixty-one interrupted.

"Yes, I'm getting to that. Jessie here, and that is her name, refused the honor. Scared, I guess. Afraid to serve her Faction and keep us all alive by winning the next Threshing."

No one spoke. Charles held them captive with his story.

"What choice did I have? I had to convince her that she was making a mistake. Didn't I?"

The Numbered nodded.

"So yes, I sentenced her to the Shaming, and she's been plugged like the rest of you, and she works the lines with you, but I can assure you that she is not a Numbered. You see, there is one difference between her and the rest of you."

He paused for several seconds.

"**This girl can leave whenever she would like.** She came here by her own petulant choice when I offered her a way out. Even when she was Shamed, I offered her a way out. Instead, she put you all at risk when she stupidly tried to escape. She's the reason Eighty-three looks like that, not me! And all she had to do at any time was agree to go to Aeta and she'd be unplugged, free, and promoted. Eating delicious food and doing what she was meant to do from birth! Code!"

As the mayor spoke, Jessie could feel the air in the room shift. She glanced out of the corner of her eyes to the Numbered in the room. At some point their eyes moved away from him. Now they were on her.

"So while she may sleep and eat and work alongside you, she's just slumming it. Trying this little outfit of yours on for size until she's good and ready to assume her spot among the Elite. There's a word for that kind of thing. Isn't there Sixty-one?"

Charles looked down at her.

"She can leave anytime she wants."

With that, Charles made for the door, **his guards** lockstep behind him.

Jessie's eyes focused on a tiny crack on the floor.

"Is that true?" Sixty-one asked. "Look at me!"

She owed him that.

When she did, his face was red with rage. He was shaking.

"Tell me!" he screamed at her.

Jessie nodded.

He let out a growl and kicked the cot in front of him, sending it skittering across the floor. He stalked out of the room and the noise grew. The other Numbered all started shouting at the same time. Some of them to each other, and some directly at her.

After a few moments, Jessie shifted her eyes to where Eighty-three lay. They locked eyes. Tears were streaming down her blistered and cracked face.

CHAPTER FIFTEEN

Analyzing the Scene

A STORY EVENT is an active change of life value for one or more characters as a result of conflict (one character's desires clash with another's).

A WORKING SCENE contains at least one Story Event. To determine a Scene's Story Event, answer the following four questions:

1. What are the characters doing?

Jessie and Sixty-one are caring for Eighty-three after her day in the climate. Mayor Charles comes in and lets out Jessie's secret – that she can leave anytime she wants.

2. What is the essential action of what the characters are doing in this scene?

Mayor Charles is trying to force Jessie to go to Aeta.

3. What life value has changed for one or more of the characters in the scene?

Jessie goes from feeling guilty but accepted by Sixty-one and the other Numbered to being outcast by them.

4. Which life value should I highlight on my Story Grid Spreadsheet?

Accepted to Outcast.

HOW THE SCENE ABIDES BY THE FIVE COMMANDMENTS OF STORYTELLING

Inciting Incident: Mayor Charles enters while Sixty-one is ranting against the Faction.

Progressive Complication: Mayor Charles announces that Jessie can leave the Numbered whenever she wants.

Crisis: Best bad choice. Jessie can admit that Mayor Charles is telling the truth *or* she can deny it.

Climax: Jessie admits that Mayor Charles is telling the truth.

Resolution: Sixty-one and the rest of the Numbered are enraged and Eighty-three is hurt.

NOTES:

Jessie's ability to run away from her destiny is now exhausted. She can no longer refuse the challenge put in front of her, as she's been alienated from the very last social class in the city. This scene represents the climax of the beginning hook of the story, 'Agreeing to fight.' The resolution, Jessie's acceptance of a 'fix it and forget it mission' resolves the beginning hook and is off-stage.

THE SEVERING

CHAPTER SIXTEEN

The craft shook violently as the wind whipped around the side of the transport. Jessie squeezed her eyes shut. Her right hand gripped the armrest until her knuckles shown a pale white. Her left hand was in her pocket, her thumb rubbing furiously at the domino.

She had avoided looking out of the windows since liftoff. She'd never been further off the ground than the high rises and, even though she had seen the transports coming and going in the distance, she'd never understood how they stayed in the air.

The turbulence settled. After a few seconds, she relaxed her grip and opened her eyes but kept them locked onto the seatback in front of her.

After a breath, she glanced to her right and across the empty row. Then she looked over her shoulder. All of the seats were empty except for one.

In the very back a **hawk-faced boy** with slicked-back hair sat calmly in his seat with his eyes glued to the tablet in his hands.

With a smirk on his face, he glanced up at her, and Jessie quickly turned away.

She heard the snap of his seatbelt unbuckling moments before he appeared in the aisle. He sat down across from her and snapped the seat belt around his waist. She glanced over at him. He wore the tight-fitting greys that **legacy Faction Elites** tended to wear. He also had a flat green sickle pin attached to his chest.

As soon as he'd secured himself, the craft started shaking again. Jessie squeezed her eyes shut as her hand returned to her pocket.

"First time flying?" he asked.

She nodded and forced her eyes back open so as not to seem like such a baby.

The boy laughed.

"You'll get used to it."

He checked his watch.

"We'll be there soon. It's almost over. My name is Az."

"Jessie," she said through clenched teeth.

The craft settled again, and Jessie let out a long breath.

"So you've never been to the Stack before?"

Jessie looked at him, her eyebrows raised.

"The Stack?"

"Yeah, well, it's the city of Aeta, Capital of the Americas Faction. But everyone calls it the Stack."

"Why?"

"It's where everything is. The grid code runs from there. All of the electricity to the major cities comes from Aeta. All of the coding and training. It all happens in the Stack."

"You've been there before?"

The boy laughed.

"Just about my entire life," he said. "My father is **Prefect Alacar**. He is the top AGI programmer for the Faction and reports directly to **President Marcus**. He's currently in Chicago overseeing a major upgrade to the grid infrastructure there. That's where I'm returning from."

"You live in the cap—in the Stack?"

He nodded. Jessie tensed again when the transport shuddered.

"So what's your story?" he asked.

"What do you mean?"

"At first I thought you were **a Numbered**, what with the shaved head and all, but that would mean you'd be in the cargo hold. The thing is, until I sat down, I thought you were a boy."

Jessie ran her hand over her scalp.

"So what happened?" he asked.

Jessie looked at Az, unsure of what to say. **Mark** and **Libby**, let alone **her father** and **mother**, always told her to keep her mouth shut—even from **other kids.** It only took one person with loose lips for everything to unravel. How much did she know about this kid? And his dad worked for the Faction. That couldn't be good.

Jessie shrugged.

"Where are you from?" Az asked.

"New York."

"The city?"

Jessie nodded.

"I hear **Mayor Charles** is a real hard ass. He do that to you?"

Az motioned to her head.

Jessie nodded.

"Sent you to the Numbered then?"

Jessie nodded again.

Az whistled through his teeth.

"I'm surprised you didn't get eaten. The Numbered in the cities are savages. Cannibals I'm told. So hungry they eat their dead."

He paused for a beat, waiting for a reaction, which was not forthcoming.

"What's waiting for you in the Stack?"

"The Preparing."

Az turned his head to look directly at Jessie. He studied her for a moment, his eyes narrowed.

"Oh yeah?" he laughed. "It's a little late for that. What genius recruited you?"

"Charles."

Az became very still, but Jessie didn't notice. She kept her eyes glued directly ahead of her. She was taking deep, slow breaths.

"You're a little young. Aren't you?"

Jessie shrugged.

"You know you're crazy late. Right? We started our training six months ago. Nobody's ever dropped in at this stage. **The last one** was three months ago. What kept you?"

Jessie gestured toward her head.

"What? You were with the Numbered. So?"

"Charles Shamed me and sent me to the Numbered because I refused the tap." No reason not to tell him something he probably already knew.

"What do you mean?"

Jessie shrugged.

Az opened his mouth but then stopped, thinking for a moment.

"I'm sure there's a line of **a hundred other recruits** who were dying to get tapped. Probably recruits from **better families** and actually of age. Why you?"

Again, Jessie shrugged.

"You don't seem to know much about how you ended up here or why you refused the only way a person like you...no offense...could make it to **lifetime Elite.**"

"I just wanted to stay home."

"In New York? It's a cesspool."

"It's not so bad. If you know the cracks."

Az didn't say anything else, but his jaw was working as he stared at Jessie, trying to figure out why she was here, now, on this transport and why the powers that be diverted his plane to pick her up. He opened his mouth to ask the next question but was cut off when the transport banked hard starboard.

Jessie screamed and looked toward Az. Behind him she saw something streak past the window as the pilots yelled and cursed from the front of the plane. She could feel herself rise out of her seat as they all became momentarily weightless.

The transport nosed toward the ground, and they started spiraling. Jessie hung from her restraints and smacked her head against something above her. She forced her head toward Az and immediately wished she hadn't.

Fear clung to his face, and his eyes were squeezed shut. He was more terrified than she was.

And just as quickly as it had started, everything stopped. The transport leveled out, and everything was calm.

Jessie looked around wildly and could see they weren't far above actual treetops, even more beautiful than the ones in the grid. The plane now held steady and straight as she heard relieved and angry chatter from the front.

She glanced at Az. He had opened his eyes and was trying to look relaxed, though sweat clung in little droplets to his brow and upper lip.

"What happened? What was that? I saw something fly by the window."

"The Scavengers."

"What'd they do?"

"Must have shot at us. They're always cobbling together stuff that was abandoned during the Burning. Their attacks have been ramping up again. They always do in the year of the Threshing. They'll do anything to get acknowledgment on the news nets. They know they can't make it into the Stack, so they go after the transports."

He shook his head, disgusted.

"They're like cockroaches. They scurry around avoiding the light, live off the garbage of us higher life forms, and, worst of all, refuse to plug in. Parasites."

A few seconds later, the ship slowed considerably and started descending. Jessie watched the trees go by as they touched down lightly to the ground.

Az unbuckled his restraint and stood quickly, rushed into the front of the plane and ducked into the storage compartment. He came back a few minutes later dressed in fresh greys. Behind him, Jessie could see the two pilots whispering to each other and smirking.

Az motioned for Jessie to follow him.

The door at the front of the ship slid open, and Jessie glanced around Az to look out. Several of the Faction guards stood just outside the doorway on either side as Az began to leave.

"What about our bags?" Jessie asked.

Az looked at her, confused.

"The Numbered get those," he said. "They'll be in your room by the time you make it there."

"What about them?" Jessie said, motioning to the guards.

Az shook his head and motioned at her to follow him. As he stepped out onto the ramp, the guards snapped to attention. He nodded to them as he passed while Jessie hurried to keep up, her eyes glued to the back of his feet.

Just as she stepped out of the hangar and into the hallway, Az turned abruptly. Jessie skidded to a halt, almost running into him. Az slid up against the wall and motioned for her to join him.

"Look, Jessie, it's obvious you don't know what you're getting into here. Once you step into Aeta and start training for the Severings, all bets are off. The only way out is by being flushed out, making it to the Threshing or winning the Threshing, which I think we can both agree isn't in the cards for you."

Jessie's eyes were wide, waiting for Az to continue.

"See that transport over there?" Az motioned across the hangar to a ship identical to the one they just arrived on.

Jessie nodded.

"It's taking off in just a few minutes. It's heading directly back to New York City. I could sneak you on board if you wanted. I've done it before. You'd have to hide out for a while once you get back, but in eight months, after the Threshing is over, nobody will care about you anymore."

Jessie stared at the transport, her hand back in her pocket.

"It's now or never, Jessie."

Jessie continued to stare at the transport, weighing the odds in her mind. Could she avoid Charles or would he track her down again? The Numbered probably wasn't a possibility a second time around. Running would be true, direct treason. The Threshing was not something any of the Faction members took lightly. Would the Rats even let her stay with them? What about her parents? Maybe she could convince her dad this time.

"Jessie?"

"Okay, yeah, let's do it," she said.

"What are you doing?"

Jessie jumped back. **A man dressed in grey** with a bright orange shield pin on his chest had appeared in front of them.

"Why are you still here?" he demanded.

Jessie's mouth was stuck open, but nothing came out.

"We're just looking around," Az said, stepping forward. He turned so the man could see the green pin on his own chest.

"She's never seen an Aeta transport before."

The man's eyes narrowed. "She's seen enough. Keep moving."

CHAPTER SIXTEEN

Analyzing the Scene

A STORY EVENT is an active change of life value for one or more characters as a result of conflict (one character's desires clash with another's).

A WORKING SCENE contains at least one Story Event. To determine a Scene's Story Event, answer the following four questions:

1. What are the characters doing?

Jessie and Az are on a transport to Aeta. He's asking her a bunch of questions and then tries to give her a way to leave.

2. What is the essential action of what the characters are doing in this scene?

Az wants to know what is really going on with Jessie.

3. What life value has changed for one or more of the characters in the scene?

Jessie is resigned to go to Aeta, but Az offers her a way to go home. Before she can decide, the opportunity is gone and she's trapped in Aeta.

4. Which life value should I highlight on my Story Grid Spreadsheet?

Trapped to Hope of Escape and back to Trapped

HOW THE SCENE ABIDES BY THE FIVE COMMANDMENTS OF STORYTELLING

Inciting Incident: Az begins talking to her on the transport.

Progressive Complication: Az offers Jessie a way to go back home.

Crisis: Irreconcilable goods. Jessie can stay the course on what she's agreed to do *or* she can try to escape back home.

Climax: The decision is made for her by the environmental inescapability of the surveillance. She is forced to stay.

Resolution: Jessie and Az are sent into the Aeta.

NOTES:

This scene represents the shift from what Joseph Campbell (The Hero's Journey) described as the ordinary world to the extraordinary world. Jessie meets an archetypical player in a heroic journey story, the threshold guardian. Az is the person who introduces Jessie to the extraordinary world of Aeta. He will also play additional archetypical roles in the rest of the story. This scene represents the inciting incident of middle build one, 'a whole new world.'

CHAPTER SEVENTEEN

They walked up a short flight of concrete stairs that ended at two large doors that slid open as they approached.

"Missed your chance," **Az** said, not looking at her.

Jessie didn't answer as they stepped into the hangar.

People shuffled around, all seemingly intent on some serious purpose. Most of them were in the same form-fitting grey outfits of pants and long-sleeved shirts. She could see the **Faction guards** with their faceless masks and semi-automatic weapons stationed at the corners of the hallways like one of those stupid old sci-fi shows they made before The Burning that **Libby** found on the dark grid.

The most shocking part was to actually see **the Numbered**. Here they moved among the people who didn't seem to worry about being "infected" by their low status, as if **the Elites** were by their very nature immune to falling so low.

She could, of course, tell the Numbered by their shorn heads but they also wore long, pale robes without any protective gear. They kept their heads bowed as they walked through the crowd, ignored by everyone else.

Az led them straight through the crowded hallways. He approached another set of doors that opened as he neared.

Jessie stopped in her tracks.

What she saw didn't make sense.

Sunlight streamed in through the doors. There was a small, open square directly in front of the building. Green grass made up most of the area, though paths of crushed rock crossed the quadrangle where people were walking. A few of the people dressed in grey sat on benches along the walkway chatting and sipping drinks. Jessie could see another building across the square pushing up into the sky.

Az stopped and looked back at her.

"What?"

"How? The sun—" she stammered.

Az laughed again.

"Yeah, I forget how most of the cities still live," he said. "Come on out. Take a look up."

Jessie stuck her foot out into the sunlight and waited a few seconds. Then she stuck her hand out and slowly stepped fully into the light.

It was warm against her face but pleasant, not searing. It was just a bit higher in temperature than it was indoors. She looked up toward the sky, shielding the direct sun with her hand.

At first it looked like the sky was set against a grid. There were large squares of the sky outlined by thick grey lines. Her eyes moved down, and she saw the squares disappear behind the buildings toward the edge of the city.

"It's a dome," Az said. "Built specifically to filter out excessive heat and UV light. It allows us to keep the temperature controlled both at night and during the day."

"It's amazing," Jessie whispered to herself as she looked back up toward the sky.

She lowered her eyes back to Az.

"Why don't all the cities have these?"

Az barked out a laugh.

"Well, they're a bit expensive to build. Plus, **the field hands** in the cities need to be harvesting, not hanging out in the fresh air. If they don't harvest, all of this," he said motioning around him, "goes away pretty quickly. The heat keeps them plugged in where they belong."

"Come on," he said, turning and walking again. "I've got more to show you. There would have been a lot more ceremony to it if you had come in with the **other recruits**, but since you came in alone, I'll do what I can. Here, put this on."

Az handed her a green sickle pin that matched his.

"What's this?"

"It's your ticket in the Stack."

"Ticket?"

"You're here to train for the Threshing. And obviously, everybody in the Stack desperately wants us to win. You're **a coding recruit**, the choice level, which means you're their hope to maintain their standard of living. That means you can get away with pretty much whatever you want. It's why that prick **security guard** back there let us go without detaining us for four hours. Hungry?"

"Starving," Jessie said as she attached the pin to her chest.

"We'll grab you something to go so I can get you up to your room. Wait here."

Jessie nodded but mostly ignored Az as he stepped through a small door off the path.

Jessie turned and slowly looked around, taking it all in. She'd never seen so many colors in her life. It wasn't just the grass, but there were little plants with leaves on top that were pink and blue and yellow. People weren't running from the sunlight, either. They were enjoying it.

Jessie's eyes caught **a little girl** running across the small field. She couldn't have been more than three or four years old. Her blonde hair was secured back into a ponytail with a big pink ribbon tied into a bow. Her dress was the same shade of pink and bounced as she ran. **Two of the Numbered** hurried after her, their robes flowing behind them. One finally caught up and took the girl's hand in hers.

The little girl looked up at the Numbered and smiled, breathing hard. The Numbered smiled back.

"Jessie!"

She turned to find Az standing with a brown sack in his hand. He passed it to her.

"Let's get you to your quarters. **Your mentor** will probably be waiting for you there."

She nodded and glanced back one last time at the small girl. Jessie couldn't help but smile before continuing after Az as he moved through the crowd. Az pulled out a small brown wrap covered in silver paper, crumbled up the sack, and tossed it at **one of the Numbered** walking the other way down the street.

Jessie glanced back to see the Numbered scurrying to pick up the trash. Jessie pulled her food out but kept the sack shoved under her arm. She scarfed down the wrap in a few bites. It was full of flavor. Absolutely delicious.

As they continued walking, Jessie looked down the street to where it dead-ended at a large building. It wasn't as big as the skyscrapers Jessie was used to, but it was somehow more imposing. The facade was all black glass, and the entrance was a single large door flanked by **Faction guards** with two long yellow banners hanging on either side.

As they got closer, she could see the building took up the entire block. The density of Faction guards had gone up as well. Some were posted at street corners and in front of buildings. Others were making their rounds through the street.

Jessie kept her eyes away from them. The body armor and the weapons didn't bother her, but the faceless, flat masks always staring and watching everyone truly freaked her out. It was like they were cyborgs.

"Okay," Az said as they approached the building. He stopped across the street from the entrance.

"This is the Americas Faction headquarters. This is where you'll sleep and train for the Threshing. I should probably take you up to your room and get you settled," he looked at the small digital display on his wrist, "but I've got to see a man about a server. Think you can make it on your own?"

Jessie nodded slowly, looking again at the guards and the yellow banners.

"Good."

He turned to face Jessie. He was more than a head taller than her.

"I know this is going to be overwhelming for you, so stick by me in the training. I'll keep an eye on you. And I'll make sure you know what to do. It's pretty intense."

Jessie nodded.

"You can trust me, Jessie. I know this place. If you need anything, just ask. We'll watch each other's back. Right? We aren't just trying to survive the Preparing. We have to be on the lookout for spies from the other Factions. I'll keep you safe, and you let me know anything you come across. Okay?"

Jessie nodded again.

"Great! Now all you need to do is walk through the front entrance. That pin is matched to the body scan they did before you left New York. You'll be scanned as you walk in and matched to the pin's data. Go straight forward through the entrance to the lifts in the back. They'll scan your pin again and take you straight to your floor. Your mentor will be waiting for you there."

Az looked down at Jessie.

"Got it?" he asked.

Jessie nodded again, but Az hadn't waited for a response. He had already turned and started walking away through the crowd.

She took a deep breath and began walking across the street. As she stepped off the sidewalk onto the concrete steps that rose to the front entrance, the **four Faction guards** manning the door all turned their faceless masks toward her.

She stopped, her heart pounding. She looked down at the pin on her chest and back up at the banners. Now that she was closer, she could see the banners were covered in small ones and zeros running up and down and sideways.

She eyed the Faction guards. Back in the city, she never approached them. It always felt like those masks could look straight through her into her mind and extract everything she knew. Maybe they could.

A metallic voice cut across the noise of the crowd.

"New recruit?"

Jessie's head snapped back down to the guards. She had no idea which one had spoken. She had never even heard them speak before. She swallowed hard and nodded.

"You may enter."

Jessie finished walking up the steps unsteadily. As she approached the doors, they slid open. Another metallic voice spoke as she walked through.

"Recruit NY3847. Marston, Jessica."

Jessie stepped through the second set of doors into the lobby and froze.

The room was huge, stark, and silent with white marble making up the floor. Where the outside of the building was black glass, the inside of the windows let in all of the light, filling the room and reflecting off the white floor and ceilings.

At least **three hundred plugged-in people** were in the room. They all sat with their eyes closed in long rows of large, plush chairs.

Jessie spotted the elevators directly across from her, but she would have to walk between all of the bodies lined up in chairs. She glanced behind her and could see the backs of the guards through the glass.

She turned back around and took a tentative step forward. Then another. After a few steps, one of the people stirred in the chairs directly next to her. Out of instinct, Jessie ran down the aisle. She raced up to the elevators, which immediately opened as she approached. She jumped through and backed up to the rear of the elevator, breathing heavily.

From this perspective, she could see all of the plugs running up from the floor through the headrests of the chairs. They must be the **peripherals**...players in the game chosen to operate with a single directive, like zombies, against all of the trainees.

The door slid closed, and the elevator began ascending.

Jessie forced herself to control her breathing, an old Coder trick that steadied her heart rate when she was inside the virtual grid. She wondered if anyone had seen her running through the lobby. How stupid did she look? She'd been around people plugged in for years, so why did she get so freaked out about these?

The elevator came to a stop and the doors slid open. The wall in front of her was covered from floor to ceiling with a portrait of **President Marcus** dressed all in black.

She stepped out into the hallway. It was just as stark as the lobby—marble floors and white walls empty except for the portrait. Harsh white light poured from the ceiling.

Jessie looked both directions and then started walking to her right. Doors were spaced every couple of yards. About halfway down, one of the doors beeped. She heard the same metallic voice say her name as the door unlatched. She pushed on it, and it swung open.

The room was small with just enough room for a twin bed, a toilet, a sink, a tiny shower behind an opaque glass wall, and a ledge that served as a desk with a chair pushed underneath. And of course, a plug-in panel. Floor-to-ceiling windows on the far side of the room took her breath away again. She could see across the tops of the other buildings, through the dome, and out into the expanse of an actual green forest in the distance.

"This godforsaken cesspool," someone muttered behind her. "I can't believe I'm back here."

Jessie gasped, turned around, and put a hand over her mouth.

"**Sixty-one?**"

CHAPTER SEVENTEEN

Analyzing the Scene

A STORY EVENT is an active change of life value for one or more characters as a result of conflict (one character's desires clash with another's).

A WORKING SCENE contains at least one Story Event. To determine a Scene's Story Event, answer the following four questions:

1. What are the characters doing?

Az is introducing Jessie to the city and her status as a Recruit as they walk. The introduction ends when she enters the training building by herself and makes her way to her room.

2. What is the essential action of what the characters are doing in this scene?

Jessie is trying to get her bearings in this new, strange city.

3. What life value has changed for one or more of the characters in the scene?

Jessie is lost with all the newness but eventually finds her way to her home in Aeta.

4. Which life value should I highlight on my Story Grid Spreadsheet?

Lost to Home.

HOW THE SCENE ABIDES BY THE FIVE COMMANDMENTS OF STORYTELLING

Inciting Incident: Az begins walking toward the city.

Progressive Complication: Jessie is sent to face the Faction guards alone.

Crisis: Best bad choice. Jessie can Az to help her get to her room *or* she can face the guards alone.

Climax: Jessie faces the guards.

Resolution: She makes it into the capital building and up to her room to meet her mentor.

NOTES:

Another convention of the Hero's Journey is to have clearly delineated mentor figures to indoctrinate the hero into the extraordinarily world. Sixty-one's return to the scene serves that purpose.

CHAPTER EIGHTEEN

Sixty-one stood. All cleaned up with a perfectly shaved head, he wore form-fitting white pants and a loose cream-colored shirt. A purple pin fastened to his chest had a white "M" on it.

"Sorry, kid. I ain't **a Numbered** no more, even though I do like being bald," he rubbed his dome. "So I suppose you can call me **Harry**."

"Harry? That's your name?"

"Nope. That's just what you can call me. Come on."

He turned and walked out the door.

"Where are we going? Why are you here? How's **Eighty-three**? How are the rest of **them**?" Jessie asked.

"We have to get your training started. We're already six months behind, and **your new team** is waiting for you. I'll fill you in on the rest later. You have almost zero time to prepare."

Jessie hurried out the door after him.

"Team? What do you mean?"

They entered the elevator, and he tapped a couple of keys on the panel, causing the elevator to begin moving downward.

"Your team! You're a Coder. You get plugged in. But to train and fight in the Severings...let's not even think about the Threshing...you need **a Comms and Medic**."

"What for?"

The elevator stopped, and the doors slid open. The hallway was crammed with **people** but orderly. Everyone seemed in a huge hurry. There were **Faction guards**, but lots of others too. **Jessie** saw several dressed like her with the same green pins. A few older people had the "M" pins like Sixty-one—Harry—but others she didn't recognize.

Harry stepped out into the crowd, just about knocking over someone. He ignored them and started walking down the hallway. Jessie hesitated, trying to find an opening, but finally just had to push into the crowd.

She kept her eyes on his bald head and hurried to catch up with him.

He stopped in front of a door with a large window and motioned for Jessie to look through. She stood on her tiptoes to peer inside.

A long table inside had **a boy** lying on it. He was plugged in, but he also had a needle in the back of his hand that ran up into some tubing and a large bag of liquid hanging on a rack. Wires were running from inside of his clothes out to a small monitor that had all kinds of graphs and data scrolling across it. Next to him was a refrigerator with a glass door filled with rows of vials and small bottles. **A girl** was in the middle of emptying the contents of a small vial into a syringe. She then stuck that into the tubing that ran into the boy's hand.

On the opposite side of the table was a large black cabinet. It was lined from top to bottom with rack-mounted servers blinking with green and orange lights. Hooked directly into the server was a terminal, which a boy was leaned over and quickly tapped keys.

"The only version of the grid you've seen is for **the field hands** and the city **Elites**. It's heavily firewalled and runs a high-end graphics interface that allows them to harvest. The Threshing is different.

Coders get plugged directly into the core code of the grid. It will feed you a graphical interface, but for you to function in that environment, you need a Comms to communicate with and help you load and run software. Everything moves way too fast for you to process on your own. You'll have no time to keystroke."

"What about her?" Jessie motioned to the girl with the syringes and vials.

"She's the Medic. It's her job to keep the Coder conscious and alive while she works."

He looked down at her.

"Remember what happened to me when you ran off?"

Shame passed over Jessie's face, and she nodded.

"That's just the start of it in here," he said. "But a good Medic can keep you moving even after you make a mistake and get fried."

Harry turned back down the hallway and kept walking with Jessie following closely behind.

The crowd had thinned out some, and Jessie kept glancing through the windows as they passed the doors. They were all replicants of the first one she'd seen. Some of them had people working in them and others were empty.

The hallway came to a T, and Harry turned to the right. Jessie glanced down the other passageway. She saw a large iron door with no discernible way to open it. Next to the door was a keypad and a small camera and monitor. The light above the door was a bright red. Two Faction guards stood at attention on either side.

"What's that?" Jessie asked.

He stopped and looked back. He shrugged.

"Dunno. That's been there since I was here before. It's always heavily guarded, and I've never seen anyone come or go. No point obsessing about it. There's plenty of other crap to freak out about."

"And you don't know what's behind it?"

"Nope. There are rumors—"

"Like what?"

"Oh, I dunno. Stupid stuff. Like that's where they keep the mainframe. Or **the recruits** that get fried end up back there as test subjects for future upgrades to the grid. It's all made up, though. Nobody really knows. Come on."

Harry turned back down the hallway and Jessie reluctantly followed.

"Okay here we go," Harry said pausing at a bay door.

Harry cut his eyes down the corridor in both directions.

He slid his hand in his pocket and pulled out a tiny drive. Jessie had used similar ones in her work with **the Rats.**

"Hang on to this," he said, reaching over and slipping it into Jessie's pocket.

"What's it for?"

"Just a little help. I'll tell you later."

He turned toward the door, but Jessie grabbed his arm.

"I don't understand what is going on here. Why did you get sent back with me? Why are you Harry now?"

"You needed **a mentor**," he said. "It's one of the rules."

"Yeah, but why you?" she asked. "I thought you were sent to the Numbered because of what you did last time you were here. Why would they pick you?"

Harry smiled at her and pushed the bay door open. It was similar to the other bays she had seen but much smaller. Everything was smaller. The server cabinet was half the size and only half-filled with server racks. The refrigerator was smaller, and there wasn't even a monitor with wires running to the bed.

Two boys were waiting inside. They looked to be about the same height, but one was skinny and kind of hunched over. The first leaned against the wall, his arms folded. He had long greasy hair that fell over his glasses. He barely looked up when they entered. The other boy was more filled out, stocky even, with buzzed hair and bright blue eyes. He sat on the bed, his legs dangling over the side.

"Alright, boys, here's your new Coder. From my briefing on the way here, it looks like you already lost your first Coder, so **the Faction** has assigned you a replacement."

Harry looked at his monitor. "Jessie, this is **Alex Hughes**," he motioned to the boy on the table. "He's your Medic. And that's **Ernst Evans**, your Comms."

Jessie had hung out behind Harry, but he reached back and pushed her in front of him. She stumbled a bit but then stopped, eyes glued to the ground.

"This is Jessie Marston, fresh from the New York City Numbered—thus the unusual haircut."

Harry paused for a bit and then looked at the clock on the wall.

"Okay, you three get to know each other. I've got to, ah, catch up with someone. I'll be around later to check on you."

He turned and pushed through the door into the hallway, leaving the three of them alone.

They all waited in silence for a full minute before Jessie finally looked up and spoke.

"Hi, um, what should we—"

Before she could finish, Ernst pushed away from the wall, shoved past her, and left through the door. Jessie's eyes followed him, and then she looked back at Alex.

He shrugged as if there was nothing he could do and then hopped off the table and followed Ernst out the door.

CHAPTER EIGHTEEN

Analyzing the Scene

A STORY EVENT is an active change of life value for one or more characters as a result of conflict (one character's desires clash with another's).

A WORKING SCENE contains at least one Story Event. To determine a Scene's Story Event, answer the following four questions:

1. What are the characters doing?

Harry is taking Jessie through the building and introducing her to the way things work and the people she will work with. He ends by introducing her to her new team and then leaves.

2. What is the essential action of what the characters are doing in this scene?

Harry is providing Jessie with the minimum amount of knowledge she needs to get started.

3. What life value has changed for one or more of the characters in the scene?

Jessie starts to gain an understanding of how things will work in her training and then her team immediately abandons her.

4. Which life value should I highlight on my Story Grid Spreadsheet?

Confused to Abandoned.

HOW THE SCENE ABIDES BY THE FIVE COMMANDMENTS OF STORYTELLING

Inciting Incident: Harry has Jessie follow him as he leaves her room.

Progressive Complication: Harry introduces her to her new team and then leaves her with them.

Crisis: Best bad choice. Do Ernst and Alex stay and try to train a recruit they know is going to lose or do they give up before they start?

Climax: Ernst and Alex give up before they start.

Resolution: They leave Jessie alone in the bay.

NOTES:

Another convention of the Hero's Journey is to introduce allies and enemies and to allow for the hero to determine which character is which. This introduction to her team is confusing to Jessie, as these are supposedly her allies but they are acting like enemies.

CHAPTER NINETEEN

Jessie could barely sleep that night. She didn't like being alone when she slept. Even before **the Numbered**, she rarely slept in her tiny room at **her parents'** apartment. It was so quiet having her own space. Too quiet, and getting up with daybreak was completely weird too. She'd never felt so out of whack.

She desperately missed **Libby** and **Mark**. She missed The Booth where she never slept alone, always curled up amongst the other **Rats**.

She wondered how they were doing. Did her getting sent to the Numbered affect them? Did they miss her? Did they know what happened?

As she thought about her past, she would start to drift off in her own mind. And then she'd hear **Harry** scream something. She'd jolt awake with the rush of fear that she'd screw something up.

She hadn't eaten breakfast either. Not because she wasn't hungry but because she had no idea where she was supposed to get food inside the building. She had thought about going back out into the city to get something where **Az** had gotten them food, but the thought of walking back through the lobby and past the **Faction guards** was enough to keep her inside.

She also had no idea where she should be or what time she should be there.

So she just waited, sitting on her bed and looking out over the city. In her left hand she clutched her domino, and in the right, she spun the small drive Harry had given her.

She had plugged it into the terminal in her room and accessed it, but there was just a single encrypted file that she couldn't open.

Somewhere around 0530, the intercom lit up green.

"Where are you?"

The voice boomed in the tiny room, startling Jessie.

"Here. In my room." Jessie paused briefly. "Who is this?"

"It's **Alex**. Why aren't you at the bay?"

"You never told me I had to be there."

"Harry didn't?"

"No, I haven't seen him since yesterday."

"Oh, right. Well, training starts at 0500. Me and **Ernst** have been waiting."

"Training for what?"

There was a long pause.

Another voice filtered from the background.

"You have got to be kidding me." Ernst said.

Alex sighed.

"Well get your greys on and get down here. We're already way behind and need to get started. Harry's really pissed off about yesterday. He went out for coffee and if you're not here when he gets back, we're going to be in deep."

Jessie nodded but then realized they couldn't see her. She was already up, stripping off her clothes and reaching for the greys.

"Okay, yeah. I'll be right there."

The light above the intercom clicked off.

Jessie finished dressing and hurried down the hall to the elevator.

She stared at the panel of buttons but had no idea which controls to use. How had Harry called the lift? She should have been paying more attention.

She felt along the wall, wondering if there was some kind of reader. She jumped, startled when the door dinged and it slid open. It immediately shut behind her and started moving down. After a few seconds, the door slid open to reveal another hallway, this one with **lots of people** moving back and forth.

Jessie stepped off and recognized it as the same corridor Harry had brought her to the day before. She watched the people for a few seconds and noticed again the variety of pins they wore. She looked down at her own.

It must be what the building was reading to send her to the correct floor.

She stepped into the swift-moving flow of people and, after a couple of wrong turns, finally made it to the small bay assigned to her team. As she approached the door, it slid open, and she stepped inside.

Ernst was sitting at the terminal pecking away at the keyboard. He didn't look up when she came in. Alex was leaning against the wall, his arms folded.

"Alright then," he said, "let's get you prepped. Up on the table."

Jessie nodded and climbed up.

Alex started separating the multitude of wires running from behind the blinking terminal next to the bed. At the end of each one was a round sticky pad with an exposed wire.

He started putting these at various points on her body.

"What are these for?" Jessie asked.

"I have to track your vitals while you're plugged in. It can get pretty rough in there, and my job is to keep your body from shutting down with the stress."

"Get pretty rough in where?"

"The Trainings. The Severings. And the Threshing, but it's not as if we're going to make it there."

Ernst let out a short, bitter laugh at this, and Jessie just stared at Alex.

"You know what the Severings are?"

Jessie shook her head.

"The Threshing?"

"Well yeah, that's where we win the favor of **the Reapers.**"

"Right, but do you know what actually goes on in there?"

This time Jessie didn't even bother shaking her head. It was obvious to both of them that she had no idea what was going on.

Alex took a deep breath and slowly released it. "Okay, the Threshing is less than six months away. We'll get into what that is later. Last I checked, there are **forty-three four-person teams.** Coders," he jerked his head up to indicate Jessie, "Medics," he put his hand on his chest to indicate himself, "Comms," he pointed at Ernst, whose head was still bent over the terminal, "and Mentors."

Alex gestured over his shoulder at the door. Jessie assumed he meant Harry would be back at any minute.

"The number of Coders changes every day as some Coders get fried. When they do, their Medics and Comms have to wait for reassignment to a new Coder. Once the Severings start, that number will drop a lot faster, and there are no reassignments. Coder goes...so does the Medic and Comms."

"**The Faction** is only allowed to send three Coders into the Threshing. In order to figure out which three Coders should represent the Americas, **President Marcus** runs three different Severings— extremely intense and dangerous trials meant to burn out the subpar Coders and leave the best standing. The first Severing hasn't been announced yet, but the rumor is that it will be coming any day now."

Jessie heard a long sigh behind her.

"You got something on your mind?" Alex said.

Ernst started in. "Yeah. What's the point of all this? She's brand new, no training and too young. Not to mention our equipment's been heavily downgraded after what happened to **Manson.**"

Jessie kept her eyes on the floor as he spoke.

"Right, so you think we should just give up before we get started?" Alex asked.

Ernst shrugged.

"The Severing *is* any day," Ernst said. "What could we possibly hope to teach her?"

Ernst stood up, looked at the two of them, and started toward the door. It slid open as he approached, but then he stopped short.

Harry stood in the doorway. His eyes were swollen and bloodshot. He looked like he'd had a very rough night.

"Where you going?" he asked Ernst with a slight slur to his speech.

"I'm leaving. She's too green. I'm bowing out. I'll try to find a new Coder."

"You're our Comms," Harry responded.

"Well, get another Comms cause I don't want nothing to do—"

Harry stepped closer to Ernst, grabbed a fistful of the front of his uniform and slammed the skinny boy against the wall. Jessie jumped at the sudden movement.

"**You listen up, kid,**" Harry yelled, spittle speckling the young boy's face. "I don't know what kind of **Mentor** you had before but you don't get to just walk out when I tell you to work. So shut your mouth and do what you're told."

He threw Ernst toward the server rack. The boy lost his feet and hit the floor. He scrambled up quickly into the chair at the terminal.

Harry turned to face Alex, whose eyes were wide with fright.

"We going to have a problem?" Harry barked at him.

Alex shook his head.

Jessie still sat on the table, her eyes wide at the sudden outburst.

Harry looked slowly around the room. "Okay, let's get her hooked up and loaded in. Right, you," he pointed at Alex, "finish getting her hooked up. And you," he pointed at Ernst who had sat up, but was still on the floor, "load up the training sim I gave you and get her started."

He looked at Jessie, gave her a nod, and then turned and left the bay.

CHAPTER NINETEEN

Analyzing the Scene

A STORY EVENT is an active change of life value for one or more

characters as a result of conflict (one character's desires clash with another's).

A WORKING SCENE contains at least one Story Event. To determine a Scene's Story Event, answer the following four questions:

1. What are the characters doing?

Jessie is sitting in her room, unable to sleep. She is waiting because she doesn't know what to do. Alex calls her to tell her that she is supposed to be in the bay, so she goes down to meet them. Ernst, fed up with how unprepared Jessie is, tries to leave, but Harry doesn't let him.

2. What is the essential action of what the characters are doing in this scene?

Jessie is trying to understand what is required of her in this new world.

3. What life value has changed for one or more of the characters in the scene?

Jessie's team continues to try to abandon her, until Harry threatens them into compliance.

4. Which life value should I highlight on my Story Grid Spreadsheet?

Defiant to Compliant.

HOW THE SCENE ABIDES BY THE FIVE COMMANDMENTS OF STORYTELLING

Inciting Incident: Alex calls Jessie to tell her she is late.

Progressive Complication: Ernst tries to leave the bay.

Crisis: Best bad choice. Will Harry let Ernst leave or try to get him to stay?

Climax: Harry physically threatens Ernst – and, by extension, Alex.

Resolution: Ernst and Alex agree to help Jessie with her training.

CHAPTER TWENTY

"They really didn't tell you anything. Did they?" **Alex** said.

Jessie shook her head nervously. She had crawled up on the table and lain down.

"We're going to have to adjust the whole table," **Ernst** said. "Get down."

For the next couple of minutes, Ernst and Alex fought with the table, figuring out how to make it as short as possible. By the end, they had something that more or less fit Jessie's height.

"Okay, up you go," Alex said.

Jessie climbed back up and lay down. She put her feet firmly in the footholds and laid her arms out on the armrests so she looked like a little capital T.

"Ready?" Alex asked.

Jessie nodded.

He turned to the IV stand and the small control panel attached to it. He tapped a couple of buttons, and the chair began to whir softly beneath her.

Padded straps slid out from under her ankles and locked her legs into place. Two more straps slid under her armpits and tightened down around her shoulders. Another went across her waist. Finally, two more straps slid out from the armrests and locked her forearms down firmly.

Alex had already pulled out several round leads with wires running out from them. He gently lifted her shirt and stuck three of them to various points on her chest. Both Alex and Jessie were relieved that she hadn't started developing yet. Then he put the last two on her forehead.

"What are these?" she asked, her voice shaking a bit.

"We have to track your vitals while you're logged in. Don't we?"

"We never had to do this back home."

Alex opened one of the drawers next to him and pulled out a small plastic pouch. He ripped it open with his teeth and produced a long, thin needle.

"Yeah," he said, spitting the plastic into the trashcan next to him, "there's not much point in tracking the vitals of **field hands**. Is there? **The Faction** considers them easily replaceable if they freak out in the grid or get scrambled. The grid they're in is a joke anyway. You have to be really stupid to lose your mind in there. We only have a small number of **Coders**, though, so you get a **Medic** to try and keep you alive."

Alex moved down to her hand and positioned the needle above it.

Jessie jerked her hand, trying to pull it back from the needle, but the straps held her tightly.

"I've got to do this, Jessie. If we don't have an IV running, I won't be able to give you the meds you need during your training, and your body will give out pretty quickly."

Most of the blood had left Jessie's face by this point, but she nodded to him. He moved the needle back to her hand. She held her breath against the sting as he slid it in. Alex deftly taped it in place and connected the tube that ran up to the IV drip bag on the stand.

"All done. You good?" Alex said.

Jessie let out her breath and nodded. She hated not being able to wipe away the tears that had pooled in her eyes, but Alex pretended not to notice.

"Okay," Ernst was talking now, "once we get you logged in to the training, you'll be able to communicate directly with me. It's a little weird at first for newbies because you won't really hear me. You'll just know what I'm saying. It's like I'm inside your head talking to you. Plus, you don't need to talk to answer. Just think about what you want to say to me, and it will show up on my screen here."

Ernst tapped the large monitor in front of him.

"Now, I'm blind to what you can see and what you're doing while you're logged in, so you have to communicate with me while you're in there. Think it to me. Remember, I can't see anything. I've uplinked the training ground Harry gave me. It should give you a taste of what it's like. We'll need to upgrade the training software pretty quickly, though, if we're going to have a chance during the Severings."

Jessie nodded.

"Okay, so this is basically an obstacle course. Your job is to get through it as quickly as possible. There shouldn't be much you need from me on this one, but just talk me through it as you work so I can keep track of where you're at."

"Ready?"

Jessie nodded, Ernst tapped a button, and she felt the plug slide into the back of her head and engage.

CHAPTER TWENTY

Analyzing the Scene

A STORY EVENT is an active change of life value for one or more characters as a result of conflict (one character's desires clash with another's).

A WORKING SCENE contains at least one Story Event. To determine a Scene's Story Event, answer the following four questions:

1. What are the characters doing?

Ernst and Alex are getting everything set up for Jessie so they can plug her into the training.

2. What is the essential action of what the characters are doing in this scene?

Preparing someone for a major challenge.

3. What life value has changed for one or more of the characters in the scene?

Jessie finally has her team behind her, and they are teaching her and helping her to get ready.

4. Which life value should I highlight on my Story Grid Spreadsheet?

On Her Own to Part of a Team

HOW THE SCENE ABIDES BY THE FIVE COMMANDMENTS OF STORYTELLING

Inciting Incident: Ernst makes Jessie get off the table so they can adjust it to her size.

Progressive Complication: Ernst explains what the training simulation will be.

Crisis: Best bad choice. Jessie can agree to be loaded into the training *or* she can refuse.

Climax: Jessie says she's ready.

Resolution: Jessie is plugged into the simulation.

CHAPTER TWENTY-ONE

Everything went white, and then **Jessie** found herself standing in front of a large black door.

Are you in? Can you hear me?

Yes. All I see is a door, though. Is that right?

I think so. Hold on.

A few seconds passed as **Ernst** sorted through the code.

Yeah, looks that way. Go ahead and open the door.

Jessie put out her hand, pulled on the handle and then stepped through the doorway.

There was another room and another door. This one had a padlock on it. She turned around to check the door she had just come through, but it was gone, replaced with a solid wall.

Okay, another door. Now it's got a lock on it.

You've got to get through the lock. Is it a keyed or combination lock?

Keyed.

Okay, have you ever broken through a keyed lock?

Jessie rolled her eyes and didn't answer.

So how do I get the tools I need? I don't see my toolbox.

That's part of the test. This isn't like harvesting where you're given your toolbox when you log in. You have to code up your own tools and use them. That's what we're testing here.

There's no terminal. How am I supposed to do that?

Just send them to me, and I'll run them in real time.

Okay.

Jessie shut her eyes.

Woah! Ernst said.

Jessie opened her eyes.

What?

Nothing. Keep going.

Her eyes shut again for just a few seconds.

Okay, you get that? Jessie said.

Yeah. It's almost...okay, there you go. Should be in the room with you. Are you sure about this?

Jessie turned around and saw what she was looking for. She walked to the corner of the room and grabbed the handle. She pulled on it and slid it across the room to the door.

She grimaced under the weight as she lifted the twenty-pound sledgehammer but managed to get it moving and brought it down hard on the lock. The lock shattered under the weight and Jessie jumped back, letting the hammer drop.

She undid the latch that was hanging at an angle now and pulled the door open enough for her to slip through into the next room.

Okay, I'm through.

Silence.

Ernst?

Sorry, Jessie.

I'm through to the next room, she said.

I'm logging you off.

What? Why?

Instead of getting an answer, **the room disappeared** and everything went white again.

Jessie felt the plug release from her head and she opened her eyes.

"Was that it?"

She looked at Ernst. His face was white and his mouth was open but nothing came out.

She looked at **Alex.** He was quickly pulling the leads off her head and chest. She could hear Harry out in the hallway screaming at someone.

"What's going on?"

Alex wouldn't meet her eyes. He concentrated on removing the IV catheter from her hand and taping a small bit of gauze in place over the tiny droplet of blood that emerged.

"All **trainee** meeting," he said. "We have to get to the briefing room."

"Okay," she said. "Is that bad?"

"It's not good," Ernst said.

CHAPTER TWENTY-ONE

Analyzing the Scene

A STORY EVENT is an active change of life value for one or more characters as a result of conflict (one character's desires clash with another's).

A WORKING SCENE contains at least one Story Event. To determine a Scene's Story Event, answer the following four questions:

1. What are the characters doing?

Jessie is loaded into the training and she starts working through it. She only gets a little way in before she is abruptly pulled out of the training and told they have to go to a meeting.

2. What is the essential action of what the characters are doing in this scene?

Jessie is trying to get ready for the Severings.

212 | TIM GRAHL

3. What life value has changed for one or more of the characters in the scene?

Jessie finally has her team behind her and is starting her training when a meeting is called. We don't know what the meeting is, but Ernst and Alex are scared.

4. Which life value should I highlight on my Story Grid Spreadsheet?

Focused to Fearful.

HOW THE SCENE ABIDES BY THE FIVE COMMANDMENTS OF STORYTELLING

Inciting Incident: Ernst abruptly logs Jessie out of the training.

Progressive Complication: Alex tells Jessie it's an 'all hands' meeting.

Crisis: Best bad choice. Jessie can ask for more information *or* not ask.

Climax: Jessie asks if it's a bad sign.

Resolution: Ernst says it's not good.

CHAPTER TWENTY-TWO

The **forty-three teams** crowded into a small white room filled with tight rows of metal chairs. The **trainees** in their grey uniforms and green sickle pins stayed within their own groups of three. Most of the groups had their **mentor** with them too.

"Where's **Harry**?" **Alex** asked.

Ernst ignored him. **Jessie** shrugged her shoulders.

Alex shook his head.

They were waiting their turn to herd into the back row. Jessie saw **Az** across the room, coming in through another door that led to the front rows. Her face lit up, and she waved. He started to lift his hand too, but then his eyes fell on Alex and Ernst. His face hardened, and he dropped his hand, looking away.

Jessie stared after him. What was going on? He had been so nice yesterday.

"What's wrong?" Alex said as they finally took their seats.

"Nothing, it's just. I saw the boy that I flew in with. And—"

"Which one?"

Jessie pointed down front to the back of his head.

"Him. Two chairs in. Second row."

Alex's face went hard and started to turn red.

"What?" Jessie said.

"What was his name?" Alex asked, his voice a little shaky.

"Az, um, I can't remember his last name."

"Alacar?"

"Yeah, that's it. His dad—" Jessie stopped. "What is it?"

Alex just shook his head, his face a deep red now, and kept silent. Ernst slumped down in his seat on the other side of him.

The room's light flipped off, and a projector turned on in the back. The picture of **President Marcus** filled the flat wall in front of them.

A man came onto the stage dressed head to toe in bright red robes.

"Who's that?" Jessie asked Ernst.

"**Bishop Pierre.** He's our Faction's connection to **the Reapers.** He's always the one doing the briefings."

"Welcome, recruits," Bishop Pierre's voice was almost comically high pitched, "to the first Severing."

Jessie gasped and looked around at Alex and Ernst. They kept their eyes forward. Jessie looked around the room.

"After six months of Preparing, your first chance to prove you belong is here. At 0600 hours tomorrow morning, **Coders** must be logged in to the main grid. Access codes and instructions are being delivered to your **Comms** now. As you know, each Severing is designed by President Marcus to test your abilities inside the grid. To have any chance at winning the Threshing, we must work harder, work smarter, and refuse to accept incompetents. This cycle's Threshing is sure to test all of you like never before. The Americas Faction is the only Faction with a single-digit net loss of life of the past four years. If you're wondering, just 6.7 percent of our population has been lost to resource scarcity these past three and a half years. **The Europa Faction** lost 12.3 percent. **The Far East Faction** lost 16.2 percent and **the Southern Faction** was decimated by a loss of 21.3 percent. Our competition is hungry for a win in ways we cannot begin to imagine. They're constantly trying to sneak spies into our midst.

This first Severing will focus on stealth and speed. Needless to say, you are expected to move quickly through the grid without being detected. This is a first-in elimination Severing. There are currently forty-three triads. Only the first sixteen that finish will move on to the second Severing. Good luck, trainees. We will see you in the morning."

Pierre walked off the stage. The picture of President Marcus disappeared, and the lights came back on.

Alex and Ernst immediately stood and pushed past Jessie.

"What is it?" she said.

They ignored her as they pushed out of their chairs and started out of the room. Jessie hurried to catch up. She was moving so fast that she almost ran into them as she came through the doors into the corridor. They stood frozen in place.

Az blocked the way flanked by two other boys, both wearing green pins. Both were imposing figures—tall and thick through the chest with broad faces. One had slicked-back dark hair like Az. The other had a close-cropped stubble of blond.

"Hi there, Jessie," Az spoke to her, actively ignoring Alex and Ernst. "Seems like you picked quite the loser of a team here."

"I didn't pick them," Jessie said. Ernst and Alex shot her angry looks. "I mean, I was assigned to them. I didn't know—"

Az barked out a laugh.

"Well, I already felt sorry for you before, Jessie, knowing you had no training. The thing is that these two couldn't protect their last Coder, **Lucas.** He ended up wasted and scrambled. I can't imagine you'll end up any different."

"Go to hell, Az," Alex barked, taking a step forward. One of Az's team stepped forward to block his way.

"Have they told you about Lucas? I'm sure he'd love to meet you if he was doing something besides drooling into a cup."

Ernst let out a high-pitched scream at this and lunged at Az. Az quickly stepped out the way and shoved Ernst, who hit the floor in a heap. Az kicked him viciously in the ribs, and Jessie shrank back at the sudden violence.

Az pulled back for another kick, but before he could connect, Harry appeared and barreled into Az. The boy hit the floor and skidded a few feet.

Az's two cronies backed up under the presence of the older man. Harry stepped forward and loomed over Az.

"Who do you think you are!" Az screamed, still on his back. "My father will—"

Az's voice cut off as Harry put his boot on the boy's cheek and pressed his face into the floor. He knelt down close and spoke just over a whisper.

"Sorry about that. Lost my balance there." He held the boy's eyes for a moment. "I could care less who you or your jackass of a father is. If you touch anyone on my team again, I will rip you apart with my bare hands."

He stepped back, turned to Ernst, and helped the boy up.

"Let's go," he said gruffly and stalked off down the hall.

Alex, Ernst, and Jessie fell in line behind him as he pushed through the gathering crowd.

Jessie glanced back over her shoulder to see Az struggling to his feet.

"I'm going to find you and eject you myself!" he yelled as Jessie and her team disappeared around the corner.

Harry escorted the three of them to their bay.

"Get in and set things up," he said to Ernst and Alex. They nodded, not quite making eye contact with him, and went to work.

"Are you coming in to help?" Jessie asked.

"No," he said, looking around the hallway at nothing in particular. "No, I gotta go."

"Oh," Jessie responded, "I was hoping—"

"There's not much I can do for you at this point," he said.

He turned his head back to Jessie, who hadn't stopped staring at him. She met his eyes and held them.

"So I'm on my own? You're still not going to explain anything? Or help me in the Severing?" Jessie asked.

"What can I do? Once you're in, it's all on you."

"I'm not going to make it. Am I?"

Harry snorted, but Jessie couldn't tell if it was a laugh or not. He knelt in front of her and locked his eyes on hers.

"Your job is to keep your head down. Don't come in first. Don't come in last. Just somewhere in the first sixteen. Don't do anything flashy. Try not to hurt anyone. Don't make any more enemies. You want to get out of this Severing without anyone caring who you are. You're invisible. Got it?"

Jessie nodded, though she was more confused than ever.

"Good," Harry stood, turned, and walked away without another word. Jessie watched him until he turned the corner and then went into the bay to join the boys. She wanted to get as much time on the grid as she could before the next morning.

CHAPTER TWENTY-TWO

Analyzing the Scene

A STORY EVENT is an active change of life value for one or more characters as a result of conflict (one character's desires clash with another's).

A WORKING SCENE contains at least one Story Event. To determine a Scene's Story Event, answer the following four questions:

1. What are the characters doing?

Jessie, Alex, and Ernst attend a meeting with all the other recruits. The Severing is announced for the following morning. After the meeting, Az confronts them and picks a fight with them. Harry breaks up the fight and escorts the team back to the training bay.

2. What is the essential action of what the characters are doing in this scene?

Jessie is trying to get support from someone – her team, Az, and Harry.

3. What life value has changed for one or more of the characters in the scene?

Jessie is scared after the meeting and is grasping for support. She talks to Harry, who isn't scared that she is going to lose. In fact, he's encouraging her to not try too hard.

4. Which life value should I highlight on my Story Grid Spreadsheet?

Scared to Confused.

HOW THE SCENE ABIDES BY THE FIVE COMMANDMENTS OF STORYTELLING

Inciting Incident: Jessie tells Ernst and Alex that she knows Az.

Progressive Complication: Harry refuses to stay and help with Jessie's training.

Crisis: Best bad choice. Will Harry encourage Jessie, at the risk of giving away too much information *or* will he keep being aloof, leaving Jessie to suffer in fear?

Climax: Harry encourages Jessie to get through the Severing without causing a fuss.

Resolution: Jessie is left confused as she enters her training.

NOTES:

This is a scene that makes more sense in the context of more information later on in the book. Harry isn't worried about Jessie making it through the Severing – he knows she is going to make it. He's actually more worried about her doing it so well that she will get on the radar of the Faction.

CHAPTER TWENTY-THREE

The elevator doors opened. **Jessie** stared at the image of **Marcus** emblazoned on the wall across from her before slowly leaning out and looking down the corridor. No one was in sight. She knew somewhere in the bowels of the building someone or something had her under surveillance. There was too much automation involved and the Threshing's stakes were so high not to be. She hoped no alarms triggered. She reasoned she had little choice but to take every measure to do what **Harry** asked.

She was back on the bay floor where Harry had introduced her to her team, but it was empty now. And dark, long past midnight. Eerily quiet.

She scanned her pin at the first bay. It beeped, and the light turned red. The door stayed locked.

"Duh," she thought. Her card probably only opened her team's bay.

She kept moving down the corridor. As she approached the end of the hallway, she realized that the secured door, the one Harry said he knew nothing about, would be there and would probably be heavily guarded.

She slowed as she reached the intersection, slid along the wall and peeked around the corner.

No guards. The door was still there with the small screen, keypad, and camera, but it was unattended. Jessie glanced over her shoulder again, checked the other way down the hallway, and then turned to make her way to the door.

She stood there for a moment expecting something, anything to happen, but everything remained quiet. She reached out and tapped the green button on the keypad. The screen lit up with seven green underscores. She touched the 1 on the keypad, and the first of the underscores lit up as a 1. She hit the 1 six more times, and they filled in the spaces. She tapped the green button again. The screen turned briefly red and reset to the seven spaces.

Jessie looked up at the camera and then down at her watch. She needed to get moving. Her watch ticked down to 00:03:12. She hurried down the corridor, glancing back once more at the imposing door. She found her team's bay and scanned her pin. The light above the handle turned green, and she entered. She rechecked her watch, sat down at the terminal, and began tapping commands.

From what she could pick up from Harry and watching **Ernst** work, the **trainees** had way more access to the grid than the typical city **field hand** or **Elite,** but it was still locked down tightly.

She pulled a small flash drive, roughly the size of her thumb, from her waistband and walked to the back of the server cabinet. She inserted the drive and sat back down at the terminal. Nothing. She used all of her offline tools to get it open, her random algorithmic generator she'd coded for other break-ins and everything she could think of about **Sixty-one** before he became Harry, but it remained ironclad.

And then, duh again, she realized she could use the drive itself to help her out.

She opened up the executable titled Ricefield that she had just finished coding up in her room and ran the code on the terminal. Then she entered an IP address and got up on the table.

She lay back and waited as the table straps wrapped around her and the plug inserted into her skull. Then everything went white.

She was back in Times Square.

The lights were off. It was the middle of the night, and everything was silent. Of course, it was quiet, she told herself. She was embedded in a simulation.

She turned around slowly, taking it all in. It was a full minute before she realized what was bothering her.

The simulation was too real. All of the images were crisp and sharp. It was up to date. It had only been a week before that she'd been in the square, and the recruiting billboard had the same dead spots in the LEDs. She had put in the initial commands to build out Times Square as the meeting place—it only made sense—but was surprised the grid was able to build it to such detail.

Jessie walked to the middle of the square and stood where her Shaming had been. Then she sat down on the lip of the circle.

She was hoping it wouldn't take too long.

Five minutes passed. Jessie told herself they'd be there any second, but then another ten minutes passed. She looked over her shoulder and around the square with more fury. She coded up the signal herself, so it shouldn't be taking this long.

What if they'd been caught? Were they Numbered now? Did Charles go back on his promise to leave them out of it if she went to Aeta?

"Hey, girl," **Mark** said. "You okay?"

Jessie grabbed **Libby** first and even turned and hugged Mark too. He awkwardly embraced her and then quickly let go.

"When did you check the drop spot?" Jessie said. "I was so worried you would forget. We set that up so long ago."

"We waited a few days to make sure it was safe, but as soon as we knew you had disappeared, it's the first thing Mark thought to do," Libby said.

She paused.

"What happened? And where are you?" Libby said.

"And where is your hair?" Mark added.

Jessie's hand instinctively went to her head. The stubble of new growth was just starting to show through after a week away from the Numbered.

"Mayor Charles sent me to **the Numbered**."

Libby's hand went to her mouth.

"Oh no. I'm so sorry, Jessie."

"It's not your fault."

"Of course, it's my fault. Security is my job. I should have checked behind you better. I had no idea Charles was going to be there."

"I don't think that's it," Jessie said. "He was waiting for me. He knew I would be there."

"But how?"

Jessie shrugged. "No idea. But when he found me, he offered me a place at the Preparing instead of getting punished."

Mark snorted out a laugh.

"If only he knew," he said.

"Right?" Libby agreed.

"So he sent me to the Numbered, which is how I got the new haircut."

Mark's eyes dilated. Even with all the sarcasm and teasing over the two years they'd been **Rats** together, Jessie suspected he cared for her. But this was the first time his emotion gave him away.

Just the mention of the Numbered terrified him.

"And you survived? They didn't eat you?" he said.

Libby backhanded him on the chest.

"Apparently not. How many times have we told you those are just rumors the Faction spreads around?"

"But **my cousin's friend**! They only found his bones!"

Libby rolled her eyes and turned back to Jessie.

"So that's where you are now?"

Jessie shook her head.

"That—" Jessie paused, trying to find the words. "It didn't work out. I ended up at Aeta."

Libby gasped.

"You're at the Preparing? In the Capital?"

Jessie nodded. Tears were welling up in her eyes.

"Oh god," Libby embraced Jessie again. "I'm so sorry."

Jessie rubbed at her eyes and pushed back from the older girl.

"It doesn't matter. What I need now is to figure out the best way to get home. In one piece."

"What are you going to do?" Mark asked.

"That's why I'm here. Is there anything you can do to help?"

Mark and Libby exchanged glances.

"I don't think so. I have no idea what we could do. We have no access to the Faction's grid outside of the city. Even if we did, I have no idea what we could do that would get you back to the city."

"What about **Balaam**?" Jessie got right to the point.

Libby shook her head, and annoyance flashed across her face.

"We haven't heard from him since you disappeared," Mark said. "He keeps a low profile anyway as a **Scavenger**, so I'm sure once he picked up that you were compromised, he disappeared."

Jessie let out a growl of frustration.

"So what am I supposed to do here? If I go into the Severing and lose, I'm dead. If I win, I'm forced to go into the next Severing, where I definitely won't survive. There's no way out!

Jessie sat back down on the lip of the platform. She dropped her head and let the tears flow. "Why can't I just come back? Why are they making me stay?"

Libby sat down next to her and wrapped an arm around the smaller girl's shoulders. Mark stayed standing, awkwardly shifting his weight from foot to foot.

"I wish there were a way out too," Libby whispered.

Silence fell between them for a few moments.

"Maybe there is," Mark said.

Libby and Jessie both raised their heads to look at him.

"You said there were two options, right? Lose the Severing, or win and get pushed to the next one. But what if there was a third option?"

"What are you talking about Mark?" Libby asked, cutting her eyes at Jessie who was looking at him skeptically.

"Remember the uptown job we pulled a couple of years back? The one you were running security on?"

"Yeah—" Jessie said slowly, thinking. She looked at Libby.

"It could work," Libby confirmed.

"If you're going to die anyway, you might as well make it interesting," Mark said.

CHAPTER TWENTY-THREE

Analyzing the Scene

A STORY EVENT is an active change of life value for one or more characters as a result of conflict (one character's desires clash with another's).

A WORKING SCENE contains at least one Story Event. To determine a Scene's Story Event, answer the following four questions:

1. What are the characters doing?

Jessie sneaks down to the training bay and logs into the grid to meet with Libby and Mark. Jessie is giving them an update on what happened to her and they discuss ways for her to get back home.

2. What is the essential action of what the characters are doing in this scene?

Jessie is trying to find a way back home.

3. What life value has changed for one or more of the characters in the scene?

After talking, they reach an impasse as to what to do next and Jessie is feeling resigned to her fate. Mark reminds them of an old job and alludes to a third option.

4. Which life value should I highlight on my Story Grid Spreadsheet?

Resigned to Empowered.

HOW THE SCENE ABIDES BY THE FIVE COMMANDMENTS OF STORYTELLING

Inciting Incident: Libby and Mark meet Jessie in the simulation of Times Square.

Progressive Complication: Mark reminds them of a job they did previously that has implications for Jessie's current situation.

Crisis: Best bad choice. Jessie can play by the rules of the Severing *or* she can take an option Mark is alluding to.

Climax: Jessie agrees that Mark's idea is a good one.

Resolution: Mark confirms his idea is a way to make it interesting.

CHAPTER TWENTY-FOUR

Lightning flashed, illuminating enormous clouds hidden by the darkness of a moonless sky. A loud clap of thunder immediately followed. **Jessie** crouched down and backed further into the shadows to survey her surroundings. The rain came, obscuring her vision as the water dripped down her stubbled head. She wiped her eyes, made a canopy with her hands on her forehead, and peered through the blinders to focus on the middle distance ahead.

Where are you? **Ernst** asked.

Can't you tell me? Jessie asked.

No, like I told you before, that's not how it works. I run the code for you and can only follow your instructions. You have to keep me up to speed on where you are, what you see, and what you need.

Jessie nodded as if Ernst could see her and then made the mental shift to tell him everything she experienced as quickly as she could.

I'm on top of a hill. The grass is tall, and it gets dark the further I look down, so it's hard to make out what it is. Something's definitely there, though. Have the instructions come through yet?

They're downloading now. Okay, here they are. Can you see a red blinking light in front of you?

Jessie wiped her eyes, made the hand blinders again and peered toward the horizon. A faint red light blinked on for a second and then back off. A few seconds later, it showed again.

Yeah. Yeah, I see it.

That's your goal. You have to be one of the first sixteen Coders to make it to the beacon.

What if I'm not one of the first sixteen?

Silence followed her question.

Ernst?

Jessie, there's only two ways out of the Severing. You either make it through, or you get a forced eject.

So...Lucas...your last Coder...was a forced eject?

Yeah, Lucas washed out. Wait, yeah, Alex is reminding me. The other way you can get a forced eject is if one of the other Coders gets to you first.

What do you mean?

Come on! This is life and death, Jessie. And everyone in the Severing knows that one less Coder is less competition for the other Severings. If you see another Coder, run. They're going to try to force an eject by killing you inside the grid.

Jessie stayed silent, processing this new information.

Jessie?

I'm here.

You, okay?

Yeah.

Then get moving. That beacon is over five miles away, and right now every other Coder is racing to get there.

Jessie nodded to herself, stood up, and began walking down the hill. A few steps in, her foot slipped out from underneath her, and she sat down hard on the wet grass. She began to get up, but something stopped her. Then she heard squishy footsteps running her way.

She hunkered down lower in the wet grass, hoping her soaking grey uniform would be enough to hide her in the darkness.

Lightning flashed again, and she made out a tall boy just twenty feet away. He was scanning the hill around him. A voice called out from further away, but Jessie couldn't make it out over the rain. She could hear the response, though.

"Yeah, I saw someone. It had to be her. She's the shortest Coder."

Again, the garbled voice from further away.

"I don't know. Maybe she already made it to the woods."

The boy turned around and started heading down the hill. Jessie tentatively raised herself out of the grass and watched the boy head toward the black blob at the bottom. He joined up with **someone else**, and they kept moving together as allies.

Jessie got to her feet and moved in a crouched position, careful to follow the noises of the boys ahead as she stepped. As she made it to the bottom of the hill, she could finally make out the dark blob she'd seen from above. It was trees. Hundreds of them. Thousands. She'd never seen so many trees all in one place.

Her dad used to tell her about how green Central Park once was, and she always imagined it looked like this. But that was before the rebellion. A few years before she was born, a bunch of the **field hands** tried to overthrow **the Faction's** stranglehold on the city by hiding out in the park and messing with the grid undercover. Instead of sending the Faction guards in to find them, **Charles** decided just to burn everything down. And when **the rebels** ran out of the park to escape the fires, those who didn't succumb to their burns were immediately captured, paraded down Seventh Avenue, and publicly executed in Times Square. A few of **the women** were saved to be Shamed and sent to **the Numbered**.

Her father had always used the story to warn her about stepping out of line with the Faction.

Now she wished she had listened.

Jessie reached the forest's edge. The two other Coders had entered just a couple of minutes ahead of her.

She stepped tentatively beside the first tree, touched the slippery bark to keep her balance, and then took another step. Hoping to hide the sounds of her movement, she stepped in time to the patter of the rain.

Never having had to navigate so many roots and rocks before, she seemed to slip on every other step. She anticipated the slips and was then able to pick up her pace. Step. Step. Slip. Recover. Step. Step. Slip.

Recover. She hadn't caught up to the two other Coders yet, but she was confident those behind her wouldn't be able to move as quickly as she did. Being the shortest Coder had its advantages in this terrain as she didn't have to duck under and evade half as many obstacles as those just a few inches taller.

After a few more minutes, she reached a thick felled tree blocking the thin path. She scrambled up on top of it, but as she tried to slide down the other end, she lost control. After hitting the ground hard, several sticks cracked underneath her.

Jessie froze, waiting, listening.

All she could hear was the rain against the trees above and thunder, now rolling in from a distance.

She rose carefully to her feet and moved forward only to come upon an even larger fallen tree. This time, she shimmied to the top and peered over it before beginning her slide.

Just on the other side, maybe ten feet away, stood the Coder she had seen on the hill. She could make out his features now. He was taller than she initially perceived in the darkness with brown hair hanging shaggily over his ears. His back was to her, but he was not moving.

What was he doing? Where was the other Coder?

Jessie waited and watched. He didn't seem to be doing anything. His hands were at his side, and he just stared off into the woods.

"Got ya!"

Suddenly, she felt hands on her. She screamed and fought to free herself, but a pair of arms wrapped around her shoulders and held her tightly in place.

Jessie scooted backward, put her feet against the fallen tree, and kicked hard, sending both her and her assailant to the ground. She kicked and rolled and snarled, but the arms held fast.

"Ben! A little help?" the boy holding her called out. The shaggy-haired boy was already clambering over the log and now held Jessie too. He secured her kicking legs and held them tightly as his partner held her arms and shoulders immobile.

Jessie soon realized she wasn't going to overpower these two boys, so she stopped fighting to collect her thoughts. The two boys relaxed their grip.

She screamed to pull in other Coders to their location.

Ben dropped her legs and grabbed for her face, but she immediately kicked him in the stomach with both her feet. He let out a loud gurgling sound and doubled over to the ground.

The other one holding her rolled her over, pushed her face down onto the ground, and sat up on top of her. She tried to buck him off, but when that didn't work, she screamed again.

Her assailant cupped her mouth with one hand and pushed her head down with the other.

"Shut up!" he whispered harshly, "or you'll get us all ejected."

Jessie heard movement as Ben worked his way to his feet, his hand clutching his stomach.

"Turn her over," Ben said.

Jessie was roughly turned over, but the boy on top of her stayed seated, mounted on her. He kept a hand over her mouth too.

Ben laughed when he saw her.

"It's the newbie. Jessie, right?"

Jessie didn't answer. She just glared at him.

"I'm gonna eject her now so we can keep moving," the boy on top of her said. Though his weight was far too much for her to move, Jessie started bucking again underneath him.

"Wait a sec," Ben said. He squatted down next to Jessie. She stopped moving, breathing hard against the boy's hand.

"You've got a choice here," Ben said. "You can keep your mouth shut when **Clifton** takes his hand off your mouth, or you can scream again, and he'll eject you right here and now. Understand?"

Jessie nodded, and Clifton removed his hand slowly, though he kept his weight on top of her.

"I can help," Jessie gasped.

"How's that?" Ben said.

"I can help you move faster through the woods."

"She'll just slow us down," Clifton said.

"No!" Jessie answered. "**I'll be your scout.** I'll go ahead of you so you won't have to worry about running into other Coders along the way. If I get caught, you can just go in a different direction."

"She's got a point," Ben said.

"What's going to keep her from running off? Or exposing our position?"

Ben looked down at her.

"We can code up something to fix that."

He motioned for Clifton to get off of her and helped Jessie to her feet.

"Welcome to the team," he smacked her on the back and then pointed into the woods. "Let's get moving."

CHAPTER TWENTY-FOUR

Analyzing the Scene

A STORY EVENT is an active change of life value for one or more characters as a result of conflict (one character's desires clash with another's).

A WORKING SCENE contains at least one Story Event. To determine a Scene's Story Event, answer the following four questions:

1. What are the characters doing?

Jessie is in the Severing and trying to get her bearings. She follows two boys who were looking for her and then gets caught by them.

2. What is the essential action of what the characters are doing in this scene?

Jessie is trying to survive.

3. What life value has changed for one or more of the characters in the scene?

Jessie has been following the boys but they have caught her. They are going to eject her, but she talks them into keeping her on with them as a scout.

4. Which life value should I highlight on my Story Grid Spreadsheet?

Caught to Assimilated.

HOW THE SCENE ABIDES BY THE FIVE COMMANDMENTS OF STORYTELLING

Inciting Incident: Jessie begins following the boys into the woods.

Progressive Complication: Clifton wants to eject her and keep moving.

Crisis: Irreconcilable goods. Do Clifton and Ben eject Jessie so they don't have to worry about her *or* do they keep her alive and use her as a scout?

Climax: They decide to use her as a scout.

Resolution: They send her off ahead of them so they can keep moving.

CHAPTER TWENTY-FIVE

Jessie glanced up through the trees again to make sure she was heading in the right direction and then kept moving forward, trying to stay as low as possible.

Clifton and **Ben** stayed close enough to make sure she didn't run off, but far enough behind so they wouldn't be in danger if someone came across her. **Ernst** was none too happy about her teaming up with them, but what choice did she have?

They'd been making steady progress for the past few hours. Jessie kept Ernst up to date, and Ernst kept **Alex** up to date along the way. She'd slowly creep forward through the forest for twenty minutes, and then she would wait as the two boys caught up. In the last meetup they had scolded her for going too slowly. They were sure others were going to make it to the tower before them since they had spent so much time meeting up and then dealing with Jessie at the beginning.

To make up time, instead of crawling and using the ground as cover, she now stayed on her feet and used the trees and their larger limbs to hide her position. It was a gamble, but not as much of a gamble to her as it was to Clifton and Ben, who were much taller and far more easily seen.

But now she had a dilemma.

She came upon a large clearing. The quickest route would be to walk right through it in the direction of the tower, but she would be exposed and vulnerable even if she ran.

However, working her way around the forest's edges to the tower would take considerable time. So much time they'd risk not making the cut. She knew she'd hear about it from Clifton and Ben if she chose the conservative way.

The big problem was that the closer they got to the beacon, the more likely they were to run into **other Coders**. Should she wait up for Clifton and Ben and figure it out then?

Jessie cleared her mind, waited a few more seconds and scanned her eyes around the edge of the clearing while listening intently. After a full minute, she crouched forward, readied herself and then leaped out from behind her tree and began sprinting across the opening. She cursed her short legs with every step.

But then miraculously, she found herself ten yards away from a patch of tree cover. And then five. Just as she was about to dive into the tree line, a log swung into her view and smashed against her forehead. The force stopped Jessie cold, forcing her back into the clearing where she slid to a stop.

Jessie quickly rolled onto her stomach and popped to her feet, but the world around her started spinning violently and her knees buckled. She face-planted into the mud.

Bile rose in her throat as she fought the urge to throw up.

Laughter floated across the clearing, waking her out of her stupor. Jessie knew the voice. She rolled to her side and looked back in the direction she'd been knocked down.

"I told you I'd find you and eject you myself. I'm still not sure why they brought you to the Preparing, but at least now they'll know it was a mistake." **Az** stepped out of the darkness. He held the thick branch he'd used to knock her down, tossing it from one hand to the other.

Jessie's world had stopped spinning and settled into a rhythmic sway. She tried to blink away the double vision as Az started walking slowly toward her like someone putting a wounded animal out of its misery.

Jessie collected herself as best she could and pushed against the ground with her feet as her hands slithered backward like a crab away from Az.

"I see you!" she yelled. "You're right here across the clearing!"

Az stopped and cocked his head to the side quizzically.

"I must have hit you pretty hard. You're not even making any sense."

What the hell is going on, Jessie? Your vitals are all over the place here.

Az attacked me.

Az? Ernst cursed bitterly. *Are you okay?*

I dunno yet.

Okay, Alex is giving you something. Hang in there a few more seconds.

Jessie continued to scamper back away from Az, and he let her go for a few more yards. She was getting closer to the side of the clearing where she had emerged.

"Look how cute you are," Az said. "Thinking you can get away."

In that microsecond, Jessie's vision cleared. Her thinking snapped back into focus, and she felt the strength surge back into her muscles. Whatever Alex had given her must have been kicking in.

Jessie jumped to her feet and turned to run out of the clearing, but before she could escape, Az grabbed the back of her collar.

He flung her back to the mud, and she rolled over to find him raising the branch over his head. She threw her arms in front of her face just in time to take the brunt of the impact. She heard a crack and felt pain knife up her left forearm as Az lifted the branch again. She closed her eyes and put up her one good arm, trying to protect herself.

A scream erupted behind her and she opened her eyes in time to see a boy's body flying over her. She heard the impact and lifted her head to see Ben rolling across the ground, tangled up with Az.

Jessie struggled to her feet, cradling her arm against her body. She saw Az reverse his disadvantage. He was now on top of Ben, pummeling him with his fists. She tried to take a step toward the fighting but immediately staggered and fell to her knees. Stars floated again in her vision as she struggled back to her feet.

Az was on his feet now. He kicked Ben viciously in the ribs and Jessie heard several loud pops. Then Az stomped on the boy's stomach.

Something gurgled in Ben's throat, and blood spilled from the corners of his mouth.

Jessie took a few uneasy steps toward Az, still fighting to keep her balance, when his eyes lifted back to her. A smile grew across his face as he took a step toward her, but then a rustling came from behind her. She glanced back as Clifton emerged from the bushes into the clearing.

Az took a look at the much larger boy, took two steps back and then turned, sprinted back across the clearing into the woods in the direction of the beacon.

Clifton rushed over and dropped down next to Ben in the mud. Jessie stumbled over and joined him.

"Oh god," Clifton whispered.

Ben's face was cut and bruised and bleeding. His breath was coming in rough gurgles.

"Ben."

The boy's eyes pried open, and he tried to focus on Clifton.

"Ben," he said, "we have to go. Can you move?"

The boy made a half attempt to sit up but groaned in pain and relaxed back into the mud.

Ben shook his head slightly and coughed again. Blood spilled out of the corners of his mouth.

"Clifton," Jessie said. "We have to leave him. We have to go."

Clifton shook his head.

"No...No we can't. If we make it to the beacon and he's not there..."

"I know, but if we wait, all three of us won't make it. I'm so sorry," Jessie said after a few moments.

"He was all I had here. We were the only two from our town to make the cut. His mom..."

Clifton gently pulled Ben into his lap and hugged him closely.

Jessie kept scanning her eyes around the clearing as Clifton rocked back and forth, holding Ben.

"Clifton, we have to keep moving," she said, tugging at his shirt sleeve.

He stayed on his knees beside Ben, his hands gently holding him. The boy was still breathing but had slipped into unconsciousness.

Finally, Clifton stood and looked at Jessie.

"Can you run?"

"I think so." Jessie nodded.

"Then let's go."

CHAPTER TWENTY-FIVE

Analyzing the Scene

A STORY EVENT is an active change of life value for one or more characters as a result of conflict (one character's desires clash with another's).

A WORKING SCENE contains at least one Story Event. To determine a Scene's Story Event, answer the following four questions:

1. What are the characters doing?

Jessie is leading the way through the woods for Ben and Clifton. Az attacks them. Ben is critically wounded, Az gets away, and Jessie and Clifton start out toward the beacon on their own.

2. What is the essential action of what the characters are doing in this scene?

Jessie is trying to stay alive while figuring out a plan.

3. What life value has changed for one or more of the characters in the scene?

Jessie is attacked and almost killed by Az, but she escapes when Ben gives his life for her.

4. Which life value should I highlight on my Story Grid Spreadsheet?

Attacked to Rescued.

HOW THE SCENE ABIDES BY THE FIVE COMMANDMENTS OF STORYTELLING

Inciting Incident: Jessie reaches the large clearing.

Progressive Complication: Jessie is injured and unable to protect herself from Az.

Crisis: Best bad choice. Will the boys help Jessie *or* will they leave her on her own?

Climax: Ben attacks Az, saving Jessie.

Resolution: Ben is critically wounded and they are forced to leave him behind.

CHAPTER TWENTY-SIX

We're getting close, **Jessie** said.

Clifton and she hurried through the thicket. At first, they were far more careful, continually scanning for **rival Coders** ready to take them out. But after a bit their worry that other Coders were going to make it to the beacon pushed their pace.

It was hard and delicate work, though. Everything was slippery and hard to see. Tripping and sliding and banging into trees became the norm, each one bringing a sharp stab of pain through her arm, but she merely gritted her teeth, stayed silent and kept moving.

Several times Clifton could have torn away after Jessie had fallen, but he had, instead, stayed with her, helped her up and kept her moving.

How're you holding up? **Ernst** asked.

I'm okay. But the pain is getting bad again. I'm definitely slowing down.

A few seconds later, the pain in her arm began to fade, and she felt her heart beating harder against her chest.

Alex gave you another dose of pain meds and adrenaline. He's saying it better last until you're out because you probably can't handle anymore without your heart misfiring.

Jessie nodded to herself and kept pushing forward. Time seemed to stretch and contract. She had no idea how far they'd already traveled. On the one hand, everything was moving so fast, and yet she struggled to remember a time when she wasn't pushing her way through a dense, wet forest. She put those thoughts out of her mind, kept her head down and moved forward.

Clifton, twenty feet ahead of her, suddenly dropped into a crouch and stopped. He waved Jessie up to meet him. She crawled up alongside him and then saw what had given him pause.

They'd made it.

The beacon was on top of a tall, wooden structure at least a hundred feet high. Down through the center of the lighthouse ran a shaft that ended at a doorway on the ground. She assumed it was the entrance to the elevator to the top.

The entire structure stood at the center of a vast and open clearing, at least a couple hundred yards across. Clifton and Jessie now knelt on the boundary between the wooded landscape and the field, assessing the situation. Oil lamps hung from tree trunks around the edge of the clearing, casting the expanse in an eerie glow.

"It looks like no one else has made it yet," Clifton said.

He began to stand, but Jessie reached out and tugged on his sleeve to pull him back down beside her.

"What?" he asked.

"It doesn't make sense," Jessie replied. "Az took off ahead of us. Why isn't he here?"

Clifton shrugged.

"Who knows? Maybe someone else got him."

His face darkened.

"We can only hope."

Jessie shook her head.

"Something is up. I'm the smallest Coder, and I'm injured and was slow moving through the woods. How did we beat everybody here?"

"Who cares," Clifton said, standing again. "If we sit here talking about it instead of getting to the top of that tower, we won't survive this Severing."

Jessie stood up beside him.

"Okay, fine. We'll go. But first, grab that lantern," she pointed at the tree several yards away. "I'll grab this one."

"What for? There's plenty of light." Clifton asked.

"So we can... for a weapon if someone comes at us."

"Good idea!" Clifton said and headed over to get the lantern.

Jessie went to the lantern closest to her and stood on her tippy toes, reaching for it. She was just able to push the bottom of the lantern up, so it came off the hook, and she gently pulled it down.

Clifton came over with his.

"Okay," Jessie said. "Let's put some space between us so if Az comes at us, we can defend each other."

"You're not going to run off to the beacon without me. Are you?" Clifton asked.

Jessie shook her head. "I couldn't ever do that."

Clifton nodded and turned his head toward the beacon.

"Ready?" he asked.

Jessie nodded.

Clifton stepped into the clearing.

"Clifton," Jessie said, stopping him. He looked at her. "Thanks for saving me back there. I know you didn't have to do that."

He shrugged. "What else could I do?"

Their lamps bounced against their legs as they moved and they continually turned their heads to scan the edges. Jessie couldn't understand why no one else was around them. How were they possibly so far ahead of the others? And where was Az? He should have made it to the beacon ages ago.

Just halfway there, the two of them subconsciously sped up. They were almost jogging now as the lamps continued to bang against their legs. Just when Jessie thought they were going to make it, that all her fears were self-defeating paranoia, **five figures** stepped out of the darkness.

Jessie and Clifton stumbled and stopped. They still had to navigate thirty yards to the lift.

Az emerged from the shadows, and four other Coders flanked him.

Jessie had seen many of the Coders following Az around Aeta. His dad was powerful, which gave him power.

"Hey, Jessie," he said, smiling. "I see you've still got your bodyguard with you."

Jessie remained quiet, but Clifton spoke up.

"What are you doing? Why didn't you go up?"

"Because," Az answered, "sixteen teams are going to make it through this first Severing."

"You are the first ones! You'll get the first five spots. There are still nine spots left after Jessie and I make it."

"That's the problem," Az said. "Actually," he said, pointing at Jessie, "she's the problem."

"What?" Clifton said. "Why?"

"She doesn't belong here. This whole thing is a joke to her. She tried to escape to go back home as soon as she got here. She's a coward and doesn't deserve to represent **our Faction**."

Clifton looked at Jessie.

"Is that true? Did you try to desert the Faction?"

Jessie didn't respond. She didn't have to. She just dropped her head.

"Come join us, Clifton," Az said. "We'll pull in another ten Coders and then we'll all go up together."

Clifton pulled his gaze from Jessie, switched the lantern to his left hand, and stepped into the space between them and the other Coders. As he walked toward Az, Jessie lost hope.

She wasn't going to make it. There was no way she could get through those massive boy Coders. Any one of them could take her out by themselves, and there were five of them—six now with Clifton.

Clifton approached Az, towering over him by at least a head.

Jessie's mind raced, trying to work a way out of this situation.

"You've made the right choice," Az said as Clifton approached.

But Clifton never broke stride. Instead, he shot an uppercut from his hip that landed with a loud crack against Az's chin. The smaller boy's head snapped back, and he toppled backward over and into the mud.

"Jessie, run!" he shouted over his shoulder. The Coder standing closest to Az lunged at Clifton, but he was already swinging the lantern and it connected against the boy's shoulder. The lantern shattered, spraying the oil over the Coder's head and chest, which immediately ignited. The boy started screaming and dropped to the wet earth, rolling around trying to put it out.

Everyone stayed frozen in place except for Clifton.

Clifton tackled the second Coder into the mud and hammered his fist down on the boy's face several times. He looked up at Jessie and pointed at the doorway.

"Go!" he shouted.

Finally, Jessie broke loose, but the three remaining Coders jumped into action. One of them started toward Clifton, and the others moved to cut off Jessie's approach to the tower. Before the ones giving chase to Jessie could make any progress, though, Clifton came up behind him and hurled them into the mud. The remaining Coder dove into the melee and they all savagely flailed and kicked at Clifton.

Jessie ran as fast as her legs could take her, cradling her broken arm against her chest and holding the lantern higher so it wouldn't impede her running.

As she approached, she saw **a half dozen other Coders** come into the clearing. They must have all been waiting on Az to take her out, but now there was no way they could get to her in time.

Jessie slowed as she approached the tower doors but stopped several yards away. She turned back to check on Clifton. He had subdued one of the Coders but was still grappling with the remaining two. He glanced at her.

"Go!" he screamed. "I'll make it."

But Jessie backed up from the entryway.

Clifton turned again toward Jessie.

"What are you doing?"

Jessie looked down at the lantern in her hand and swung her arm back as far as it would go.

"Jessie! No!" Clifton yelled.

Jessie launched the lantern as hard as she could into the lighthouse's wooden doors. The glass shattered, and the oil exploded against the door. The fire quickly engulfed the only way to the top of the tower.

Jessie felt Clifton sprint by her, but he stopped a few yards from the door to cover his face against the heat.

Other Coders came upon them now, but it was too late. The flames had already spread up the face of the tower as it crackled and smoked.

All the Coders could do was stand and watch the flames continue to climb and engulf the tower. Clifton stood next to her, watching their only escape from the Severing burn, and began quietly laughing.

And then whiteness filled Jessie's field of vision.

Jessie kept her eyes shut as she felt the restraints loosen and the plug disengage from the back of her skull.

When she finally opened her eyes, she saw Alex and Ernst hovering above her.

"What the hell did you do?" Alex demanded.

CHAPTER TWENTY-SIX

Analyzing the Scene

A STORY EVENT is an active change of life value for one or more characters as a result of conflict (one character's desires clash with another's).

A WORKING SCENE contains at least one Story Event. To determine a Scene's Story Event, answer the following four questions:

1. What are the characters doing?

Jessie and Clifton make it to the final clearing with the tower. As they approach the tower, Az emerges with several others. A fight breaks out, and Jessie is the first one to make it to the tower. However, instead of going inside, she burns the tower down.

2. What is the essential action of what the characters are doing in this scene?

Jessie is trying to make it out alive without winning the Severing.

3. What life value has changed for one or more of the characters in the scene?

Jessie knows something is wrong as they enter the clearing. Her premonition is confirmed when Az emerges with several others. She is sure she is going to die when Az invites Clifton to join them. Instead, Clifton attacks Az's group and makes space for Jessie to make it to the tower first.

4. Which life value should I highlight on my Story Grid Spreadsheet?

Certain Death to Saved

HOW THE SCENE ABIDES BY THE FIVE COMMANDMENTS OF STORYTELLING

Inciting Incident: Clifton and Jessie enter the final clearing where the tower is located.

Progressive Complication: Clifton clears the way for Jessie to make it to the tower first.

Crisis: Best bad choice. Jessie can enter the tower and win the Severing *or* she can burn the tower down so no one can win.

Climax: Jessie throws her lantern against the tower, burning it down.

Resolution: All the Coders are logged out of the Severing.

NOTES:

This scene represents the turning point progressive complication of middle build one, 'the protagonist becomes the target of the antagonist.'

CHAPTER TWENTY-SEVEN

Jessie sat up slowly, flexing her left arm. **Alex** was pressing his shoulder into the door and holding the handle as shouts came from the other side.

Ernst was stuffing equipment into his bag and then snapped it shut, throwing it over his shoulder. Empty bottles and papers lay across the floor.

"You ready?" Alex asked.

Ernst looked back at Jessie, annoyed, and then grabbed her wrist and yanked her off the table. She stumbled to take her place next to his side. His hand was like a vise around her wrist, and his hair hung down in front of his face.

He nodded to Alex.

"Okay, stay close. This isn't going to be pretty." Alex opened the door, and the noise immediately became deafening. Jessie saw **angry faces** crowded around the door, screaming and yelling in her direction.

"Back up," Alex bellowed, but the crowd pressed forward. He shoved **the one closest to him**, which pushed the whole group back a fraction, but nowhere near enough to escape the room.

One of the most powerful recruits stepped through the crowd to face Alex.

"What the hell did your Coder do? We were almost to the tower!"

"Back up, **Shaw**," Alex warned, "let us through!"

"Not until she answers for what she did!"

Alex pushed Shaw back.

"One more chance," Alex said.

Shaw stepped forward to shove Alex, but just as his hands were going to connect, Alex stepped to the side and swung his right fist. It connected hard with Shaw's jaw in a loud crack. The large boy slumped to the floor at Alex's feet.

Alex stepped close to the crowd, who backed up under his glare. Ernst hurried out of the room, dragging Jessie alongside him. They stepped over Shaw's motionless body as they exited.

Alex shoved the person closest to him, who stumbled back and fell to the floor, opening a swath in the crowd of trainees. Alex pushed his way through the rest of the people with Ernst and Jessie staying close behind him.

As soon as they broke free of the crowd, **the three ran down the hallway**. They had made it halfway to the turn when Jessie looked back.

She saw Shaw on his hands and knees struggling to stand, and a part of the crowd had already broken off to follow them.

"They're coming!" Jessie yelled at Alex and Ernst, but they ignored her and kept running.

They turned the corner at the iron door and kept running past the empty bays. A few of the trainees and mentors were in the hallway, but the trio flew by before they could react.

Jessie started to slow at the elevators, but the boys kept going full speed, so Jessie hurried to stay up with them.

Alex crashed into the door at the end of the hallway, sending it flying open. The three of them poured into the stairwell. The metal rails and concrete steps ran up and down. Alex took off down the steps.

"No!" Ernst yelled, stopping Alex. "Up! We have to go up!"

Alex nodded and turned to follow as Ernst dragged Jessie up the first few steps. Alex passed them easily. Jessie missed a step and slammed her shin on the edge of the concrete, but she got back on her feet and kept moving, barely allowing herself to register the pain.

After ascending two floors, they heard a loud crash below them as the door swung open again. The trainees must have gathered themselves enough to start following in earnest.

"Here!" Ernst said in a hushed tone.

He had stopped at a landing and was opening the door. Alex was already several steps ahead of him and had to turn back. Ernst held the door open as Jessie and Alex dove through and then quickly, quietly closed the door behind him.

They were in a brightly lit hallway bustling with activity, but none of the **people** were dressed in the greys of the **trainees**. Many of them wore long white coats, **the women** pushing carts full of small tools and equipment around.

They forced themselves to calmly walk down the hallway, fighting to keep from gasping for air.

"Where are we—" Jessie started to ask, but Ernst and Alex shushed her simultaneously.

Halfway down the hall, Ernst glanced into a room and then opened the door for Alex and Jessie to enter.

The furniture inside was not too dissimilar from the training bays. There was a bed and an IV kit, plus some other medical equipment, but there were no servers or terminals.

"What are we going to do?" Ernst asked Alex.

"I don't know, but we have to get her out of here. If they find her—"

"I know."

"If they find me, what?" Jessie asked.

They both turned to Jessie.

"Are you really that dense?" Alex asked.

"What?" Jessie said.

"You just hijacked the Severing," Ernst said. "I—I don't think anyone has ever done that." He looked at Alex, who shook his head in agreement. Ernst stopped talking and just stared into space.

"So," Jessie said, shrugging her shoulders. "They should have built it better."

"They?" Alex shouted.

Ernst immediately shushed him. They ducked down below the window in the door and waited for a few people to pass by.

Alex lowered his voice and kept going.

"**President Marcus** himself coded up that Severing! And the only reason we're here, the only reason the Faction is even functioning, is that we won the last Threshing because of how good a Coder he is! And we have to win it again. We have to. And the only way they figure out who should be in the Threshing is the Severings. And you broke it! Oh my god, I can't believe this happened. Why did you do that? How did you even think of that?"

"**Libby** and **Mark**—" Jessie cut herself off.

"Who the hell are Libby and Mark?" Alex asked.

Jessie considered the two of them before speaking but realized that she was helpless without them and needed their trust.

"I snuck down to the bay last night after hours."

"What?" Ernst hissed out. "You can't—"

"I was freaking out!" Jessie said. "I needed some advice, so I reached out to my friends back home. It got me thinking about a job we did a couple of years ago."

"You mean like the jobs that got you Shamed. Right?" Alex said, sarcastically.

Jessie ignored him and kept talking.

"I was in charge of hacking the security system. I was supposed to keep the cameras looking the wrong way and the right doors locked and unlocked. But instead of coding up a hack that deleted the security infrastructure of the entire city, I found a hole in their code. So I just exploited it. I figured it would be funny to really screw with them without them even knowing how they'd been screwed."

"What happened?" Ernst asked.

"Well, we were able to finish the job, but we also had to disband for three months and move our hideout because it brought down so much heat on us."

"And what? They told you to do it again?"

"Yes. Well, not really. I just thought..."

Alex turned around and started pacing with his hands on his head.

"We have to get her out of here," Ernst said again.

"Get me out of here? Why?" Jessie said.

They both looked at her incredulously.

"Trainees have been banished for far less, not just ejected, but banished!" Alex said. "They'll put you out of the city into the wild on your own. You wouldn't last twenty-four hours with **the Scavengers**."

Jessie shut her eyes as if to block out the very idea. She opened her mouth to speak but then closed it again.

"Where are we going to take her?" Alex asked.

Ernst shook his head.

"I have no idea. There have to be places in Aeta to hide, but before we can even think of those, we have to get her out of this building first."

"How long do you think we have?" Alex said.

"I don't know. How could I possibly know? This isn't something that has ever happened before. And she's not exactly easy to hide," Ernst said motioning to Jessie's stubbled head.

"Okay, okay." Alex took control. "Here's what we're going to do. I'll go out first to check the corridor, and then we get her to the stairwell— not the one by the elevator, but the emergency one at the back of the building. I can't imagine many people use that one. From there, we—I guess we just try to get to the first floor and figure it out from there. Okay?"

Ernst and Jessie both nodded.

Alex took a deep breath and reached for the door handle, but before he touched it, the door swung open from the outside, revealing two Faction guards.

CHAPTER TWENTY-SEVEN

Analyzing the Scene

A STORY EVENT is an active change of life value for one or more characters as a result of conflict (one character's desires clash with another's).

A WORKING SCENE contains at least one Story Event. To determine a Scene's Story Event, answer the following four questions:

1. What are the characters doing?

Alex and Ernst are trying to escape the building to put Jessie into hiding.

2. What is the essential action of what the characters are doing in this scene?

Alex and Ernst are trying to keep Jessie safe.

3. What life value has changed for one or more of the characters in the scene?

Jessie is in denial that what she did is that big of a deal, until Alex takes control with a plan to get her out of the building and she agrees to go along with it.

4. Which life value should I highlight on my Story Grid Spreadsheet?

Denial to Acceptance

HOW THE SCENE ABIDES BY THE FIVE COMMANDMENTS OF STORYTELLING

Inciting Incident: Alex opens the door to leave the bay.

Progressive Complication: Ernst says this has never happened before and he has no idea what the Faction is going to do.

Crisis: Best bad choice. Do they stay and hide *or* do they try to escape?

Climax: Alex makes the decision to try to smuggle Jessie out of the building.

Resolution: Before they can act, two Faction guards show up.

CHAPTER TWENTY-EIGHT

Jessie saw her reflection in the dark masks of the **two Faction guards** as they towered over her. Odd, she thought, two fake Jessies and one real. Which one was she? They reached out simultaneously, grabbed her arms, and yanked her out of her hiding place. **Alex** stepped forward and reached toward one of the guards, but **Ernst** grabbed him and pulled him back.

The guards pulled her down the hallway and started marching quickly. Like a ragdoll, Jessie's toes dragged across the ground as they effortlessly pulled her to her destiny. She didn't bother to struggle. She just dropped her head and let them carry her, focusing on the squeaking sound her toes made on the polished floor.

They made their way through the large sterile corridors featuring the portraits of the president. Each one seemed to appear just as the last one faded from memory. Did they watch her as she passed or was that just her imagination? Many of the **other trainees** lined the hallway and glared at her, but she ignored them. None of it mattered anymore, and she was sure she'd never see them again.

There was no way she was going home. She wasn't going back to New York City and **her parents'** house. She wasn't going to see **Mark** and **Libby**. She'd probably be dead within a day.

Ernst and Alex had made that perfectly clear.

Would she become a **Numbered** here in the Capital? Or were they right and she'd be banned and tossed on her ear outside the city to become another sacrifice to **the Scavengers**?

The guards approached the end of the hallway and dragged her into a waiting elevator. They let go of her arms, and Jessie tumbled over her feet, slamming her knees into the floor. The doors closed, and the metal box began to descend.

Once the elevator began moving, it was impossible to tell how fast or how far they were traveling. There were no lights or buttons on the panels—just a weird sinking sensation.

Jessie struggled back to her feet and glanced up at the guards. From what she could tell from their posture, they were looking directly forward, neither of them moving in the slightest.

Eventually, the elevator began to slow and came to a stop, the doors sliding open to reveal a concrete room with low ceilings and harsh fluorescent lighting. Old, broken-down equipment was stacked haphazardly to the ceiling in towered configurations with only a small pathway down its middle, which led to a door on the opposite side.

Jessie looked up at the guards, unsure of what to do. They both nodded at her to go through the door. Jessie stepped out of the elevator. As soon as she was clear of the doors, they snapped closed behind her, and she heard the elevator start to ascend.

Jessie stood, not wanting to approach the door. Was she banished down here? It seemed like a weird way to punish her. Jessie heard a rattle across the room, and the door opened.

A tall, thin man with wispy grey hair appeared in the doorway. He pushed the glasses on the end of his long nose up and smiled. He wore an old pair of dirty jeans and a bulky sweatshirt.

She immediately recognized him.

"Hi, Jessie, come on in."

Jessie stepped tentatively through the room.

"Don't worry, dear. I won't bite."

He held the door open as she stepped through.

"Have a seat. I'll be right with you."

This room was even more of a wreck.

Old, beaten-up tables lined the walls, and every surface was covered. To the right, ancient computers were stacked so high they threatened to fall over—all in varying states of disassembly. Wires hung out of cases beside stacks of cooling fans, motherboards, and various other circuitry Jessie didn't recognize.

Along the back wall were working computers. Several different ones seemed to all be chaotically wired together and whirred loudly. Two large monitors sat next to each other on the desk amid the stack of hardware. Windows were popping up, moving around and disappearing on the screen. Commands fired while the cursor flew around the screen seemingly on its own.

The man was rattling and fighting with an old coffee maker. The entire desk overflowed with junk that Jessie had only ever seen hawked in the town square by the scroungers. Several coffee makers sat stacked in the corner with at least half a dozen toasters. Jessie recognized a microwave, but she'd never seen one actually plugged in and turned on.

"Ah!" he said. He did something else to the coffee maker that Jessie couldn't see and then turned around.

His thick, bifocal glasses sat on the end of his nose, and he hunched slightly over.

"Have you ever had real coffee, Jessie?"

She shook her head slowly.

"Ah, ah! Well, you're in for a treat! I don't suppose there's much available in the cities these days. It'll be ready shortly. Why don't you have a seat?"

He motioned to the middle of the room where an old couch and several loungers sat all facing each other around a small table. The carpet was red and shaggy with stains overwhelming several spots. Papers and stacks of folders were piled everywhere.

"Um…"

"Yes, dear?"

"You look different."

"Different? Well, yes. All those portraits you see everywhere were taken a long time ago. And a bit touched up I have to admit. I'm still **President Marcus**, though I'd rather you call me Barry. That's my first name, and I much prefer it. Now, sit, sit. I'll get the coffee and then we have a few things to talk about."

Jessie moved over and took her seat on one of the couches, sitting just on the edge of the cushion.

Barry puttered around with the coffee a few more minutes and then brought two steaming cups over. He sat one on the table in front of Jessie and took a seat in the lounger across from her. He lifted his cup to his face, dropped his nose to the edge, and inhaled deeply. "Nothing quite like it," he said and then took a sip before placing it back on the table.

"Now, dear, I was greatly impressed by your performance in the Severing. I've been doing this for, well, much longer than I care to think about, and never has someone exploited a vulnerability in the game quite like you did. Sure, a few always try some last-ditch efforts when they know they're going to lose, but you...you could have won the entire simulation...and yet you burned it down. Care to explain why?"

Jessie shrugged. "Seemed like a good idea."

"But you could have killed yourself and all of the other trainees."

"That wasn't how it was coded."

Barry's eyebrows lifted at this.

"And how did you know that?"

Jessie pressed her lips together and looked away from him.

"Very well. Now you've left me with a bit of a problem. That Severing was supposed to cut the number of teams down to sixteen and I coded the next one for only that many teams."

Jessie raised an eyebrow.

"It's easy enough to fix—a minor inconvenience, really. I'll still be able to pare the teams down to the number we need for the Threshing."

Jessie's eyes cut at him.

"You have a problem with that?"

"Why do the trainees have to die in the process? I don't understand that."

Barry let out a deep sigh.

"I hate it. I really do. But it's the only way to test you truly. We can only send the best to the Threshing. Also," Barry shrugged, "it's what **the Reapers** require."

"Then why send me here? I have no training. Why force me here instead of just recruit me for the next one? Or bring someone in who actually wants to be here."

Barry paused for a long moment.

"That's not really up to me. Is it? I didn't know you existed until a few minutes ago. I rely on the **city mayors** to send me their best and brightest."

"That doesn't make any sense! I—"

Barry raised his hand to silence her.

"It doesn't matter. All I've seen so far suggests your mayor was right in his insistence. You say you have no training, and yet you were one of the first to make it to the tower. That shows me you're more prepared than most of **the Coders** who are much older and experienced. And your burning down of the tower shows me you're thinking far outside the bounds of what is presented to you, which is what we'll need to win the Threshing."

Fear seized Jessie. She dropped her head and tried to keep from shaking. "You're sending me to the Threshing?" she asked quietly.

"Well, we don't know that yet. Do we? There are still two more Severings left."

"And what if I don't want this? What if I refuse to play?"

Barry paused for a moment and then motioned to Jessie's cup. She leaned down, picked it up, and took a sip of the steaming liquid.

Her face screwed up as the taste hit her tongue.

"Ah yes, it's a bit bitter at first. It's an acquired taste." He paused. "Now, tell me, dear, what do you want? What would make you happy?"

"I just want to go home," she said.

"All of the other candidates see it as an honor to be here. They're the best of the best. And their families are rewarded with extra credits. And yet, you want to go back to the city. Why is that?"

"**My brother**," she said.

"Your brother? What do you mean?"

"He came to Aeta, to the last Preparing."

"What happened?"

"He made it all the way to the Threshing. Mom and Dad were so excited."

Barry became very still.

"Surely you got a report back?"

"We were told he died, but we never saw a picture or got a certificate of death. It was never in the news reports."

"What was his name?"

"**Randy.**"

Barry froze, his coffee cup halfway to his mouth. He sat for a few seconds and then slowly put the cup back down on the saucer.

"Randy Marston?"

"No, his last name is—was—different from mine. We have different dads. Randy Teller."

Barry let out a deep sigh and sat back into the old couch. He lifted the mug to his lips and sipped on the hot liquid while staring at the ceiling.

Jessie sat quietly, waiting.

"Okay," Barry said. "How about this. You stay for now and keep training. I'll look into what happened with your brother and will get you a definitive answer before the next Severing. If you still want to go home, I'll get you on the next transport back to New York. But if I can change your mind, you stay on as a candidate, and we'll see how you do in the next Severing. How does that sound?"

Jessie smiled at him. "Really? You'd send me back?"

"Of course! We only want candidates who want to be here. Lots of psychological research proves that an invested candidate is better than someone only doing it out of duty. So let me do some digging for you, and I'll get back with you in a few days. Deal?"

Barry stood and reached out his hand. Jessie stood and shook it.

"Deal!" she said.

Jessie turned back toward the elevator.

"Oh, one more thing," Barry said.

Jessie turned back.

"Yes?"

"Let's keep this meeting between us. We can't go having everyone think I'm playing favorites. I want to make sure you can go home if you want to."

Jessie nodded and turned back toward the elevator.

CHAPTER TWENTY-EIGHT

Analyzing the Scene

A STORY EVENT is an active change of life value for one or more characters as a result of conflict (one character's desires clash with another's).

A WORKING SCENE contains at least one Story Event. To determine a Scene's Story Event, answer the following four questions:

1. What are the characters doing?

The Faction guards are taking Jessie to meet with President Marcus.

2. What is the essential action of what the characters are doing in this scene?

Jessie is trying to work out what her punishment will be.

3. What life value has changed for one or more of the characters in the scene?

Jessie starts out assuming she is getting punished and is trying to figure out what her punishment will be. However, she ends up making a deal with the President to eventually send her home.

4. Which life value should I highlight on my Story Grid Spreadsheet?

Scared to Relieved.

HOW THE SCENE ABIDES BY THE FIVE COMMANDMENTS OF STORYTELLING

Inciting Incident: Jessie is taken by the guards.

Progressive Complication: Barry offers to find out what happened to Randy and to send Jessie home if she wants to go.

Crisis: Irreconcilable goods. Jessie can agree to take the deal with Barry and go home *or* she can stay and finish the task she came to Aeta to do.

Climax: Jessie agrees to take the deal.

Resolution: Barry dismisses her with a warning not to tell anyone about their meeting.

NOTES:

This scene represents the crisis of middle build one, 'comply or defy?'

CHAPTER TWENTY-NINE

The two guards were waiting when **Jessie** returned to the elevator. This time there was no need to hold on to her. She stared into the distance as they made their way back down the corridor.

When the doors opened again, the guards let her take the lead. Jessie began to make her way to her bay room as if nothing had happened. She fought to keep her face blank as she navigated through the corridors like it was totally normal that she was walking to her room with two Faction guards behind her. **The other trainees** were obviously still angry with her, but they couldn't do anything to stop her now. They made a show of inching away from her as she came near them and followed her with their eyes as she passed, their faces screwed up in disgust. But they stayed quiet and kept their distance.

They turned the corner, but when she slowed down in front of her room, the guards kept moving. She opened her mouth to ask, but before she could speak, the guards indicated to her to follow them. She shrugged and followed.

Soon, they came to a new door. One of the guards swiped his hand across the key lock, and it buzzed open. Jessie took a look at the guards, their blank masks pointed directly forward, and then pushed the bay door open. **Alex** and **Ernst** were waiting for her inside.

Their eyes lit up when they saw her.

"Jessie! Where have you been?" Alex asked.

Excitedly, he continued before she could answer. "Oh, man! I wish you could have seen it! **Pierre** read everyone the Riot Act. Railed about how this new recruit with no training was able to pull off such an upset. He individually called out mistakes each and every one of **the Coders** made, and oh man, **Az**—that was the best part! He pulled Az to the front and chewed him out for a good five minutes about letting you not only reach the tower before him but burn it down while he was standing there. It was amazing!"

Ernst and Alex beamed at her, unable to contain their excitement.

"What about everyone else? They're still glaring at me as I walk down the halls," Jessie said.

"Oh that," Ernst waved his hands as if that didn't matter. "They're just jealous. Pierre warned everyone that they better keep their hands off you, and instead of attacking you, they should probably try to learn something from you."

Alex laughed at that. "Man, you should have seen the other Coders' faces! They loved being told to learn from the youngest recruit who's been here for a week."

"And here's the best part," Ernst said. "Our equipment and credits were seriously upgraded. It's pretty standard for the teams that pass the Severings to get new installs, but since we were considered the only winners, we got a bigger upgrade than normal."

"Yeah, we have a brand-new private bay with bigger stacks and much nicer medical equipment," Alex said.

"Come on, let's go take a look at it," Ernst said, turning to the door.

"Wait," Alex said to Ernst and then looked down at Jessie. "Where'd you go during the briefing? Where'd those guards take you?"

Jessie paused. Everything **Barry** had said raced through her head, and she struggled to speak.

Should she tell them what he had said? Shame shot through her, a palpable queasiness in her stomach. She thought of **Ernst's and Alex's families.** What would happen to them when she went home before the Threshing? But she couldn't think about that now. Barry had said to keep their agreement a secret, and that meant keeping the fact that she'd met the president of the Faction a secret too.

She looked between the boys' excited faces. They had no idea their fates were even more tied to hers now and they had no control over their future.

"Um," she said, trying to keep her voice relaxed. "Apparently, Pierre knew the other trainees weren't happy with me, so he sent the guards to get me before anything happened. They just sat me in a room. I had no idea what was going on until I saw you two."

She forced a smile on her face. "This is great, though. We're one step closer to the Threshing. Let's go take a look at the upgrades."

The door slid open again, and **Harry** walked in. His face was almost purple with rage.

"What kind of stunt was that?" he screamed at Jessie.

Jessie couldn't find words to speak, but Alex stepped in between them.

"She won," Alex said.

"She didn't win! She melted down the entire Severing!"

"Didn't you see Pierre's debrief?" Alex asked, still incredulous at Harry's anger.

"You have no idea! No idea!" Harry screamed and slammed his fist down on the counter nearest him, rattling everything inside. "What the hell were you thinking?"

Jessie finally found her voice.

"I survived!" she yelled. "Those Coders wanted to kill me, and I made it out! Who cares how I did it? What else do you want from me? And I got us a brand-new bay and equipment!"

Harry took two deep breaths in and slowly exhaled.

"You're on his radar now."

"Whose?"

"**Marcus.** *Everybody.* They're watching you now. You were supposed to lay low, get through the Severing but not make a splash. Remember me telling you that? Just move on to the next round. And not only didn't you do that, but you've also become the only thing everyone in the entire city can talk about."

"So?"

At this, Harry's face went purple again, and the three of them instinctively backed away. But instead of exploding again, he slumped into one of the office chairs nearby. He pressed on either side of his temples with his thumbs, closing his eyes against the pain.

"Why are you here, Jessie?" he asked, just above a whisper.

Jessie looked at Ernst and Alex, confused. They shrugged at her.

"Because of the Threshing. Because **Mayor Charles** sent me."

"Yeah?" Harry asked, opening his eyes. "You haven't wondered why you're the youngest of all the recruits or why you were late to the party? Or even why you're the second in your family to be recruited?"

Jessie's eyes narrowed.

"What do you mean?"

Harry stood.

"It's not for me to tell you, especially if you haven't figured it out yourself."

"No," Jessie yelled, taking a step toward him. "You can't just say that and then not explain."

Harry smirked.

"Unfortunately for you, I can."

"But—"

Harry waved his hand, cutting her off. "The only thing we can do now is get you ready for the next Severing. It'll be coming in the next couple of weeks. Since you've already got everyone's attention, we'll need to figure out how to use that to our advantage."

"And how are we going to do that?" Jessie asked. "I still don't understand most of what happened in the first Severing."

"What do you mean?"

"How did **Clifton** and **Ben** find each other? How did Az find me? How did he recruit the Coders to help him? I feel like I'm playing a game when I don't know all the rules."

Harry looked at Jessie like she was crazy and then back at Ernst and Alex. They all looked back at him, confused.

"Are you serious?" Harry asked Jessie. She just stared.

"And you two don't know?"

Ernst and Alex shook their heads.

"It's no wonder **Lucas** didn't even make it to the first Severing."

Alex's face darkened at this, but he kept quiet.

"Do none of you even know how we won the last Threshing?"

Their blank stares answered his question.

"Come with me," he said and walked out of the bay.

CHAPTER TWENTY-NINE

Analyzing the Scene

A STORY EVENT is an active change of life value for one or more characters as a result of conflict (one character's desires clash with another's).

A WORKING SCENE contains at least one Story Event. To determine a Scene's Story Event, answer the following four questions:

1. What are the characters doing?

The guards take Jessie to meet with Alex and Ernst, who tell her everything that happened – all good stuff – since she was taken. Harry joins them and is very angry about what Jessie did, but he doesn't fully explain why.

2. What is the essential action of what the characters are doing in this scene?

Jessie is trying to acclimate to the changes, while contending with the knowledge she gained while meeting with President Marcus.

3. What life value has changed for one or more of the characters in the scene?

Jessie is relieved that everything is okay for Ernst and Alex, but she ends up defending herself to Harry in the face of his rage.

4. Which life value should I highlight on my Story Grid Spreadsheet?

Knowing to Ignorant.

HOW THE SCENE ABIDES BY THE FIVE COMMANDMENTS OF STORYTELLING

Inciting Incident: The guards take her to a new place to meet with Alex and Ernst.

Progressive Complication: Harry explodes in anger instead of congratulating Jessie on her performance.

Crisis: Best bad choice. Does Harry answer Jessie's questions about the Severing *or* does he keep evading her?

Climax: He agrees to answer Jessie's questions.

Resolution: He leaves the room and has them follow behind him.

CHAPTER THIRTY

The white light faded into almost complete blackness. **Jessie** turned around slowly to get her bearings. Another training simulation. **Harry** had been pushing the three of them hard over previous two weeks. Sixteen and seventeen-hour days. Some of the sims were just a few minutes while others lasted more than six hours.

I'm in a weird cavern—one I've never imagined before, she said.

Right, said **Ernst**, *this is an evade and avoid simulation. **Five Faction guards** will be hunting you, and you have to survive for the full hour to pass the sim.*

And if they catch me?

Then you log out once one has you in its grasp. It's like a big game of tag. Don't let the guards touch you until the hour is up.

Jessie took a step further into the tunnel and rocks shifted under her feet. She stopped, listened, and then began to move forward again.

She was generally anxious—not so much from the simulation because this was just like all the others. But she hadn't heard from **President Marcus**. At all.

He told her at their coffee meeting to give him a few days to sort things out about what happened to her brother, and it had been two weeks. The next Severing could come any day, and he had promised to get back with her before she was required to perform. What was taking so long?

Jessie took a deep breath and let it out slowly.

Marcus was a busy man, and he had promised Jessie she would hear from him. So she just needed to be patient. She put him as far out of her mind as she could.

So, what's the play here? Do I just find a place to hide or stay on the move?

Where are you now?

In the middle of the tunnel.

Then I would say at least keep moving until you find a good place to hide.

Jessie nodded and kept walking. She hugged the sides of the tunnel, trying to keep her feet light and make as little noise as possible. She took a few steps and then stopped to listen. As she moved, she ran her hand along the rocky wall to keep her bearings.

She had only been moving a few minutes when she heard the sound of boots crunching on shifting rock heading her way. Quickly, she backtracked a few steps to a small indention in the wall she'd felt a minute before and crouched down, tightening herself into as small a ball as possible.

The boots continued to get louder as they approached, but Jessie remained motionless as they came by her position. She ventured a peek as they went by and shivered when she saw the familiar black helmets and weapons of the Faction guards.

Two Faction guards just passed by, she said.

Did they see you?

I'm still here. Aren't I?

Okay, good. Can you stay where you are?

I don't think so. I got lucky they didn't see me. They'll definitely find me if they come back through.

Keep moving then.

It was hard to tell how far she had gone, but it must have been at least a couple of hundred feet when she saw flickering light coming from ahead. She crept closer and saw some kind of chamber. Her tunnel connected to it and several others seemed to branch off of it.

Large, ornate carvings decorated each of the doorways into what she assumed were the branching tunnels, but Jessie couldn't quite make out what the figures were from her position.

She froze as a shadow cast across the wall. **A figure** had stepped into the chamber and stopped.

What are these things? she thought to Ernst.

What do you mean? I think they're just Faction guards. You already saw them. Right?

Jessie looked ahead at the shadow. If it was a guard, it was down on its knees for some reason. The shadow kept jumping with the flickering light, but the image was only a few feet tall.

Suddenly, whatever it was raised onto its hind legs and stuck what looked like a dog's snout into the air for a few seconds before dropping back down and disappearing.

Jessie froze in place. What was that thing? When it was on its hind legs, it looked to be about seven feet tall unless the light was playing tricks. She was unsure what to do next, but the sound of boots behind her spurred her into action. She walked quickly forward, hugging the wall and avoiding the loose rocks wherever she could. She lost her footing now and then but quickly recovered on her next step.

She surveyed the chamber as she approached and then stepped in, looking around wildly for the best direction to go. Four other tunnels branched off from the inner sanctum besides the one she just exited. Now that she could see them better, the carvings above each of the doorways were terrifying depictions of monstrous beasts with serrating fangs, ragged claws, and enormous eyes.

The sound of boots was getting closer behind her. With the position of the torchlight, whatever shadow she had seen must have moved to one of the tunnels on her left, so she turned and entered the closest tunnel on her right. She kept moving for a while, hugging the wall and staying silent.

Forty-five minutes down, Jessie, Ernst said. Keep going. You're almost there.

Jessie didn't know whether to be relieved or not. On the one hand, she had only had one brush with the Faction guards. On the other hand, this place with the crazy drawings of horrific monsters gave her the creeps. The carvings on the wall and whatever that beast was that she saw reflected in the corridor ran through her mind repeatedly.

She continued to move farther into her new tunnel until her hand found a large crack in the wall to her right. It was too dark to see, but she felt her way along the edges and found that the space was a little over a foot wide. It would be a tight squeeze, but she could fit. It'd make a good hiding spot.

She decided to wait in the recess in case more Faction guards followed down the same tunnel.

She crouched down by the crack in the wall, waiting and listening. She had gone around a small bend right at the beginning of the tunnel, but she could still make out the corridor in the firelight.

The sound of boots hitting the hard, smooth rock of the corridor soon followed, and she heard voices. They must have been discussing which way to go next.

Suddenly, there was **a loud yell of alarm** and then a quick pop-pop-pop. Jessie had heard that sound before. It took her back to Times Square and the sound of executions.

Jessie remembered how closely packed the square had been that day. She hadn't been able to see over the heads of the adults, but she knew what was happening. Someone had been caught stealing food, attacking one of the Faction guards or one of the other myriads of reasons an adult faced the death sentence.

They would be hung by their hands and tied to the tops of ten-foot poles. Their crimes were recited over the loudspeaker and then Jessie would hear the pop-pop-pop of the Faction weapons, and she knew the people were dead.

This time, though, the pop-pop-pop kept coming as the guards screamed. Jessie crawled up the tunnel to see what was going on. She saw shadows moving quickly, and she saw the strange beast jump on and sink its giant teeth into one of the guards. The scream was super high pitched before a loud crunch and everything went silent.

Jessie gasped and started scrambling backward toward her crack in the wall again, yelling at herself internally about being so stupid to go back. But the shadow heard her movement. She could see it leave the dead Faction guard's body and turn toward her tunnel, a low growl rumbling.

She turned, scampered back to the crack and pushed herself as deeply into it as she could.

What is that thing?

What is what? Ernst replied.

Jessie pressed her body as far as she could into the space. She heard the scratching of the rocks as the thing started down the tunnel after her. She froze as she listened to the monster approach and then bypass her hidden crevasse.

There's something here.

Right, the guards.

No, it's something else.

There's nothing else. Just the guards patrolling. All you have to do is evade them for another few minutes.

No! I'm telling you. Something just jumped the guards and killed them.

What?

And it's stalking—

A loud growl filled Jessie's ears, and a searing pain ripped down her arm. Jessie screamed and shoved back so tightly that the back of her head and arms began to ache. She heard more growls and snarling followed by claws scraping against the rock.

The claws found her leg and tore through her flesh with little effort. Jessie screamed in pain, but there was no more room in the crack. It had grown too tight to shove herself in any more deeply.

The claws found her leg again, and she screamed, kicking at the invisible attacker, but she hit nothing. She pushed with all her might into the crack and clamped her eyes shut, trying to block the sound of the monster as she pushed as hard as she could.

A loud tearing sound rent the air, and she toppled out of her hiding place away from the monster. She slammed her head as she hit the ground, stars exploding in her vision.

She shook her head, trying to clear her thoughts, and finally became aware that Ernst was yelling into her head.

Jessie! What is going on? Jessie, answer me!

I'm—I'm still here.

She could hear **the beast** still growling and its claws scraping against the stone as it frantically reached for her, but it was farther away now. She must have pushed her way into a hidden cave somehow. She rolled over and tried to push herself up, but pain shot through her right arm, and she collapsed back down to the ground. The pain from her leg and arm overtook her mind, and she began to moan.

With her unharmed arm, she reached down and felt along her leg. She could feel the wide wounds where the claws had torn through and the sticky warmth of the blood.

Ernst, I'm—

Her head began to swim again. She couldn't tell if the blackness was the lack of light in the tunnel or her vision disappearing.

I'm trying to log you out, Jessie, but the grid won't let me.

There is— When am— Jessie paused. Home?

Jessie, hang on! Alex is giving you something. You've got to stay awake just a minute longer.

Jessie nodded her head limply but realized she'd closed her eyes. She forced them open, but she couldn't tell if she'd been successful. She could only see black. Was it the darkness in the cave? Or had she lost her sight? Thankfully, she sensed that the monster's noises receded farther and farther away from her.

Thirty seconds, Jessie. You're almost there.

Jessie closed her eyes again, leaning into the blackness until everything went white.

CHAPTER THIRTY

Analyzing the Scene

A STORY EVENT is an active change of life value for one or more characters as a result of conflict (one character's desires clash with another's).

A WORKING SCENE contains at least one Story Event. To determine a Scene's Story Event, answer the following four questions:

1. What are the characters doing?

Jessie is in a training simulation where she has to evade Faction guards. A monster shows up, attacks her, and almost kills her.

2. What is the essential action of what the characters are doing in this scene?

Jessie is trying to build her skills.

3. What life value has changed for one or more of the characters in the scene?

Jessie is at first more stressed by Marcus's lack of communication than by the simulation. However, the simulation quickly turns to terrifying when a monster shows up and almost kills her.

4. Which life value should I highlight on my Story Grid Spreadsheet?

Safety to Extreme Danger

HOW THE SCENE ABIDES BY THE FIVE COMMANDMENTS OF STORYTELLING

Inciting Incident: Jessie is logged into the simulation.

Progressive Complication: The monster attacks the Faction guards in the simulation.

Crisis: Best bad choice. Jessie can give up and let the monster finish her off *or* she can keep pushing into the crack and try to get away.

Climax: Jessie pushes through the crack.

Resolution: Jessie falls out of reach of the monster, buying herself enough time to let the simulation end before she dies.

NOTES:

This scene represents the climax of middle build one, 'the shadow agent asserts their dominant power.'

CHAPTER THIRTY-ONE

"What the hell was that?" **Alex** yelled. "She almost died! She flatlined right there at the end!"

"I don't know!" **Ernst** screamed back. "It was just a training sim. Avoid and evade. It was the caverns with **the Faction** guards. If they found you, you lose and get logged out. That's it."

Jessie was sitting up on the edge of the bench, shaking her head. She kept gripping her arm and leg, making sure they were still intact. The sounds of **the snarling monster** and raking claws still reverberated through her head.

"What happened in there?" Ernst asked.

Jessie squeezed her eyes shut and tried to picture the cavern again. So many of these things would float away like dreams if she didn't concentrate.

She began recounting what had happened in the cavern—hiding from the guards and seeing the shadow of the monster.

The door to their bay slammed open, and **Harry** came in.

"You two, out!" he demanded.

"Why? She was telling us—"

"Out!" Harry screamed. He grabbed Alex by the shoulder and

shoved him toward the door. Alex shot him an ugly look but left with Ernst hurrying to catch up.

"Tell me everything," Harry said.

"Couldn't you watch in the public logs?" she asked.

"I did. But the public logs cut out halfway through. That's when Ernst called me freaking out. So. You tell me."

Jessie told Harry everything she could remember about the entire sim. She had to fight for the last few minutes before she finally logged off. Harry's face remained emotionless as Jessie walked through the ordeal step by step.

After she finished, Harry stood in silence for several long moments, his eyes darting back and forth before he spoke.

"I inspected the coding of that sim myself before Ernst ran it. There was no monster demon dog thing. It was just Faction guards on patrol."

"Then how—"

"I don't know. There shouldn't be a way for anyone to get into our sim code. However this happened, it came from someone very, very savvy."

"You mean somebody powerful in the Faction?" Jessie said, thinking of **Az** and his attacks on her.

"Maybe," Harry said.

"He tried to have me killed?" Jessie asked.

"This is why I told you to stay under the radar," Harry said, frustration thick in his voice. "Now they know you're a threat."

"Let's report it to **President Marcus**," she said. "He'll take care of it. He doesn't want the candidates trying to kill each other outside of the Severings."

"Marcus? That's who probably did this! Who were you talking about?"

"Az! He tried to kill me in the last Severing."

Harry rolled his eyes. "There's no way he would have the access to hack into our training sim. This has to be Marcus. It's retribution for what you did in the last Severing."

"I don't believe it. **Barry** said—"

Jessie cut herself off, but Harry's eyes narrowed.

"Barry? You mean President Marcus?"

Jessie didn't answer.

"What's really going on, Jessie?"

"Nothing. I just think Marcus will take care of the candidates."

"You mean **the man who churns through candidates** every four years? The man who has kept a stranglehold on the **Americas Faction** for forty years? You lived, like I did, as **a Numbered.** And we probably will again. You should know what he's capable of."

"He didn't do this," Jessie said. "Az did. He came after me. Not Marcus. That's who we should be worried about."

Harry sighed. "I guess it doesn't matter. You survived and either way you have to get ready for the next Severing."

Jessie nodded and hopped off the table.

"What's next?"

CHAPTER THIRTY-ONE

Analyzing the Scene

A STORY EVENT is an active change of life value for one or more characters as a result of conflict (one character's desires clash with another's).

A WORKING SCENE contains at least one Story Event. To determine a Scene's Story Event, answer the following four questions:

1. What are the characters doing?

Alex and Ernst are debriefing Harry on what happened, but Harry interrupts and talks to Jessie alone. She shares what happened, and they argue over who is responsible.

2. What is the essential action of what the characters are doing in this scene?

Jessie wants to blame Az, so she can protect her hope in President Marcus.

3. What life value has changed for one or more of the characters in the scene?

Jessie is forced to choose the person she is going to trust more in this game, Harry or President Marcus. Until now, she's trusted Harry because of their history together, and she has needed him. However, she now feels like she has President Marcus to take care of her.

4. Which life value should I highlight on my Story Grid Spreadsheet?

Trusting to Suspicious.

HOW THE SCENE ABIDES BY THE FIVE COMMANDMENTS OF STORYTELLING

Inciting Incident: Harry enters the room and kicks Alex and Ernst out.

Progressive Complication: Jessie refers to President Marcus by his first name.

Crisis: Irreconcilable goods. Jessie can stand her ground in her defense of President Marcus *or* she can side with Harry.

Climax: She stands her ground in support of President Marcus.

Resolution: Harry realizes he can't change her mind and lets it go.

CHAPTER THIRTY-TWO

Jessie shuffled in behind **Ernst** and **Alex** and took a seat on the aisle. The three of them were in the very back row of the small auditorium where a dozen rows of plush red seats folded down and faced a big white screen.

Jessie looked at the rest of the boys and nudged Ernst and his unwavering gaze.

"What?" he whispered.

"Knock it off. Staring at **Az** won't do anything but piss off **Harry**. He wants us to move on."

Ernst pulled his eyes away from the boy and poked Alex, getting him to break his intense stare as well.

Harry had reluctantly let Jessie share what she thought had happened in the sim a few days before with Alex and Ernst. But at the same time, he swore to do all kinds of awful things to them if they went after Az in any way.

"He's getting away with it!" Ernst said, unable to keep his eyes from glancing to the back of Az's head.

"Harry told us we'd have our time to go after him, but we can't do it now. It'll just cause more trouble," Jessie said.

"The little prick needs to be cut out of the program for good," Alex said. He nodded at Jessie. "You'll get him in the next Severing. I'm sure of it."

Jessie forced a smile and nodded before turning her head to face the screen.

The next Severing loomed large.

Everyone was whispering that it would happen in the next couple of days, yet Jessie still hadn't heard from **President Marcus**. Despite herself, she was getting worried. She had been brainstorming since the disaster in the sim how she could get a message to him, but nothing seemed probable of success. She couldn't ask Harry or the boys for help seeing as she'd promised to keep her agreement with Marcus a secret.

The night before she'd chanced sneaking out of her room and made her way down to the elevator she had ridden to Marcus's office, but nothing came of it. There were no buttons or panels, and she couldn't remember how **the Faction guard** had even opened the door.

She squeezed her eyes shut and took a deep breath, calming herself as best she could. No matter how hard she prepared for the next Severing, she couldn't get it out of her mind that she could get a free ticket home before she had to perform.

Marcus was the president of the **Americas Faction** and ran the entire Severing process. He wrote all the software and personally oversaw the progress of **the recruits.** If he was waiting to get back to her, there must have been a very good reason. She forced herself to relax again, assuming he'd definitely reach out to her before the next Severing and let her go home.

She'd made a good show of continuing her training, putting in the hours and pushing hard. Even though she knew she wouldn't be facing the Severing, she didn't want to disappoint Ernst and Alex in the process.

Feeling a bit better, Jessie opened her eyes just as the lights began to dim.

A projector somewhere overhead flipped on, and an image of the Americas flag with its vertical red and white stripes and its single blue star imposed in the middle began flapping on the screen. It faded out to show President Marcus standing at attention, his brow creased as if he was thinking very hard about something important.

Ever since she had arrived in Aeta and started the training, the Monday morning routine required all of the recruits to attend the video presentations. The first one had been all about the history of the Americas. It was similar to ones shown to her when she was younger and still logging in for her school lessons every day. That was a few years before she figured out how to reroute the coding to hide the fact that she was skipping.

The story was always the same—back way before she was born, way before even **her parents** were born, as the Burning first swept across the world, war broke out over the last remaining resources. At stake were the land areas that could actually sustain crop growth—way up north at the top of the world.

At the worst of it, when it was unsafe to unlatch your door for fear of a **marauding band of killers** breaking in and taking what little food you had left, **the Reapers** emerged.

The small group of **military hackers** was able to pull together the scattershot automated systems of defeated military operations into a single overpowering force that put an end to the fighting. Since they controlled not just the weapons systems but the food and water resources, the power lines and what oil reserves remained, they quickly put down any opposition.

They organized the global community into divisions, which gave rise to the northern urban-dominated Factions. **People** flocked to the northern cities of the world as the food was almost nonexistent outside of the cities. They soon relied entirely on the Reapers to deliver it.

Before long, the cities had become unmanageable. With too many people packed into too small of spaces, chaos and violence resurfaced every time food shipments arrived.

To solve the problem, the Reapers developed the grid.

It calmed the swelling population with virtual reality, one practically indistinguishable from what the world looked like before its destruction. The vision was so captivating that it turned the people's attention away from their physical starving long enough so tens of millions of people could live in close proximity without violence. Food was distributed at specific times without fear of riots as the people were reluctant to leave the tranquil online universe.

Nevertheless, the first few iterations of the grid failed spectacularly. They would calm the crowds for a short time, but before long the unrest would start up again as starvation would eventually seize the attention of even the most enthralled, and things would begin to unravel again.

And then the Threshing was born.

It solved two problems at once for the Reapers.

First, it allowed them to find the best and the brightest minds of the younger generations. The **premier children** had the choice of joining the ruling Reaper class and be put to work improving the grid. Those who failed never made it home and left **their families** to live with the disgrace.

Even more importantly, the Threshing gave the people a purpose.

Now since people farmed in the grid, they no longer just hung out in bliss. Instead, they were put to work doing virtual chores that wired directly into the machinery that grew the food in the temperate climates. The more credits they built up for their Faction by doing these chores, the better the Faction's resources, and the more likely they were to win the next Threshing. The credits conferred privileges to their teams.

The Faction that won the Threshing got a double portion of food and resources for the next four years. They'd be well-fed for four years while the other three Factions would live on the brink of starvation.

The Reapers had figured out the perfect sweet spot to keep the population purposeful and complacent. Most spent twenty hours a day plugged into the grid farming for credits, nodding off and even sleeping inside the virtual world. Every credit they farmed put a little more food on their table. And those who were exceptionally successful were granted **Elite** status.

The Coder who won the Threshing was the elitist of the Elite. He or she fast-tracked straight into Reaper status.

Except for the last Threshing.

Jessie shook her head and tried to pay attention to the latest video. The screen darkened, and then an image of a chair appeared. The image flickered for a moment and a man, who looked to be in his forties, materialized in the chair. He faced his young audience. Jessie swore he was looking directly at her even though she knew this recording was many years old.

"I'm **mentor M9385**. Toronto is my home city. I'm here to walk you through my second Threshing as mentor."

As the man began talking, the background behind him filled up. It now looked like he was in some kind of large hangar. She couldn't make out a ceiling, though, and behind him, people moved in and out among the equipment. Now that she had been in Aeta training for a few weeks, Jessie recognized much of it. She made out the stacks of servers, the gurneys for the Coders, and the med bay equipment, but on screen was on a whole new level. Everything was bigger, nicer, and better stocked. But the few people in the broadcast looked dejected and moved slowly.

M9385 spoke softly.

"We've just lost the Threshing."

He rubbed his face and took a deep breath, barely containing his emotion.

"My recruit was the last standing, so I've been asked to give my report on what happened as a way to help future teams. Since we were the first Faction cut this year, there's not a whole lot to say. I'll walk through our demise as succinctly as I can." He took a breath before he began.

"The setting was pre-Burn Tokyo.

"Levi—err, my Coder—was quickly overwhelmed by the intensity of the city lights and the masses of people. He loaded in on the city's outskirts like normal, but even there he encountered an insane amount of movement. In past Threshings, they've been loaded into abandoned and nearly empty cities. There were always the urban traps and pitfalls you had to watch out for, but this sim was very different. Within seconds of being loaded in, **Reaper bots** attacked my Coder by posing as people pushing to get to the commuter train.

"He was able to fend those challenges off, but not without coming away from the experience fatigued and injured, which made the rest of the journey to the city center a hard take. I know the advice is always given to be ready for anything, but it's hard to say anything else when they could load you into any city set in any time in recorded history."

M9385 slumped back in his chair. The image flickered a few times, almost as a reminder that this was archival footage.

"I suppose if I were forced to advise future mentors and Coders, it would be this. First, and foremost, be on the lookout for **spies from the other Factions** in your midst. One from the Far East Faction sabotaged our software ahead of time, which caused all kinds of trouble.

"Once in the Threshing, blend in as soon as possible even if you have to attack a bot and take their clothes or cover yourself in mud because you were loaded into an empty, bombed-out city. It doesn't matter. Figure out a way to either hide in the crowd or elude detection in the shadows. You have to avoid a fight as long as possible. An early fight will drain you mentally and physically, and you won't recover well enough. From there, find a balance between a direct route and a safe route to the target. Of course, the direct route will be heavily set and snared in some unique new form of Reaper punishment. But if you're too cautious, the other Factions will beat you to the city center, and it won't matter that you lived because nobody but the winner makes it out alive. The last thing I'll say is to work with your other Faction recruits. Decide how to signal and find each other ahead of time. Even though only one of you can win, you have to work together for the praise and preservation of Americas. So even if you've made enemies of the other Coders in your Faction, kiss and make nice because you're going to need to watch each other's backs."

Again, even though Jessie knew the image was meant to feel as if it was specially designed for her—Marcus probably had something to do with that—she felt like M9385's eyes bored through the decade that separated them and was only talking to her.

"All else I can say now is God speed, good luck, and code well."

The image flickered a couple of times as M9385 stood, his eyes still locked on Jessie, and then the screen went dark.

A few seconds passed, and then it lit up again. Once more, a chair sat in the center of the screen, but the background was different this time. It looked like it was in a small bay. Everything was a wreck. The medical supplies littered the floor, and the gurney sat upended with wires hanging haphazardly from the stack. It looked like several of them had been ripped out.

Again the flickers, and then **a woman** sat in the chair.

Jessie gasped, and her hand went to her mouth. Ernst and Alex cut their eyes at her, but she didn't notice.

She was beautiful. Long, flowing blonde hair fell around her shoulders. Even the dark, tired circles below her eyes didn't take away from the large, blue irises and high cheekbones. She also had a smile on her face.

"Mentor M3548. New York is my home city. This is my third time mentoring for the Threshing and," she paused, took a deep breath, and then continued. "We won. We actually did it." She seemed more relieved than happy.

She kept talking, but Jessie couldn't listen. Her mind was racing far too fast to take in any new information.

How could it be? Why hadn't she said anything? Why hadn't Harry? How did she end up—?

Jessie jerked as a hand touched her arm. Ernst and Alex were both staring at her, their faces questioning her.

"What is it?" Ernst whispered.

"**It's her,**" Jessie said.

"Who?"

Jessie turned back and looked at the woman one more time to confirm what she already knew.

"**Eighty-three.**"

CHAPTER THIRTY-TWO

Analyzing the Scene

A STORY EVENT is an active change of life value for one or more characters as a result of conflict (one character's desires clash with another's).

A WORKING SCENE contains at least one Story Event. To determine a Scene's Story Event, answer the following four questions:

1. What are the characters doing?

Jessie, Alex, and Ernst are sitting in a weekly briefing where they learn from participants about past Threshings.

2. What is the essential action of what the characters are doing in this scene?

Jessie is trying to stay calm because she hasn't heard from President Marcus.

3. What life value has changed for one or more of the characters in the scene?

Jessie moves from distracted and uninterested to completely shocked when Eighty-three shows up as a past mentor in the briefings.

4. Which life value should I highlight on my Story Grid Spreadsheet?

Uninterested to Shocked.

HOW THE SCENE ABIDES BY THE FIVE COMMANDMENTS OF STORYTELLING

Inciting Incident: They settle in for the weekly briefing.

Progressive Complication: A recording of Eighty-three as a Mentor starts playing during the briefing.

Crisis: Best bad choice. Jessie can stay calm *or* she can storm out.

Climax: [Off-screen] She gets up and storms out as soon as the briefing is over.

Resolution: [Off-screen] She goes to find Harry.

CHAPTER THIRTY-THREE

"When are you going to get it through your head that you cannot be bringing attention to yourself?" **Harry** barked at her.

After the film with **Eighty-three, Jessie** stood and pushed her way down the aisle past the other recruits, leaving **Ernst** and **Alex** gaping behind her. **Everyone in the auditorium** had noticed her by the time she slammed into the door, shoved it open and left.

But she didn't care. Nothing made sense anymore, and she had to get answers. Now.

She stalked the halls looking for Harry. She'd checked the bay and his bunk and even the common room, finally finding him stuffing his face in the commissary.

"What is going on?" she had yelled across the room. The various **mentors** and **officers** who were eating their late breakfast startled, looking up at her.

"I saw her! She was here! Years ago!"

Harry jumped up from his table, his chair skittering back behind him, and took two big steps toward her. He grabbed the top of her right arm hard enough to leave bruises.

"Shut. Up," he whispered harshly and then dragged Jessie out of the commissary. When they made it into the hallway, she opened her mouth to speak, but he silenced her with an intense look.

"Follow," he said, and the two of them set off down the hallway. They rode the elevator in silence, and it wasn't until they were out of the building and sitting on one of the benches in the park under the dome that he finally spoke.

He was still angry, but there were enough people within earshot that he was forced to keep his voice down.

"I saw her," Jessie said.

"Who?"

"Eighty-three! She was in one of the training videos. She was a Mentor!"

Harry's face went blank as she spoke, and he kept a stone face while he processed what she was saying.

"Did you know?" Jessie asked.

Harry didn't respond.

"Answer me, Harry, or I will make sure everyone in **the Faction** knows who I am, where I came from, and who **my brother** is."

Harry let a long pause hang before he answered. "Yes," he said. "I knew."

"And you didn't say anything?" Jessie demanded.

"No."

"Why not? Why wouldn't you tell me that?"

"Why would I?"

"Why *wouldn't* you? It's just crazy. It's like you both were trying to hide it from me when we were **Numbered**. Or something. Why would you do that? Were you there just to get me to give up and come here?"

Harry's face twitched at this.

"Harry," Jessie said, her tone softening. "Were you trying to hide this from me? Why? What would be the point? What would be the harm in me knowing that the two of you flushed out of Aeta?" Harry began to speak, slowly and carefully choosing his words.

"Jessie, did it ever occur to you that there was more going on than just the grid and the cities and the training and Threshing and all of this?"

Harry waved his hands around him as he finished.

Jessie's eyes narrowed at him.

"What do you mean?"

Harry glanced over his shoulder and eyed the others moving and relaxing in the park.

"I don't know how much I should tell you," he said.

"What does that mean? What is there to tell me?"

"You're the youngest recruit here. Did you ever wonder why that is?"

Jessie shrugged, "I guess **the mayor** thought my coding was pretty good."

Harry nodded. "Sure. Yes. It's good. But others in the city—**kids of age**—are as good as you are."

Jessie shrugged.

"And why," Harry continued, "do you think the mayor sent you to the Numbered? A kid your age has never been sent down to the Numbered. That's a pretty harsh penalty. Don't you think?"

"Well, I had been robbing **the Elites**."

"Are you the first kid to do that?"

"I'm the first kid to be that good."

Harry chuckled and took a deep breath.

"You're here because we want you to be here."

"We? Who is we?"

"I can't tell you that yet, but just know that you were brought here for a purpose."

"I know that. I'm not an idiot!" she said. "I have to win the Threshing."

"No. You're here for something else."

Jessie couldn't understand what he meant and grew more frustrated, "What?"

Harry shook his head. "I can't tell you that either."

"Why not?"

"It's too dangerous. And it's not time yet."

"Time for what?"

"You've already caused enough trouble on your own. You were

supposed to arrive, keep your head down, and make it through the Severings. We didn't plan for you to...make such a ruckus."

"Who is we?" Jessie demanded.

"I'm not going to tell you that," Harry said.

"Well, maybe I should just ask **Barry** about it."

Harry's entire body stiffened, and his voice became very rigid.

"Don't even joke about that."

"Why not? You're obviously up to something, and you won't tell me what's going on. Maybe it's my job as a member of the Americas Faction to report behavior that seems—"

Jessie's voice was cut off as Harry's palm connected with her face. The loud smack drew glances from some of the people around them, but Harry didn't notice. He had stood and was towering over her.

"You have no idea what you are playing at here, girl. I was against bringing you here. I said you were too young. Too naive. But I was overruled, and here you are. You are not going to put our lives at risk because you want to be petulant. You are to keep your head down, do your work, and win the next Severing. That's all that matters."

Jessie's cheek had turned a bright red, and she kept her hand pressed against it.

Her voice was shaky as she spoke.

"Okay. But—" Jessie tried to think of something to say to get Harry to stop yelling and smacking her. She could only think of the truth.

"But what?"

"Barry already promised to send me home before the next Severing."

"What? What are you talking about?"

"After the first Severing, **I went to see him.** I mean they took me to see him and—"

"You said they just held you to keep you safe from the other recruits."

"He told me not to say anything. He said I had to keep it between us if I wanted to keep our deal."

Harry sat down again next to her.

"Jessie," Harry's voice was now eerily calm. "I need you to tell me everything that went on in that meeting. And I need you to tell me now."

Jessie nodded and began talking.

She told him about Barry not being who they'd thought he was along with all of the odd stuff and computers in his office. She told Harry about telling Barry who her brother was, how she was scared and about the deal they made that he would look into her brother's disappearance and give her a choice to go home.

"He said it would be a few days, but that was three weeks ago, and I haven't heard from him. I tried to go back down and see him but couldn't get the elevator to move. I just keep telling myself that he said it would be fine and that he would send word to me and—"

She went silent when she realized she had started babbling.

"I'm sorry I didn't tell you, Harry. I was just scared. I want to go home, and he said he would let me, but I had to keep it a secret. He's the president after all."

His face softened now as he lifted his eyes and looked up at the sun. His eyes welled up as he spoke.

"Jessie," he said. "I know you want to go home, but President Marcus is not going to let that happen."

"But he said—"

Harry held up his hand to silence her and dropped his eyes back to meet hers.

"I know what he said. He says a lot of things. He's willing to say whatever it takes to maintain control of his Faction and to win the next Threshing. He's the same man who keeps all of **your friends and family** locked into the grid. He's the same man who codes up Severings so they will kill the **recruits**. You have no idea what he's capable of. There's no way he's going to let you go home before the next Severing."

Jessie leaned away from him.

"No," she said. "No, you're wrong about him. He was so nice. He let me try coffee. And he said he would try to find out what happened to Randy. Why would he just say that?"

Harry opened his mouth to answer but was cut off by a shout from across the courtyard. They both looked up to see **Ernst** and **Alex** hurrying toward them.

Harry stood as they approached.

"What is it?" he said.

"The Severing," Ernst gasped out and then he leaned over, putting his hands on his knees wheezing. "Sorry. Ran here," he panted.

Alex rolled his eyes.

"They announced it right after the video," Alex said. "The next Severing is tomorrow at 0600."

CHAPTER THIRTY-THREE

Analyzing the Scene

A STORY EVENT is an active change of life value for one or more characters as a result of conflict (one character's desires clash with another's).

A WORKING SCENE contains at least one Story Event. To determine a Scene's Story Event, answer the following four questions:

1. What are the characters doing?

Jessie is confronting Harry about Eighty-three.

2. What is the essential action of what the characters are doing in this scene?

Jessie wants to understand what is going on.

3. What life value has changed for one or more of the characters in the scene?

Jessie starts out defiant and demanding, but ends up telling everything to Harry.

4. Which life value should I highlight on my Story Grid Spreadsheet?

Defiant to Contrite.

HOW THE SCENE ABIDES BY THE FIVE COMMANDMENTS OF STORYTELLING

Inciting Incident: Jessie finds Harry in the commissary.

Progressive Complication: Harry smacks Jessie when she threatens to report what he is doing.

Crisis: Best bad choice. Jessie can keep hiding the truth from Harry *or* she can finally reveal her deal with President Marcus.

Climax: Jessie tells Harry everything about her meeting with President Marcus.

Resolution: Harry shows compassion to Jessie and tries to get her to see the truth.

CHAPTER THIRTY-FOUR

Jessie opened her closet and pulled out her last clean grey suit, dressing slowly in the pale light that came from the monitor. She'd been up hours before her scheduled alarm.

Her mind cycled from what happened at the first Severing to her conversation with **President Marcus** and then to the attack in the training sim. It churned over to the images of **Eighty-three** in the training video, and lastly, to her confusing conversation with **Harry**. Over and over, her mind kept trying to pick each piece of the experiences apart and make sense of them all, but it couldn't.

Most of what Harry said to her made no sense. What did he mean that she was here for something other than the Threshing? He made it sound like he was working with people to get her here, but not to compete. But that didn't make any sense. Aeta was all about competition. Why would they do that? And why would they be so mad that she burned down the first Severing if she wasn't here to compete?

She squeezed her eyes shut and pushed the palms of her hands into their sockets. And around the same cycle her mind circled again.

Time to go.

She kept her eyes on the floor as she maneuvered the hallways to the cafeteria. She avoided eye contact with everyone. After the last one, she definitely wouldn't find any **friends** in this next round of Severing. She would be entirely on her own, which meant she was for all intents and purposes, dead.

She hadn't fully appreciated how close she had already come to death in the training sim. What would have happened if she was just a couple of minutes later being logged out? She hadn't worried about it at the time because she never expected to still be in Aeta for the second Severing. She had made that deal with Barry fully intending to ask to go home no matter what he said he'd found. But he never got back to her. Not a word, and now she was unprepared.

Maybe he'd planned it this way. If he didn't have any contact with her before the next Severing started, he rightly assumed she would not make it out alive. Who knew? Maybe he even programmed it so she definitely wouldn't make it out alive.

Jessie grabbed a small bowl of pale fruit and a roll.

Alex had told her to go light on food. If the Severing got rough, it would just be something for her to vomit up and for him to clean up. After a few minutes, **Alex** and **Ernst** sat down next to her.

"You couldn't sleep either?" Ernst asked.

Jessie shook her head.

They ate for several minutes in silence.

"You're going to be fine, Jessie," Ernst said. "You've done so well so far."

Jessie shrugged as Alex stayed laser-focused on his food.

They sat in silence long after their food was gone. Finally, Alex spoke.

"Time to go."

They stood, put their trays away, and made their way down the corridor to their bay.

Ernst immediately began fiddling with the monitor and Alex started setting up his equipment and readying the IV.

A familiar electronic voice boomed through every room.

"Three minutes until the start of the Severing. All Coders are to log on now."

Alex moved next to Jessie's chair.

"You ready?"

She glanced at Ernst, who looked like he was on the edge of tears, looked back at Alex and nodded.

Jessie shut her eyes. She felt the plug attach to her skull and then everything went white. She opened her eyes again to find herself in a small, empty room. There was one door leading out with a simple doorknob that didn't appear to have a lock.

Instructions are downloading now, Ernst said. *Okay, it's a capture-the-flag scenario. Your room is your flag. As soon as another Coder finds your room and ejects you, they claim your flag, and they double their available credits.*

It looks like...he continued...you're in a large building full of hallways and rooms exactly like yours. So, the goal is to be one of the last six Coders left. When the seventh from last gets his flag taken, the Severing is over, and you'll be logged out.

How many rooms are there?

Hard to tell. Hundreds at least.

How am I supposed to find the other Coders?

That's the test, I think.

Why don't I just stay here and let them fight it out?

What kind of defenses does your room have?

None.

Precisely. You have to use your handful of credits to both defend and attack. Every time you eject another Coder, you get double the credits you started with, so each Coder you take out gives you a better chance of winning.

Jessie sighed.

She was unsure of what to do.

If she went on the hunt and ran into another Coder, she would quickly find herself overpowered physically. If she stayed put, with her current credit balance, she couldn't do much more than deadbolt her door.

What are you going to do?

I'm working on it.

Jessie grabbed the doorknob and slowly turned it. She pulled the door open an inch and peeked out. The hallway was the same stark white as her room, and there was an identical door right across the hall. She opened her door a little more and could see a line of doorways, all identical, all the way down the hallway.

She opened the door enough for her to move through and stuck her head out to see how long the hallway stretched. She heard a wet pounding noise before she figured out what she was seeing. At least a hundred feet down the corridor she saw **Az**. He had tackled **another Coder** and was straddling him and hitting him over and over in the face in quick succession. The Coder was such a bloody mess Jessie couldn't even tell who he was.

As Az lifted his hand again to land another blow, he stopped himself. As if he could feel Jessie looking at him, his head jerked upward. They locked eyes, and he smiled for a moment—a tight, wicked smile that only turned up at the edges. Az gleefully sprang to his feet and started sprinting toward her. Jessie stumbled back into her room and slammed the door. She held the doorknob with both hands and screamed coding instructions to Ernst.

Soon there was a bang against the door, and Jessie felt it shudder as Az slammed into it from the other side. The knob rattled under her grip.

Done! Ernst said.

Within two seconds, the deadbolt appeared on the door. Jessie reached up, secured it and then stepped back.

There was another slam into the door. A few seconds later, Az's body hit the door again, and Jessie heard a crack from the door frame.

I'm trapped, Jessie said.

No, no, we can get you out of there.

It doesn't matter anymore. They've already found my room. I've used most of my credits.

Jessie backed away until her back reached the sterile white wall opposite her collapsing doorway and then she slid down to the floor.

It was over.

She'd be dead for sure. Az would pummel her and feel nothing but joy to be rid of her. Ernst and Alex would be sent home with nothing for their families. And all of it was her fault. She thought she was so clever, outsmarting everyone else, but every time it only made everything worse. Now she was all alone, and the **few people** who were on her side would suffer severe consequences for her failure.

The bangs against the door continued. The cracking in the door frame grew louder.

It would only take a few more tries, and then Az would be in the room happily beating her just like the other Coder.

Jessie wiped away the tears that had formed in the corners of her eyes. She put her head down on her knees.

I'm so sorry, Ernst. Tell Alex that I'm sorry too. And tell Harry—

No, Jessie, don't give up. There's got to be some way out of there.

Jessie ignored him. She squeezed harder against her knees and clenched her teeth. Her face turned red, and the veins on her forehead stood out. She slammed her head against the wall in frustration. Pain shot through her head and stars swam in her vision.

What did it matter? Once again, she'd failed to do what was expected of her.

She lifted her head again and slammed it against the wall. Maybe she could knock herself out before Az took her apart? But this time there was a loud crack. Jessie turned and looked at the wall. An odd fissure cut through the blank white. She lifted her fist and slammed into it as hard as she could. There was a loud tearing sound as the wall seemed to crumble in front of her. It left an empty black space. She peered in, but she could see nothing.

She slowly reached her hand in, and it disappeared up to her wrist. She yanked her hand back out and took a step away. But behind her now, she heard a loud snap. She turned in time to see the door slam open. Az stood in the entryway, breathing heavily, with a smug and wicked smile on his face.

He took a step toward her but stopped in his tracks as Jessie gave him back the same smug wicked smile. She turned, stepped back, and then dove through the hole in the wall straight into the darkness.

CHAPTER THIRTY-FOUR

Analyzing the Scene

A STORY EVENT is an active change of life value for one or more characters as a result of conflict (one character's desires clash with another's).

A WORKING SCENE contains at least one Story Event. To determine a Scene's Story Event, answer the following four questions:

1. What are the characters doing?

Jessie meets Ernst and Alex for breakfast, then they head to their bay. Jessie is logged in and the Severing starts. The Severing immediately falls apart when Az sees her and she gets trapped in her room.

2. What is the essential action of what the characters are doing in this scene?

Jessie is trying to survive the second Severing.

3. What life value has changed for one or more of the characters in the scene?

Jessie starts out solemn and resigned to the idea that she is probably going to die in the second Severing. The Severing immediately falls apart, and it looks like Jessie is going to be one of the first ones ejected. However, a way out seems to magically appear.

4. Which life value should I highlight on my Story Grid Spreadsheet?

Assuming Death to Resigned to Death to Narrowly Escaping.

HOW THE SCENE ABIDES BY THE FIVE COMMANDMENTS OF STORYTELLING

Inciting Incident: Jessie logs into the second Severing.

Progressive Complication: Jessie is trapped in her room, with only moments until Az breaks through.

Crisis: Best bad choice. Jessie can stand her ground against Az *or* she can escape through the hole that has appeared in the wall.

Climax: Jessie dives through the hole in the wall.

Resolution: [Next scene] She disappears from the room.

NOTES:

This scene represents the resolution of middle build one, 'no way out/the point of no return.'

CHAPTER THIRTY-FIVE

Jessie opened her eyes to blackness. She wasn't sure if she was standing or lying face down on some kind of cushion. It felt as if she were floating. She moved her body into a position that felt upright, took a couple of steps into the darkness and then turned to look back. Light emanated from the hole she'd come through, and **Az** stood on the other side staring into it, confused. He reached out his hand as if to push it through the hole, but his fingers did not punch through. He ran it over the space as if the wall was still there for him.

Jessie watched, waiting for him to figure out how to come through the wall, but it didn't happen. It looked like he was yelling something, but she couldn't hear him.

She leaned toward the hole, squinting when he slammed his palm against the wall. She jumped backward at the movement, and her feet landed on a ledge. She began swinging her arms around wildly but eventually lost her balance and toppled over.

For a moment she struggled, terrified, waiting for the fall to abruptly end. But after a few seconds, she stopped moving. There was no wind rushing by her. She felt weightless in the dark and felt as if she were floating again.

She looked all around her, trying to find something that would give her bearings and calm her nervous stomach. After a few seconds, she noticed a soft light and discovered she was moving toward it headfirst. It was getting brighter and more prominent.

A floor appeared far below her, and without thinking, she began screaming. She was moving so fast now it was impossible to stop. She started flailing around trying to right herself, but couldn't manipulate her body in the weightless air.

As the floor sped toward her, she squeezed her eyes shut and crunched into a ball.

Just as quickly as she had accelerated, she now abruptly started slowing down. And soon she'd come to a dead stop. She peeked open one eye and saw the floor just a couple of inches below her face. She started to uncurl from her ball when whatever was holding her let go. She landed onto the floor in a heap.

Jessie pushed her way up to stand and looked around her. She was in a long, plain hallway, not unlike the one she saw Az in only minutes before.

"You have to move, Jessie," **a voice** boomed from all around her.

Jessie cowered under the voice.

"Go!"

"Who are you?" No response. "Go where?" she yelled back.

"Toward the door."

"There isn't a—"

Jessie turned around to find a single red door, like one of the old-fashioned ones **her father** showed her in an antique book he read to her when she was little, at the other end of the hallway. She knew it hadn't been there a few seconds ago.

"Who are you?"

"It doesn't matter. You have to move if you're going to make it out."

"I'm not going anywhere until—"

She heard a crackle behind her. She turned to find **a Faction guard** standing at the other end of the hallway, no more than fifty feet away. There was another loud crackle, and **another guard** appeared.

They both raised their weapons and pointed at Jessie.

"Go!" the voice boomed again.

Jessie didn't hesitate this time. She turned and ran as fast as she could to the door. She heard the report of guns behind her and dropped to her knees, covering her head with her hands and waiting to feel the impact of the bullets, but they never came.

She turned around to see the bullets floating in the air right behind her, still spinning. Many more appeared as the guards continued firing.

"They won't stay like that forever, Jessie!"

Jessie scrambled to her feet but lost her balance and fell to her knees again. She hobbled back up and sprinted for the door. She lunged at the crash bar, and the door swung open. Once on the other side, she turned back around and slammed it closed. She felt several impacts on the door as it swung shut and felt at least one bullet whiz by her.

Once she heard the audible click of the door's locking mechanism engage, the entire door disappeared. Jessie turned around to find a maze of grey staircases. Some were going down, and some were going up. Others were running along the walls and at weird angles that made them seemingly impossible actually to walk on.

She took a step forward.

"Where am I? Who are you?" she asked.

"Hold on. I'm calculating."

"What?"

"I'm trying to build an untraceable path so **the Faction programmers** can't drop in more guards."

The stairs shifted in front of her. One of the staircases split into three sections, all of them turning at odd angles. The down staircase directly in front of her slowly shifted and raised until the steps were going up. Its coloring flashed from a dull grey to the bright red the door had been previously.

"I see it," she said.

"Perfect, keep moving. You have to be fast. I'm holding them back, but they'll eventually crack my code. They know we're in here now and their computational power is well beyond ours."

"Who are you?"

"You'll know soon enough. Start heading up the stairs."

So far, this mysterious voice had saved her twice—once when Az came into her Severing cubicle and then from the digitized Faction guards in the hallway. There didn't seem a point in doing that if the voice was leading her to another trap.

Jessie took a deep breath and then began running up the red flight of stairs. She took them two at a time and reached the first landing quickly. New staircases were already forming, splitting, turning, and disintegrating in front of her. She waited a few seconds until the spiral staircase on her left flashed red, and then she began running up the red stairs again.

She was halfway up when she heard a faint crackle below her. She leaned over the edge and looked down at the landing she had just left to see two guards were standing there with their weapons readied as they scanned the area.

Before they saw her looking down, the landing disappeared from underneath them, and they fell away into the darkness.

Jessie looked up to see how far she had to go. She couldn't tell, so she just put her head down and kept climbing.

Her breath came in ragged shallow breaths now, but she kept pushing herself. She wasn't taking the stairs two at a time anymore, but she forced one foot in front of the other. She wondered what readings Alex must be getting on the other side.

Every few seconds, she would hear the crackle of **another Faction guard** popping into existence, but she didn't bother to stop. There was no point in risking being seen.

After several minutes, she finally came to another landing. As she stepped off the staircase, it disappeared from underneath her, and like a polar bear on an ice floe, she floated away on a small square piece of floor.

She put her hands on her knees and sucked in a deep breath to calm her heart.

"Are you okay?" the voice asked.

"Yes," Jessie huffed out.

"Good, okay, I'm working up this last bit of—"

The voice was cut off by another crackle and flash in front of her. Three seemingly floating Faction guards leveled their weapons at Jessie.

"We are **grid security forces N894-26**," a robotic voice came from the guard's direction. "You are in an unauthorized zone. Come with us immediately or be terminated from the system."

Jessie stood up slowly and raised her hands. She backed up slowly until she could feel the edge of the floor under her feet.

"Do not move!" the robotic voice yelled.

"Jump!" the voice boomed.

Jessie pushed herself backward and kicked off the back edge of her floating floor. She heard the report of guns above her and felt something tug at her sleeve as she fell into the darkness. She twisted around to see where she was falling.

Another red door appeared in the distance The door slammed open, and a hand shot out and caught her as she sped past it.

She swung wildly underneath the door with only the hand keeping her from falling into eternity. She screamed, reached up, and grabbed the disembodied hand to steady herself. It slowly pulled her up and through the door.

She dropped to her knees as she was pulled up onto the landing. When she looked up to see who had saved her, she lost control of her emotions.

His shaggy brown hair still hung into his eyes. His blue eyes were still as piercing as ever.

"Hey, Domino," he said.

Jessie lunged into his arms.

"I knew it," she whispered into his chest. "I knew you weren't dead. Everybody kept telling me you were gone, that we would have heard from you by now, but no, I knew it. I told them."

He squeezed her back for a few seconds but then started pushing her away. Jessie clung to him, refusing to let him break the embrace.

"You have to let go. We can't stay here long."

For the first time, Jessie looked around at their surroundings. They were in a small living room with a couple of worn-down chairs and a couch. She looked over to where she knew a little, spotless kitchen would be. The hallway ran out of the room to where she knew her parents' bedroom and her secret closet would be.

"I wanted you to know it was really me, so I coded up our old apartment," he said.

Randy pulled back some more and looked at Jessie.

"It is so good to see you. I can't believe it." He looked at her up and down as tears flowed down his face.

"I've missed you so much."

"Where are you? Where have you been?" Jessie asked. Randy checked his watch. Characters and numbers raced across the face of it. Worry spread across his face.

He reached out and grasped Jessie's arms.

"We don't have long before they break through my code and find us. I need you just to listen and trust me, okay?"

Jessie nodded.

"After I won the last Threshing, **Marcus** put me in lockdown."

Jessie opened her mouth to speak, but Randy cut her off.

"I know. You and **Mom and Dad** were told I died just after I won it four years ago. That isn't true. The truth is, Marcus had no idea how I beat the **other Factions**. He became terrified that I would take over the **Americas Faction** with my code and demanded to know the secret to how I did it. I refused to tell him. So he spent the next couple of years running experimental code on me, trying to break down my defenses so he could directly read my thoughts. He and the Faction Coders have been working on this technology for years, but they still haven't gotten it to work. In the meantime, he's kept me locked into the grid as a prisoner. He constantly beams me feeds of you and Mom and Dad and what is happening to my friends, trying to torture me into giving up what I know."

"Why don't you just tell him?"

Randy shook his head.

"I can't. What I know would destroy everything. It would put even more power into Marcus's hands. Plus he would kill me and—"

He cut off his voice looking intently at Jessie.

"This is bigger than me. Bigger than you. Jessie, we have to take Marcus down."

Jessie's eyes went wide.

"What are you talking about? We can't do that! Why..."

"Look at what he does to **people**! We're herded like cattle into the grid so he can keep control of us. He has ultimate power over the entire Faction and lives here in Aeta like a king while the rest of us suffer in the cities. Look at what he did to you! He sent you to **the Numbered** just because you refused to come here and risk your life for the Faction."

"That was **Mayor Charles**. He—"

"Who do you think Charles works for?"

"But what can we do? You're a prisoner, and I'm only a kid and about to flush out of the Severing."

"There's more than just me. There's **a whole underground** of us working to take down Marcus and overthrow the Faction. But we need you."

"What can I do? I'm just a low-level Coder in the Preparing. I've barely survived as it is."

"More than you know, Jessie. And you're still in the running for the Threshing. The only hope of taking down Marcus is if you make it to the next Threshing."

Jessie thought for a moment and then started shaking her head.

"No," she said. "Are you crazy? I can't do that. I was about to lose a minute ago and flush out. Why do we have to do this? Why don't I just come and find where they're keeping you and get you out. Then we can sneak onto the next transport and go home. Mom will be happy again. And you can even have the closet back. I'll move back in with Mom and Dad. I know they won't care."

"Jessie," Randy said softly. "You know that won't work. Marcus will hunt us down. We'll have to live on the run among **the Scavengers**, and you know he'll eventually find us. I want to go home too. I want to be back with Mom and Dad, but the only way to do that is to take down Marcus and the Faction."

Jessie dropped her head. It was ridiculous. Impossible.

"Please, Domino. Please."

Jessie looked up and then nodded her head just to make him stop insisting.

Randy let out a sigh before checking his watch again. He jumped to his feet.

"We have to go now!" he said. He grabbed Jessie's arm and pulled her up to her feet.

"But what do I do when I get back?" she asked.

"Just keep your head down and make it to the Threshing. Do whatever Harry tells you to do."

"Harry, why—"

"And I'll get you a message as soon as I can, but you have to go now."

"But, Randy, I don't want—"

There was a loud crackle from down the hall.

"No!" Randy shouted and then shoved Jessie hard. She heard the gun before she stumbled back through a hole in the wall and landed back in the Severing.

CHAPTER THIRTY-FIVE

Analyzing the Scene

A STORY EVENT is an active change of life value for one or more characters as a result of conflict (one character's desires clash with another's).

A WORKING SCENE contains at least one Story Event. To determine a Scene's Story Event, answer the following four questions:

1. What are the characters doing?

Jessie is trying to find her way out of the code she fell into. A voice is guiding her, which ends up belonging to Randy. Jessie and Randy meet and he tells Jessie his plans for her to take down Marcus.

2. What is the essential action of what the characters are doing in this scene?

Randy is trying to get Jessie on board with his plans to remove President Marcus from power.

3. What life value has changed for one or more of the characters in the scene?

Jessie is relieved to find that her brother is actually alive, but she is scared by his insistence that she help him remove President Marcus from power.

4. Which life value should I highlight on my Story Grid Spreadsheet?

Relief to Fear.

HOW THE SCENE ABIDES BY THE FIVE COMMANDMENTS OF STORYTELLING

Inciting Incident: A voice tells Jessie to go through the red door.

Progressive Complication: Randy tells her he needs her to help remove President Marcus from power.

Crisis: Best bad choice. Jessie can agree to help Randy *or* she can refuse.

Climax: Before she can make the decision, the guards show up. Randy pushes her out of the code and back into the Severing.

Resolution: She lands back inside the Severing

NOTES:

- This scene solidifies the point of no return for Jessie. She cannot go back home again. Her life is forever changed with this revelatory knowledge.
- This scene represents the inciting incident of middle build two, 'an encounter with the noumenal.'

CHAPTER THIRTY-SIX

Jessie landed hard and slid across the floor. She scrambled to her feet and ran back to the rapidly shrinking hole in the stark white wall. She tried to reach through, but an invisible wall blocked her hand. Now cupping her hands over her eyes, she peered into the darkness.

Like peering through a looking glass, she could see a facsimile of **Randy** pressed up against the backside of the kitchen counter. Hiding, he clutched his chest just as the hole in her white wall disappeared. Before he was gone completely, Jessie caught a glimpse of Randy pulling his hand away. It glistened bright red, as red as the doors and stairs in that odd other-world, as the blood ran down his arm and stained his shirt.

"No!" she yelled and slammed her fist against the now-unblemished and continuous white wall.

Jessie! Jessie, are you there?

Ernst 's voice betrayed his panic. Jessie didn't answer. Her mind was busy running through scenarios trying to figure out how to get back to Randy.

Pull me out, she said calmly. *I need to come out now.*

Where have you been? Why were you off comms?

Jessie stalked to the door of the small room. It was still hanging from one of its hinges after **Az** had kicked it in. She stepped out into a long hallway filled with doors running in either direction. She briefly looked both ways and then stepped back into the room.

I need to get out of here. How many are left?

Just seven. If one more gets taken offline, you'll make it through. Just stay where you are. The odds are in your favor. Someone else will be found before you.

But Jessie was already out the door before Ernst finished speaking.

I have to get out of here now. I don't have time to sit around and wait.

Why? If you just wait, you'll win.

Jessie ignored him. She opened the door next to hers and glanced in. No one was inside, so she stepped back into the hallway. She stepped across to the next door and did the same.

She moved at a manic pace, sprinting the steps from door to door and leaving them open. She made no effort to be quiet and behaved as if she were bulletproof.

Damn it, Jessie. What are you doing?

I'm finishing this.

Ernst started to speak again, but Jessie tuned him out and focused on moving as quickly as possible. She panted now, her breath rasping out of her throat, but she didn't slow down.

It had become a physical mantra...open a door, glance in, lunge for the next door, repeat.

After dozens of doors, Jessie stepped out of another empty room, and movement caught her eye. She looked up to see **a large boy** running full tilt down the hallway in her direction. He was over a head taller than her and had to weigh double what she did.

Suddenly the realization of her mistake flooded over her. She turned to run in the opposite direction, but tripped over her tired feet and crashed to her hands and knees. She scrambled up and started running again but knew there was no way she would outrun this stronger, faster boy with a stride twice as long as hers.

She heard the sound of his footsteps getting closer and glanced over her shoulder. The boy's face was red with exertion. He would know what she knew from his comms. If he took her out, he would survive the second Severing.

Jessie kept pumping her legs but knew it was no use. She was seconds away from him catching her. She looked back a second time. He had to be less than ten feet from her.

As she turned back forward, she heard a latch turn and saw the door she was passing swing open wide. She jumped to the side and away from the opening door, but her forward momentum caused her to lose her balance and stumble into the opposite wall.

She looked up to see the boy bearing down on her, but out of the doorway, Az's tall, lanky body lunged and connected with the boy's thighs, throwing him off balance. The two boys crashed into the door opposite Az's.

The door crashed open, and the boy fell back into **another Coder's** cubicle. Az found his footing, turned, and noticed Jessie. His eyes became predatory, and he turned to chase her. Jessie began backing up, getting ready to turn and run, but before Az could take another step, a foot shot out from the doorway and tangled up his feet enough to make him stumble and drop to a knee. Az turned to face the larger boy as he pounced. There was a loud crack as the boy's massive fist connected with Az's face. Az's head snapped back against the hard, marble floor.

Jessie stood frozen, watching the first few seconds of the fight until the opportunity of the situation dawned on her, and she turned and ran.

She ran as fast as she could, glancing over her shoulder to see the two boys, both covered in blood now. She couldn't be sure whose was whose, but she was happy none of it belonged to her. Then she grabbed the nearest doorknob, pushed through, and slammed the door behind her. She dropped her hands to her knees, panting.

After a few seconds, her head snapped up as a high-pitched scream drifted down the hallway. The cry was abruptly cut off. Jessie waited, forcing her breath to slow.

You did it! Ernst 's voice popped into her head. *It's over!*

Jessie closed her eyes briefly. The white light filled her vision, and she felt the plug disengage from the back of her skull. She fought with the straps on her arms and legs, desperate to be in the real world.

Her eyes popped open, and she could hear Ernst talking excitedly. **Alex**'s face floated into her vision.

"Get me up!" Jessie yelled.

"Hold on. I'm working on it," Alex said. "You won! You made it! Can you believe it?"

Jessie didn't answer. As soon as a hand was free, she clawed at the strap on the other hand and then sat up and started working furiously at the straps on her ankles.

Alex stepped back, the excitement turning into concern on his face.

"What's going on?" he asked.

Jessie got the last of the straps off, jumped off the table, and turned toward the bay's door. Alex grabbed her arm.

"Jessie, wait. Where are you going? What happened?"

Jessie yanked her arm out of Alex's grip and turned back to the door.

"**I have to find him**," she said.

Ernst stepped between her and the door.

"Find who?"

"Randy. He's hurt. He's still trapped in there."

"Randy? Who's Randy" Ernst said.

"He's my brother," Jessie said. "I haven't seen him since he came here four years ago."

"You mean Randy Teller?" Alex said. "The one who died winning the last Threshing?" Jessie whipped around.

"He's not dead! They've kept him locked up the past four years, and now he's hurt, and I have to find him!"

Alex held up his hands as if calming down a wild animal, but Jessie just turned and glared at Ernst.

"Get out of my way," she snarled at him.

Ernst glanced over her shoulder at Alex, hesitated for a second, and then stepped back out of the way.

Jessie brushed past him quickly, threw the door open, and turned left.

She ran down the hallway toward the giant iron door. Alex and Ernst glanced at each other but then started walking quickly after her.

Guards were posted during the day and she walked right up to them.

"Let me through," she yelled.

They ignored her.

She took a step to move past them to the keypad on the door and the guard took a step to block her.

Jessie shoved him in the stomach as hard as she could, but it was like trying to push a brick wall. The guard's hand snapped out and grabbed her neck. He stepped forward, turned her around, and slammed her into the wall. Jessie's cheek bounced off the wall and her head swam as the guard deftly caught her arms and used plastic ties to secure her wrists behind her back.

Alex and Ernst started yelling in protest as they caught up, but the guard acted as if he didn't hear. The guard grabbed her arm and dragged her kicking and screaming down the hallway toward the lift while the remaining guard blocked Alex and Ernst's path to follow.

CHAPTER THIRTY-SIX

Analyzing the Scene

A STORY EVENT is an active change of life value for one or more characters as a result of conflict (one character's desires clash with another's).

A WORKING SCENE contains at least one Story Event. To determine a Scene's Story Event, answer the following four questions:

1. What are the characters doing?

Jessie arrives back in the Severing. She is frantic to end it, which Az eventually does. When she comes out of the grid, she goes on the hunt for Randy and assaults a guard, who takes her into custody.

2. What is the essential action of what the characters are doing in this scene?

Jessie is manically trying to find her brother.

3. What life value has changed for one or more of the characters in the scene?

Jessie moves from being the victim to being the pursuer.

4. Which life value should I highlight on my Story Grid Spreadsheet?

Victim to Pursuer.

HOW THE SCENE ABIDES BY THE FIVE COMMANDMENTS OF STORYTELLING

Inciting Incident: Jessie sees her brother is injured.

Progressive Complication: Alex and Ernst try to stop her from leaving the bay.

Crisis: Best bad choice. Do the boys let her leave when she's in this wild state *or* do they try to physically restrain her?

Climax: The boys let Jessie leave.

Resolution: Jessie assaults a Faction guard and is taken into custody.

CHAPTER THIRTY-SEVEN

Jessie kicked and screamed, making as much of a scene as she could. At one point, she bucked hard enough at just the right time, and **the guard**'s grip on her arm slipped so she dropped to the floor.

Jessie struggled to get to her feet and run, but before she could make any progress, the guard was on her again. He picked her up by both arms and brought his faceless mask within inches of her nose.

"Stop it!" a mechanical whisper rasped from inside of the helmet. "Please. Stay calm or this isn't going to work."

Jessie's eyes went big and she quieted down. Being directly addressed in such a way by one of **the Faction guards** shocked her.

Jessie stopped resisting, relaxed, and let him drag her down the corridor. She gave everyone they passed sullen, hateful glares, but most **people** kept their eyes averted, acting as if they didn't notice the large man dressed in head-to-toe black dragging a small girl behind them. The **other Coders** had no idea how to handle Jessie's presence.

Jessie glanced ahead and could see the elevator bay approaching. She knew this was bad. Marcus had given her strict instructions about what it would mean if she kept acting up.

What was going to happen now? Was she going to be kicked out of the program? What if **Marcus** actually sent her home now when she'd found out her brother was so close? What if he decided to lock her up next to **Randy**?

The guard slowed and dragged her up to her feet. A few seconds later, the elevator doors opened. Another Faction guard was already on the elevator as the two of them stepped in and the door closed behind them. The lift started descending. With a ding, it stopped, but the doors didn't open. The guard that had joined them on the elevator reached toward the control panel, but then there was a loud snap behind her.

The guard's arm went rigid, and then he pitched forward. His face mask slammed into the panel, and he fell to the floor.

Jessie looked around at her guard and saw him sliding a small device back into his jacket. He reached over Jessie and waved his hand in front of the panel. The doors slid open to reveal **Harry**. He nodded to the guard and then reached in, grabbing Jessie's wrist restraints and yanking her out.

"What just happened?" Jessie said.

"I could ask you the same question," Harry said. He produced some snips from his pockets and released Jessie from her restraints.

Jessie looked around. She seemed to be on a deserted floor somewhere underground with only emergency lights casting any light. The floor looked like it hadn't had any visitors in quite a while.

"What about that guard?" Jessie asked.

"He's a friend. He'll put himself out too, so it'll look like you did it."

"How is that going to help?"

Harry started walking off down the hallway.

"Least of my worries right now."

Jessie fell in step next to him.

"What are your worries, then?" Jessie asked sarcastically.

"First up, how we're going to explain your little disappearing act in the Severing."

"What do you mean?"

"I wasn't the only one plugged into the comms. We have to assume Marcus knows you disappeared. What I want to know is where you disappeared to."

"You won't believe me."

Harry cut his eyes down at Jessie as they walked. They came to a T in the hallway, and Harry immediately took the right turn. They continued down the dark corridor.

"How is he?" Harry asked.

Jessie stopped and waited for Harry to stop and turn back toward her.

"You knew?"

"Of course. Why do you think I'm here?"

"To be my Mentor."

Harry waved that off.

"Why would Marcus need an old, broken down **Numbered** to be your Mentor? No, no. I'm here because Randy wanted me here. Just like you. We had a backup plan all along. If something happened to him in the Threshing, we'd wait four years and try again. This time, with his little sister."

"Why didn't you tell me?" she said.

"What good would that have done us? You'd just have gone off the handle as you did in the city and that little detour with the Numbered. And as you did in the first Severing when you blew up the game—and now disappearing in the second Severing. There was no way telling you would have helped anybody. Probably would have ruined the whole thing."

"What whole thing?" Jessie said.

"Come with me. I'll show you."

Jessie glared at him, her anger still running hot at the knowledge that Harry knew all along why she was here, that Randy was alive, that her whole stint as a Numbered was just to get her to do what he and whatever group he belonged to wanted. But there wasn't much she could do right now on her own. She had to figure a way out of this, not spend her time angry about how she got here.

And Harry was right. Az would have reported her disappearing act by now, and there would be a lot of questions that Jessie couldn't easily answer. Not to mention the new wrinkle of her reported attack on the guards.

Without a word, she took a step forward. Harry turned and continued down the corridor with Jessie following silently behind him.

They continued walking for several minutes and cut through a couple of offices. Eventually, Harry shoved a door open to reveal up and down staircases. He started ascending, and Jessie followed.

"I knew they would be keeping him onsite somewhere, but this building is like a huge puzzle, hard to maneuver in, and has quite the array of surveillance. So here and there as opportunities arose, I would meander through the building looking for indicators."

"Indicators?"

"Sure. Heavy power supplies. Automated security. More surveillance than usual. That sort of thing."

They had climbed two flights of stairs, and Harry headed to an entryway door. He shushed Jessie with a finger and cracked it open. Bright light showed through as Harry poked his head in and looked back and forth. He reached back and grabbed Jessie's sleeve, dragging her tightly behind him.

"Stay close and use me as a shield," he whispered. Then he stood up straight and began walking down the hall. They passed a few people dressed in Capital greys, but none of them paid any mind. Eventually, Harry stopped at an unmarked door. Jessie noticed it didn't have the typical electronic latch. It required an actual, physical key.

Harry tried the handle, but it held fast.

"Do you have the key?" Jessie's whisper was a bit strained.

Harry nodded, dug in his pocket, and produced a long flathead screwdriver. He jammed it into the keyhole and then glanced down the hallway. There was now no one in sight.

He slammed the palm of his hand into the end of the screwdriver a few times and then twisted it hard. There was a loud pop inside the lock.

Harry removed the screwdriver and slid it back into his pocket before opening the door and shoving Jessie through it.

He closed the door behind them, leaving them in inky blackness. The smells were pungent, reeking of strong chemicals. Jessie could hear Harry fumbling around, and finally, a light on the wall switched on.

The room was small, lined with shelves on three walls. Plastic bottles of various designs littered the shelves. Jessie saw a bucket and mop shoved into the corner.

"The janitor's closet?" Jessie said. "This is where you brought us."

"Shush," Harry said. "I've been working on finding access for weeks. We're only going to get one shot at this."

"One shot at what?" Jessie asked, but Harry ignored her. He grabbed the mop from the corner and reached up to the ceiling. He pushed one of the ceiling tiles up and back out of the way.

"Up you go," he said.

Harry interlaced his fingers and bent down, waiting for Jessie to step on them. She hesitated a moment, but he nodded at her reassuringly. She stepped on his hands, and he hoisted her up. She grabbed wildly as her head poked into the space above the ceiling. She grabbed at something substantial and pulled herself up.

"What about you?" she whispered down at him.

Harry was already grabbing the bucket and turning it upside down. He proved spryer than Jessie gave him credit for as he used the bucket and shelves to climb his way up to join Jessie.

She looked around as he got his other knee over the edge and settled in next to her.

There was enough room for them to crawl around, but where exactly were they going to go?

Harry started moving, and Jessie stayed close behind. They didn't go very far before Harry stopped and gently lifted another ceiling tile. He peered into the room before completely removing it and setting it aside. He lowered himself down into the room and then helped Jessie down as well.

They were in what seemed to be a surveillance room with rows of monitors all blinking between various camera feeds. Jessie didn't recognize any of the images she could see.

Harry went to the door and checked. When he seemed satisfied it was locked, he came and sat at the table with all of the monitors. He pulled out the keyboard, and the monitor directly in front of him switched from a camera feed to a blank screen with a prompt.

Harry quickly typed in a few commands, and within seconds webcam feed appeared on the screen. It showed Ernst and Alex.

"We got your message, Harry. We've been waiting," **Alex** said. "Did you get her?"

Harry slid his chair back a bit so they could see Jessie.

"I did," he said.

"So what? Are we ready to get started?" **Ernst** said.

"Just about," Harry said.

"Get started with what?" Jessie asked.

Harry turned to face her.

"I'd thought you would have worked that out by now," he said.

He tapped one of the screens behind him.

The feed only showed a door with two Faction guards positioned next to it.

"Is that..." Jessie started but then stopped.

"That's right," Harry said. "Your brother is behind that door and we're going to get him out."

CHAPTER THIRTY-SEVEN

Analyzing the Scene

A STORY EVENT is an active change of life value for one or more characters as a result of conflict (one character's desires clash with another's).

A WORKING SCENE contains at least one Story Event. To determine a Scene's Story Event, answer the following four questions:

1. What are the characters doing?

The guard delivers Jessie to Harry, who leads her through a maze in the building until they land in a control room. Harry tells her they are going to break Randy out.

2. What is the essential action of what the characters are doing in this scene?

Harry is continuing to get Jessie on board with their plan.

3. What life value has changed for one or more of the characters in the scene?

Jessie is confused about what is going on. Harry explains it to her, and several of the pieces start coming together for Jessie.

4. Which life value should I highlight on my Story Grid Spreadsheet?

Confused to Informed.

HOW THE SCENE ABIDES BY THE FIVE COMMANDMENTS OF STORYTELLING

Inciting Incident: The guard delivers Jessie to Harry.

Progressive Complication: Harry tells her that her coming to Aeta was part of a plan with Randy and that Harry was to be her Mentor.

Crisis: Best bad choice. Jessie can follow Harry and give up control of the situation *or* she can stand her ground and remain defiant.

Climax: Jessie follows Harry.

Resolution: Harry takes Jessie to a control room. He reveals where Randy is and that they are going to break him out.

CHAPTER THIRTY-EIGHT

"Where are you exactly?" **Ernst** finally broke the tension.

"We're on Basement Level 3," **Harry** said.

Ernst moved into the background on the screen and was tapping at a keyboard. **Alex** replaced him in front of the camera.

"There is no Basement Level 3," Ernst 's voice came from the background.

"He said there is no Basement—" Alex began.

"Yeah, we heard him," Harry cut him off. "But there is, and we're here. Ernst, you're not going to find this floor on the proper channels. You'll need to...dig a little."

Jessie could see Ernst over Alex's shoulder. He paused for a beat and then nodded.

"I'm on it."

"So, what next?" Alex asked.

Jessie looked at Harry. He shrugged.

"I got you here, girl, but this is up to you."

"Well," Jessie said. She moved close to the bank of monitors, her eyes roving. "I see **guards** all over the place. I'll need to see where all the corridors and rooms are."

"Yeah, the schematics," Harry said. "Ernst?"

"I'm working on it."

"I don't suppose any of those guards are friends of yours. Are they?" Jessie asked.

Harry snorted out a laugh and shook his head.

"I've walked the hallway a couple of times," he said. "All the doorways into that room with **Randy** are locked tightly and need a clearance much higher than mine."

"Has anyone ever gone in the room?" Alex asked.

"Not that I've seen."

"There," Jessie said, pointing at a monitor.

A tall man approached the door wearing a long white coat. He was pulling on a pair of gloves from his pocket. The man ignored the guards and waved his badge in front of the panel. The doors slid open and he entered.

Jessie's eyes were darting around, checking each screen.

"Okay, it looks like a little kitchen or something there."

"A break room," Harry said.

"Yeah, there's another long white coat guy in there."

"I think it's **a doctor**," Harry said. "Probably monitoring Randy's condition and that of any others like him."

Jessie turned back to Harry.

"You need to go get him."

"Who? The doctor?"

"Yes, you need to steal his clothes, and whatever badge the guard checked."

Harry nodded. "I'm on it, but where is that room?"

"Ernst!" Harry and Jessie spoke together.

"Almost there!" his voice whined from the background. "Okay, got it. How can I get it to you?"

Jessie's hands were already moving over the keyboard.

"What station bay are you in?" she asked.

"Fifth floor. 102," Alex answered.

"Got it," Jessie said. "One sec."

The screen directly in front of her jumped around a few more times, and then schematics appeared on the screen. Jessie leaned in as she continued to tap keys, and the screen image zoomed, backed out, and shifted again.

"There," she said. "There's us."

A small box was on the screen in the center of a long hall.

"And there's the break room."

Her eyes scanned the screens around her for another few seconds, and then she swiveled around to Harry.

"Go out and take a left. Walk to the end of the corridor, and then take a right. Three doors down, you'll find the break room. Once you get into Randy's bay, find a terminal, and we'll be able to communicate with you."

"What are we going to do once we get him out?" Alex asked.

"We'll get him hidden somewhere," she answered. "I'm assuming Harry can help us with that."

Harry nodded off to her left.

"We can't stay hidden forever," Ernst said.

"One thing at a time," Jessie said, "but we'll try to get him out of the building and see if we can smuggle ourselves onto a transport."

As she spoke, Harry was pulling open drawers, glancing in and then shutting them.

"What are you looking for?" Jessie asked. "You need to go."

"Ah!" Harry said, pulling out a brown sack from a drawer. He pulled out a second sack, balled it up, and then stuffed it into the first one. He clutched the bag in one hand and reached for the door with the other.

"Alrighty, see you on the other side," Harry said.

"What about the guards?" Alex's voice floated from the terminal.

"Oh, I'm fine," he said, opening the door. "They'll be looking for her."

Harry shut the door behind him, and Jessie followed his movements on the screen.

"Alex," she said. "We need you here."

"How do I get there?"

Jessie started giving him instructions.

CHAPTER THIRTY-EIGHT

Analyzing the Scene

A STORY EVENT is an active change of life value for one or more characters as a result of conflict (one character's desires clash with another's).

A WORKING SCENE contains at least one Story Event. To determine a Scene's Story Event, answer the following four questions:

1. What are the characters doing?

Alex, Ernst, Harry, and Jessie start putting a plan into action to rescue Randy.

2. What is the essential action of what the characters are doing in this scene?

Jessie is desperate to get Randy free and will do whatever it takes to make that happen.

3. What life value has changed for one or more of the characters in the scene?

Jessie switches from letting Harry be in control to taking over control of the situation.

4. Which life value should I highlight on my Story Grid Spreadsheet?

Following to Leading.

HOW THE SCENE ABIDES BY THE FIVE COMMANDMENTS OF STORYTELLING

Inciting Incident: At the end of previous chapter, Harry says he and Jessie will break Randy out.

Progressive Complication: Alex asks what they need to do next.

Crisis: Best bad choice. Jessie can keep looking to Harry to lead the way *or* she can step up as the leader.

Climax: Jessie steps in and starts making the decisions.

Resolution: Jessie, Harry, Alex, and Ernst put the first part of their plan into action.

CHAPTER THIRTY-NINE

Harry moved lazily down the hallway, his hands clasped behind his back, holding the brown sack. He nodded to **the guards** as he passed but received no reaction or response.

He got to the end of the corridor and took a right. He looked ahead to the third door on the left. The corners of his mouth turned down as he approached. The access pad glowed red.

He stood in front of the door for a moment, cast his eyes back and forth, and then knocked on the door. After a few seconds, he banged on the door again, this time with his fist.

Right as he lifted his hand to do it a third time, the door slid open.

The man on the other side was tall with dark thinning hair that he had desperately combed over his balding spot. His wire-rimmed spectacles sat high on his nose.

"What is it?" he demanded.

Harry lifted the sack up to show the man.

"I need to heat up my lunch," he said.

"This break room is for Medic Class A only."

The disgust was evident on his face as he looked Harry up and down.

"Not for **mentors**," his eyes scanned Harry's head. "And definitely not for a **Numbered**. I'm not interested in catching whatever diseases you've picked up in the sewers."

Harry lifted his sack higher and stuck it in the Medic's face.

"But what about my lunch?"

"Get that bag out—"

The words were cut off as Harry's fist connected with the man's nose through the paper bag. The man stumbled back and sat down hard on the ground. Harry stepped in and slapped the access panel, closing the door behind him.

Jessie watched the grainy footage as the Medic quickly handed over his coat and badge to Harry, who put them on. A few minutes later, Harry had tied the man's hands with the coffee maker's power cord and stuffed him into a closet.

"How are we doing, **Ernst**?" she demanded.

"Not good. I can't find anything on **Randy** in the system anywhere. I have no idea how Harry even knew he was in there."

Jessie rechecked the screens.

"He's moving," she said.

She watched as Harry moved down the hallway, her eyes jumping from screen to screen. Why did he have to walk so slowly? He nodded and smiled at every guard as he passed. Jessie wasn't sure, but she thought he might have even flashed one of them a thumbs up.

She shook her head in frustration.

Finally, he approached a heavily armored door. Randy was supposed to be behind it. He gave a friendly nod to one more guard as he passed and pulled the badge down to the access panel.

Jessie held her breath for a few seconds before the door slowly slid open. Harry stepped through, and the door closed behind him.

"Okay, he's in," Jessie said.

"So, we wait?" Ernst asked.

"Yeah," she answered. "It's on Harry now."

They waited a full minute. And then another.

Jessie had her domino in her hand, rubbing furiously along its face. If Harry was wrong, how would they get out of here? Where would they go? For that matter, they hadn't laid out a real plan for what they would do even if they did get him out.

There was a crackle, and then a tinny version of Harry's voice came from a speaker somewhere inside the terminal.

"You there? Did I put in the right code?"

Jessie tapped a button and answered.

"Yes, we're here. Did you find Randy? Is he okay?"

Harry didn't answer.

"Harry?"

"Hold on," he said.

One of the screens in front of Jessie blinked and frizzed, and a new picture showed.

"Can you see him?"

Jessie put her face close to the screen. She couldn't believe what she was seeing.

Randy was emaciated, the skin on his face pulled taut over his skull. His hair was mostly gone, but what little was left fell in long tufts.

He was strapped into a gyroscopic device that allowed each of his limbs to move independently, and he was currently standing in a somewhat upright position. His arms slowly rose up, and then down in front of him as his legs bent and stepped in what looked like a machine-induced awkward walking motion.

Tubes ran into his nose, under his shirt, and down into loose-fitting pants. The plug in the back of his head had an unusually thick cable attached to it. She couldn't tell if he was conscious.

A sob escaped Jessie's throat before she knew it was coming.

"It's bad," Harry said. "Even if we do get him out, there's no way he can travel anywhere. He won't be able to walk. I'm not even sure we'll be able to get him conscious."

"Get him out of there," Jessie all but screamed at him.

"Jessie," Ernst said, "we have to think about this. What are we going to do with him? We can come back for him later, once we—"

"No," Jessie said. "We do it now. **Marcus** may throw me in one of those today for all I know. And then what do you think he's going to do with you and **Alex** and Harry?"

She paused for a beat, thinking.

"No, we do this now. Harry, how do we get him out."

"That's the thing," Harry said. "I have no idea. I'm looking over the system, and I've never seen anything like it. I have no idea how to break this open. And if I try, I could cut off his life support somehow. I think Ernst may be right on this one, Jessie."

Jessie rubbed furiously at the domino for a few more seconds before shoving it in her pocket as she started tapping on the keys. The schematics moved, zoomed and moved again.

"Is there another plug bay in there?"

A couple of seconds passed as Harry looked.

"Yeah. Yeah, there's one here. It looks older but—"

"Okay, **I'm coming to you.** I can get him out."

"Wait, Jessie. There's no way—"

"Shut up, Ernst," she yelled. "Harry, I'm coming to you. Get ready to open the door."

Before Harry could respond, she opened the door of the security room and stepped out into the corridor.

Jessie hurried down the hallway. She had checked the security feeds before leaving the security hub, and she thought there was a chance she could make it to Randy's med bay without a guard seeing her.

As she neared the corner of the first turn and squeezed herself into a door's nook, she held her breath.

Two Faction guards rounded the corner and passed by her. As soon as they moved past, she silently stepped out from the alcove, peeked around the corner and then started walking quickly down the hallway.

She ducked into a room to avoid another patrolling guard and then made the final turn. She could see the med bay door up ahead and broke into a short jog.

"Stop!" a mechanical shout came from behind her. A guard stepped out of one of the many offices and bays she had passed along the way.

She turned deliberately with her hands in full view.

"What are you doing on this floor? You don't have access to be here."

He walked slowly toward her.

"I know. I'm so sorry. I got turned around. I'm just trying to get to the elevator."

He was now less than twenty feet from her. He reached into one of the pockets in his vest.

Jessie didn't wait to see what he found and took out of his pocket. She turned and ran. The guard yelled, and she heard the steps pick up behind her.

She made it to Randy's med bay in a few seconds, but Harry hadn't opened the door yet. She raised her fist to bang on it, but before she could connect, what felt like fire shot through her body. She screamed and dropped to the floor.

The guard stood over her with a long rod in his hand. He dug it into her ribs a second time as Jessie writhed on the floor and her vision blurred. The guard replaced the weapon on his belt and knelt down beside her. She could hear his heavy breathing as he flipped her onto her stomach and began securing her hands.

Just as he pulled the restraint tightly, Jessie heard the familiar whoosh of an opening door. She craned her neck around to see Harry standing there, surprised. The guard snatched the electric prod off his hip and lunged at Harry, but before he could connect, a body slammed into the guard.

Jessie flopped over to her side to see a mess of limbs and bodies as Alex rolled over on top of the guard.

"Grab her!" he shouted at Harry.

Jessie felt hands grab at her shirt, and she slid across the floor. The last thing she saw as Alex disappeared from her sight was the guard's cattle prod jamming into his armpit.

She tried to scream out, but no sound emerged.

Harry laid her on the ground next to the terminal and snipped off the restraints, but it didn't make much difference. She felt trapped in her own body. She fought to move her arms, but the only responses were odd twitches. Her mouth lolled open, and she could feel drool oozing over the corner of her mouth.

Harry was typing frantically at the terminal. She managed to shimmy her body just enough to see Randy. Up close, it was worse than she could have imagined. His skin seemed almost translucent. She could see open sores on his legs and arms. His face twisted in a rigor mortis of unconscious pain.

"Harry..." she managed to whisper.

"Yeah, you put us in a tight spot," he said. "They definitely know we're here by now, and who knows what they're doing with Alex."

Jessie moved her mouth but merely gaped like a fish.

"I've got the door locked, but I'm not sure how long it will last. Ernst managed to get his door secured, but I'm not sure if they'll figure out he's involved too."

Jessie tried her arms again and found she was starting to regain control. She rasped out Harry's name again and then moved her hand up and tapped at the back of her head.

"Yeah, I'm working on it," he said. "I'm not sure what the point is. Even if we get him out, Marcus will have us as soon as we try to leave."

Jessie screwed up her face at him and tapped the back of her head again.

"Okay," Harry answered. He grabbed the plug hanging on the side of the terminal and unwound some slack from the wiring. He knelt beside Jessie and rolled her up onto her side.

"Ready?"

"Ernst? Still on?"

Jessie barely recognized her own voice.

"Yeah, he's ready."

She nodded weakly.

"Do it."

Harry slid the plug in, and everything went white.

CHAPTER THIRTY-NINE

Analyzing the Scene

A STORY EVENT is an active change of life value for one or more

characters as a result of conflict (one character's desires clash with another's).

A WORKING SCENE contains at least one Story Event. To determine a Scene's Story Event, answer the following four questions:

1. What are the characters doing?

Harry makes it into the chamber with Randy and tries to talk Jessie out of finishing the job. Jessie insists that they are doing it now, and she heads to the chamber herself. She is almost caught by faction guards, but Alex saves her and Harry plugs her into the grid.

2. What is the essential action of what the characters are doing in this scene?

Jessie is intent on rescuing her brother at all costs.

3. What life value has changed for one or more of the characters in the scene?

Jessie moves from confident leadership to risky overconfidence when her team tries to talk her out of rescuing Randy.

4. Which life value should I highlight on my Story Grid Spreadsheet?

Confident to Overconfidence.

HOW THE SCENE ABIDES BY THE FIVE COMMANDMENTS OF STORYTELLING

Inciting Incident: Harry sees the current state of Randy.

Progressive Complication: Harry says that Ernst is right and they should wait to rescue Randy.

Crisis: Best bad choice. Jessie can take their practical advice and wait to rescue Randy *or* she can push forward, even though there is no clear way they can escape.

Climax: Jessie leaves the control room and heads for Randy's bay.

Resolution: She barely makes it to Randy's bay after she is attacked by faction guards and saved by Alex.

CHAPTER FORTY

Ernst?

Yeah. I'm here. I'm not sure what you want me to do.

Everything was still white. **Jessie** was inside the grid, but there was no simulation running, so it was a blank slate.

Don't worry about that, she said.

In moments, walls and floors swirled into existence. A three-walled room formed around her with a single slender door centered on each wall.

How are you doing that? asked Ernst.

I need you to open up a feed outside of the building? Can you do that?

Sure, but why?

I need you to get ready to broadcast a signal to Aeta Comm Central and the outlying cities. I need it to stream directly to all of the outlets you can get access to. I need as many people as possible to see it.

Ernst started to question again, but Jessie cut him off.

Just do it, Ernst. I need you to hurry.

Jessie walked up to one of the doors and opened it. She approached the entryway and stepped through. She immediately fell into a white abyss but closed her eyes and concentrated, reminding herself that what she was experiencing wasn't real.

After a few seconds, she began to slow down and then stopped a few inches above a new floor.

This one was tiled and dirty. Jessie observed how the tile was more soiled in the grout lines from decades of use. No bleach or mopping would make these tiles gleam again. Many of them were cracked and some even had pieces missing with the grout crumbling underneath. She was surprised at the specificity of the coding.

She turned to her left and stepped up to a large window in the wall. She peered through the blinds that were open on the other side of the window.

Randy lay in a hospital bed. A breathing tube ran down his throat, and wires ran out from underneath his ratty old gown. A brown blanket was folded at his waist, and machines on tall metal stilts next to the bed beeped and blinked.

Jessie walked to the room's door, turned the knob, and stepped inside. She locked it as she entered and closed the blinds before stepping up to his bedside.

She stared at her brother for a few seconds, a sad smile playing at her lips. This was how she wanted to remember him—full head of shaggy hair, arms strong and tanned, face full and healthy.

She blinked and Randy changed into the emancipated shell of a person from reality.

She put her hands on his shoulder and chest. She pressed into him and squeezed her eyes shut. Her hands shook slightly before his eyes popped open. He immediately jerked as his eyes searched the room to see where he'd been taken.

Jessie opened her eyes and started whispering to him while she kept a grip on his arm.

"Calm down," she said. "Stay calm. We have to move, but you've got to listen to me first."

His eyes were wide with fear, and he shook his head at her.

"Yes, I'm here, and you have to come with me. It's too late now. They know I'm here, so the only chance we have is if you come with me. Are you ready?"

Randy nodded slowly.

"Okay," Jessie said. She let go of his arm and climbed up on the bed next to him.

"I can't imagine this is going to feel too good," she said.

She grabbed the tube in his throat and slowly, forcefully dragged it out of his throat. A dull moan escaped him as she got the last of it out.

A distant bang floated in from outside of the room, and Jessie glanced over her shoulder but then put her attention back on her brother. His eyes squeezed shut, and a single tear had left a track down the side of his face. He was obviously in extraordinary pain.

"Okay, we have to get you out of bed now, and then we have to move. As soon as I disconnect the monitors from you, they're going to be able to pinpoint our location."

"Ready?" she asked.

Randy nodded.

Jessie quickly removed the IV catheter from his hand and then grabbed all the wires running under his shirt in one hand and yanked them all at once. Randy winced as the tape ripped from his chest.

The machine behind Randy immediately began screaming as Jessie helped Randy sit up. He slid off the bed and onto his feet, wavering for a second, but then nodded to Jessie.

Another bang sounded, much louder now. Jessie walked over to the wall opposite Randy's bed and placed her hand on the wall. The wall shimmered and began to fade, but a loud bang sounded, this time right next door. The wall snapped back to its solid-state.

"Concentrate," Randy choked out.

"I am!" she yelled at him, her eyes still closed.

She put both her hands on the wall this time, and the wall immediately began to fade. And then another bang came on their door. The wood cracked next to the doorknob, and the door slammed open.

Three guards stood at the opening and raised their weapons. Jessie grabbed Randy's hand, and they both fell through the wall before the guards could fire.

They were back in the three-walled room.

"That was too close," Randy choked out. "How did you even get here?"

Jessie shook her head at him as they both got to their feet and then grabbed his hand, walked to the closest door and led him through.

Jessie's eyes popped open, and she immediately turned over to look at Randy.

"Hold still," **Harry** was saying as he fumbled with her plug.

She looked up at Randy just as his eyes fluttered open.

Jessie felt the plug release and fought to sit. With the electrical shot from her run-in with the guard gone, this time, her body listened to her, and she was able to push herself up.

"Help him," she said to Harry, pointing at Randy.

Harry's face lost a bit more color when he saw Randy, but he hurried over. He put his arm around Randy's waist and begin removing the tubes and restraints to get him down.

Jessie got to her knees and crawled over to the terminal. She pulled herself up into the seat and leaned close to the microphone.

"Ernst?"

"Here!"

"You've got that feed patched to the Faction?"

"I do, but what are we going to do?"

"I need you to run our camera through the patch."

Harry made a sort of gasp behind her.

"How long will it take?" she asked.

"Just a few seconds. It's ready to go."

"Do it," she said and spun around.

Harry had Randy in his arms. Somehow her brother looked even weaker now.

"Get him in that chair and bring him over here."

"You're crazy! What are you doing?" he said.

Jessie didn't answer.

Harry gently sat Randy in the chair and then slid the chair next to Jessie. He rummaged through one of the cabinets and emerged with a blanket.

Jessie locked eyes with Randy and reached out her hand to gently stroke his face.

"It's my turn to save you," she said.

Harry wrapped the blanket around Randy and then stepped to the side.

"You're on! Live. I didn't get to all the cities, but most of them. And all of Aeta," Ernst said. "I'd say about half of **the Faction** is seeing this feed now."

Jessie nodded and leaned into the microphone.

"This is Coder Jessie Marston of the Preparing. I'm one of the last standing after the second Severing. For years we thought my brother Randy had died winning the Threshing for our Faction. But it isn't true."

She hesitated for a moment, looking at Randy and then off camera at Harry. The older man nodded at her.

"The truth is, spies from **the Europa Faction** kidnaped him and put him into a grid-induced coma. They hoped to use him as leverage against us in the upcoming Threshing. But thanks to the bravery of the **Faction Elites** and the cunning strategy of our great **President Marcus**, he has been rescued and returned home, here to Aeta where he belongs. Not only has this struck a blow to our **enemies**, but we now have his wisdom and experience back with us to help win the Threshing for Americas once again!"

Jessie paused again and stared at her brother, this time looking into his eyes as she spoke.

"He is the bravest of us all, and once he has recovered, he will address you as well. Thank you for your bravery and support of our Faction. Now, more than ever, we will win the Threshing and maintain our place in **the Reapers'** favor."

There was a brief pause before Ernst's voice came through.

"Feed is cut."

Jessie locked eyes with Randy.

"Let's hope this works," Harry said.

CHAPTER FORTY

Analyzing the Scene

A STORY EVENT is an active change of life value for one or more characters as a result of conflict (one character's desires clash with another's).

A WORKING SCENE contains at least one Story Event. To determine a Scene's Story Event, answer the following four questions:

1. What are the characters doing?

Jessie logs into the grid to rescue Randy. They both come out of the grid. Jessie addresses the entire Americas Faction, letting them know that she and Randy are both alive.

2. What is the essential action of what the characters are doing in this scene?

Jessie is trying to create a situation where President Marcus has to keep her and Randy alive and in the Preparing.

3. What life value has changed for one or more of the characters in the scene?

Jessie takes herself, Randy, and her team from a situation where their lives are threatened to one where they are temporarily safe.

4. Which life value should I highlight on my Story Grid Spreadsheet?

Threatened to Safe.

HOW THE SCENE ABIDES BY THE FIVE COMMANDMENTS OF STORYTELLING

Inciting Incident: Jessie logs into the grid.

Progressive Complication: Jessie begins her public address that is streaming to half the Faction.

Crisis: Best bad choice. Jessie can tell the truth of what is going on and ensure their capture and punishment *or* she can spin a lie that will protect them temporarily.

Climax: Jessie creates a lie that protects them.

Resolution: They turn off the feed and wait.

CHAPTER FORTY-ONE

"Open the door," **Jessie** said.

Jessie kept her arm around **Randy**, both clinging to him and keeping him propped up.

"Are you sure you want to do that?" **Harry** asked.

"He needs help, Harry. They'll help him."

Harry nodded. He tapped the keys on the door lock, and it slid open. His hands immediately shot up into the air, and he started backing up. The room filled with **guards** as they whipped their short black weapons back and forth, sweeping the room. Two kept their guns trained on Harry as they spun him around and zip tied his hands together.

As the guards moved to surround her and Randy, she kept her arms tightly around him but made sure her hands were visible. A few moments later, a guard dragged an unconscious **Alex** into the room and dropped him on the floor next to Harry. His hands and feet were all secured.

Once the room was still, the guards relaxed a bit but kept their weapons at the ready.

Everyone waited. The guards were on edge and ready to strike, but Jessie and Harry didn't dare ask any questions.

Every couple of minutes, Jessie would reposition herself, and the guards around her would tense up. She did every movement very slowly and always made sure they could see her hands.

Harry had slid down the wall and was sitting with his knees up.

After a while, Randy's eyes fluttered and opened. He lifted his head a bit and looked around the room.

"You okay?" Jessie whispered into his ear.

He opened his mouth to speak, but only a dry croak escaped. He shut his mouth and nodded.

Jessie looked up at one of the guards.

"Can we get him some water?"

The guard ignored her.

"Hello," she called at him, but he only responded by lifting his weapons when Jessie moved to stand.

She sighed and leaned back into the chair.

"I think you'll have to wait a bit for some water."

"I wonder what **Marcus** is up to," Harry said from across the room.

Another croak escaped Randy, and Jessie leaned in to listen.

She was barely able to make out what he said. "Damage control," she repeated.

"Yeah," Harry said. "Thankfully, you gave Marcus a story that made him look good, but it's still a story. He has to scramble to play it up."

Alex stirred and groaned next to Harry.

"You okay, kid?" Harry asked.

Alex opened one eye and looked up at Harry.

"Yeah, I'll live."

Harry helped him up to a sitting position.

"We just waiting?" Alex asked.

Before anyone could answer, all of the guards in the room stiffened and stood at attention. The gun muzzles that were drifting downward snapped back up and focused on their subjects.

The door slid open, and **Marcus** stalked into the room, followed by **two of his bodyguards.** The sweatpants and easy manner were gone. He was in full military dress, just like the portraits hanging on every wall in the Faction.

He scanned the room. His face was a dark red, and he was taking deep, slow breaths as he surveyed the controlled chaos around him.

When his eyes landed on Randy, something like a thin smile slid quickly across his face. He walked over to Randy and squatted down so he could look up into his face.

"Is he awake?"

"Yes, sir," the guard on his left answered.

"Said anything?"

"I don't think so, sir."

Marcus nodded and reached his hand out to Randy. Jessie instinctively batted it away.

Marcus slowly turned his head and considered her for a moment before backhanding her. The sound cracked through the room, and Jessie, surprised by Marcus's strength, toppled out of her chair. She scrambled to get to her feet, but Marcus kicked her back to the ground.

She landed on her back, and before she could move again to get up, Marcus put his black boot on her chest and held her down. He squatted down next to her, the heel of his boot driving into her sternum.

The air squeezed out of Jessie's lungs, and she began taking short ragged breaths, trying to keep breathing under the intense pressure. She felt like her chest was going to cave in under the weight of the man.

Marcus leaned over her and stared into her eyes.

"You've become a true thorn in my side. Haven't you?"

Jessie held his gaze with her jaw set and continued sucking in small breaths. She was determined to show no pain, no matter what he had planned for her.

"After the first Severing, something about you seemed familiar, but I just assumed you were another bratty recruit that got lucky and would be culled out in the next Severing. But in our little meeting you gave me the reason you were so familiar. "

He leaned in heavier on her chest, and Jessie felt something pop. She squeezed her eyes shut and moaned out her breath as pain exploded in her chest.

"Stay with me," he said, snapping his fingers in front of her face.

Jessie's eyes came back open, and she fought to keep her face passive.

"It connected you," he continued, "to the other giant pain in my ass from four years ago. I thought for sure my little hacking of your sim would take care of you—I'm still unsure how you made it out of that—and, then, I all but ensured you would be taken out early in the second Severing. Not only did you inexplicably make it out of the second Severing, but before I could even gather myself to make another plan, I heard about a disturbance on Randy's floor."

Marcus laughed, wiped his brow with the back of his hand, and then stood, releasing the pressure from Jessie's chest. Despite herself, she gasped. It seemed like the first full breath she'd had in hours. Then she pressed her hands against the place under her armpit where she'd felt the pop to see if anything was broken.

"I think my favorite part about all of this is that you solved a real problem for me."

He walked back over to Randy, grabbed the scruffs of hair on the top of his head and yanked his head back. Randy's eyes fluttered open again, and he looked up at Marcus. It was hard to tell if he was actually focusing on him.

"I've been wondering what to do with you. You had become quite useless to me. I've thought for months now that we should get rid of you, but something told me I should keep you alive for just a bit longer."

Marcus glanced over his shoulder at Jessie and then back at Randy.

"Okay, get him out of here," Marcus said, stepping back.

"No!" Jessie rolled up to her side, struggling against the pain. The guard nearest her stepped in front of her and pressed her back into the ground. She watched between his legs as Randy's chair rolled out of the room.

"Him too," Marcus said, pointing at Harry.

One of the guards grabbed Harry, who looked over at Jessie.

"It's on you now," he said.

The guard punched Harry in the stomach, forcing him to double over, and then dragged him out of the room.

Marcus headed for the door, took one look back over his shoulder at Jessie, and then stepped out into the corridor.

The guard standing over Jessie grabbed her arm and roughly dragged her to her feet. She winced, clutching her side. They released Alex's feet and he stepped over near Jessie.

The two of them looked at each other.

"What now?" Alex said.

Jessie had nothing to say.

CHAPTER FORTY-ONE

Analyzing the Scene

A STORY EVENT is an active change of life value for one or more characters as a result of conflict (one character's desires clash with another's).

A WORKING SCENE contains at least one Story Event. To determine a Scene's Story Event, answer the following four questions:

1. What are the characters doing?

All of them are waiting on President Marcus to arrive. Once he arrives, he threatens them all. He then takes Randy and Harry and leaves.

2. What is the essential action of what the characters are doing in this scene?

President Marcus is showing that he still has control over the situation and tries to imply that this actually helps him.

3. What life value has changed for one or more of the characters in the scene?

Jessie starts out in a position of perceived power but quickly realizes that she and everyone she cares about is still under President Marcus's control.

4. Which life value should I highlight on my Story Grid Spreadsheet?

Perceived Power to Weakness

HOW THE SCENE ABIDES BY THE FIVE COMMANDMENTS OF STORYTELLING

Inciting Incident: President Marcus enters the room.

Progressive Complication: President Marcus inspects Randy.

Crisis: Best bad choice. Does President Marcus leave them together *or* does he arrest them?

Climax: President Marcus takes Randy and Harry with him and leaves Alex and Jessie behind.

Resolution: Alex and Jessie are left alone to figure out what to do next.

NOTES:

This scene represents the turning point progressive complication of middle build two, 'all is lost.'

CHAPTER FORTY-TWO

Jessie stared at herself in the mirror.

Her hair had grown quite a bit in the two months since she'd come to Aeta. It was still jet black and almost long enough to tuck behind her ears.

She glanced back at the clock on the wall. The two little dots between the numbers blinked so slowly.

Five more minutes, and it would be safe.

She closed her eyes and took a deep breath. She could still feel the pain in her chest when she took in a full breath. **The Medics** said it was a dislocated rib, not a broken one. Apparently, an out-of-place bone hurt worse than a broken one, but with the two weeks of rest and some pills from the Medics, the pain had subsided a good bit. Jessie looked at the clock again.

Three more minutes.

They hadn't heard from or seen **Marcus** since he took **Randy** away. The first couple of days, Jessie, **Ernst**, and **Alex** were always on edge, waiting for more **guards** to show up and take them away.

"I guess it worked," Alex had said. "They can't touch you since you're a finalist for the last Severing."

"What about Randy?" Ernst added and then quickly regretted speaking. Jessie's anxiety over her brother's fate was palpable.

Jessie was working Ernst's guilt. She'd been trying to convince him to hack into the mainframe and help her find where they were keeping Randy. He had been resisting up until this point, but she finally got him to relent.

They had moved Randy up to the forty-third-floor infirmary. Four days before, she made her first attempt to see him but was blocked as soon as she exited the elevator and sent back down. She spent the next twenty-four hours attempting to find different ways to sneak up and see him, but she was caught and turned away every time.

Two nights before, after she waited until 0300, Jessie was once again met by a **Faction guard** as soon as the elevator opened. She had sighed and started to reach for the control panel herself to descend back to her floor, but instead, the guard stopped her. He looked both ways, checking the corridor, and then motioned for Jessie to follow. She had hesitated at first, unsure why a guard would let her pass.

The doors had begun to close on the elevator as she jumped off and hurried to catch up with the guard. He led her down the corridor to one of the nondescript infirmary rooms, unlocked the door, and let her inside.

"Ten minutes," he said and then the door clicked shut, locking her inside.

While Randy looked better than when they had found him—some color had returned to his cheeks and the sparse hair on his head had been shaved down—he was still a shell of his former self. He was skinny and pale to the point of translucence. He was breathing on his own but had an IV pumping fluids and nutrients into him since his digestion could not yet handle real food.

She moved slowly over to his side and knelt. She rested her hand on his, and he stirred slightly but remained asleep. Jessie cried. Sobbed. It was the first time in four years that she didn't have to push down all of her feelings about her brother along with her fear and loneliness. He was alive.

Every night since then, Jessie had gone to see him at the same time.

Jessie looked at the clock again just as the time blinked over to 0300 She hopped out of bed, slid open the door, and checked the corridor. Two minutes later, she was escorted down the forty-third-floor hallway to Randy's room.

As soon as his door opened, she stepped in and then stopped short.

Randy wasn't there. The sheets were off the bed, and the equipment keeping him alive had been taken out.

Instead, Harry sat on the bed.

They stood staring at each other, and Jessie's jaw was set in her defiance.

"This has to stop," Harry said.

"Why? I'm just coming to see my brother."

Harry stared at her for a few seconds. Jessie folded her arms and leaned back against the wall.

"You're going to get all of us caught and executed. You think you did something clever with the way you got Randy out, and you did, honestly. I wouldn't have thought of that. But it doesn't give you a free pass. You're not invincible."

"I'm just coming up to see—"

"Shut up," Harry whispered. "I know what is going on. You know the guards talk to me. That's the only way I was able to have them sneak me out of my cell tonight."

Jessie frowned hard, anger washing over her face.

"And it's a good thing they did," Harry continued. "Did you really think you could smuggle a man in Randy's condition out of this building, all the way through town, and onto a transport without getting noticed?"

"I had a plan," Jessie said. "I've been watching the guards, and—"

Harry stood and shook his head.

"No," he said. "Your plan is ridiculous. And *childish*. You are watched every second of every day. You are followed wherever you go. Do you really think Marcus isn't watching every single move you make? He's waiting for a reason to execute you and your brother. The only reason he can't now is that Randy's a hero, and you're a potential hero. All he needs is for you to try and escape with Randy to accuse you both of treason. Then he can execute all of us without any public outcry. He's playing the long game, just waiting for you to give him an excuse. Don't be stupid enough to give him one."

Harry sat back down.

"Which is why he's let you see your brother for the last few nights. He's just hoping you would make a mistake like this."

Jessie dropped her head and stared at her toes.

"And what were you hoping to accomplish by getting him back to New York?"

Jessie shrugged.

"You think you're going to live happily ever after? No. You'll be in hiding for a few days. Maybe a couple of weeks before somebody recognizes you and turns you in for the bounty."

"I just thought—"

"I know what you thought. You, Randy, your **mom and dad**, together and happy. You could go back to stealing credits. You'd nurse him back to health. But that's not how it works. You'd be caught and executed very quickly. So would your parents. **Alex and Ernst and their families** would be thrown in with the Numbered. I'd probably get executed too."

Jessie shifted her feet and refolded her arms.

"There's only one way out of this, Jessie."

Jessie shook her head. "No," she said. "I can't do it. I've only gotten lucky so far. There's no way I don't die in the next Severing. Then they'll kill Randy too. There's no way."

"Yeah, probably," Harry replied. "But it's the only way you have a chance. Win the Severing. Win the Threshing. Then you and Randy can go home happy and rich. Your parents will be taken care of. You'll be free."

Harry sighed.

"Or as free as we can get."

Harry stood up again.

"This is the last time you'll come up here. Your job is to prepare for the next Severing. If you want to help Randy, that's the only way."

CHAPTER FORTY-TWO

Analyzing the Scene

A STORY EVENT is an active change of life value for one or more characters as a result of conflict (one character's desires clash with another's).

A WORKING SCENE contains at least one Story Event. To determine a Scene's Story Event, answer the following four questions:

1. What are the characters doing?

Jessie is sneaking up to see Randy after Ernst helped her find him. Harry meets her and tells her that her visits to Randy have to stop.

2. What is the essential action of what the characters are doing in this scene?

Harry wants Jessie to commit to finishing the Severing and the Threshing.

3. What life value has changed for one or more of the characters in the scene?

Jessie is still avoiding her fate of going to the Severing and the Threshing. She is trying to come up with a plan to smuggle Randy out of Aeta and back to New York. Harry convinces her that her only way out is through the Severing and the Threshing.

4. Which life value should I highlight on my Story Grid Spreadsheet?

Avoidance to Acceptance.

HOW THE SCENE ABIDES BY THE FIVE COMMANDMENTS OF STORYTELLING

Inciting Incident: Harry meets Jessie when she goes to see Randy.

Progressive Complication: Harry points out that her plan to escape is ridiculous and will never work.

Crisis: Best bad choice. Jessie can keep fighting her fate to go to the Threshing or she can finally accept it as the only path.

Climax: [Next Scene] Jessie is in the final Severing, so we see what she has chosen.

Resolution: [Next Scene] Jessie arrives in the final Severing.

NOTES:

This scene represents the crisis of middle build two, 'meaning making of life.'

CHAPTER FORTY-THREE

As the white faded, **Jessie** found herself in the middle of a large field. The grass blew in the wind and brushed against her knees as she turned to take in the surroundings. **Az** faded in next and then **the rest of the Coders** appeared.

They stood in a circle in a small clearing with a dark forest surrounding them. The trees towered above and Jessie looked up to see the heavy limbs pressing down overhead.

Light came from flickering torches that stood next to each Coder.

She turned and squinted into the darkness of the woods. She swore she could make out a shadow of movement, and as Jessie leaned closer into the blackness, she swore she could hear low growls within.

A spotlight snapped on from somewhere in the sky and cast down into the middle of the clearing to reveal a beautifully carved, round wooden table. Across the top of the table were one-inch squares in alternating green and black colors—the edges of each of the squares outlined in gold. Seven chairs were arranged around the table.

One seat was occupied. It was **Marcus.**

He was quietly shuffling and reshuffling a small deck of cards.

"Welcome," he said, opening his hands with a flourish, "to the final Severing."

"As you know, I code up all of the Severings," Marcus continued, "and I have put together a straightforward final test to see who should represent our great **Americas Faction** in the upcoming Threshing. Please, have a seat."

Each of the Coders took their designated seat. Jessie took her place to the left of the only other girl Coder, **Catherine**, who was seated next to Marcus. As they took their chairs, twenty-one figurines appeared on the table in front of each of them, all arranged in the squares closest to their seats. Eighteen figures were dressed in armor and three in common clothes.

Marcus continued shuffling the small deck of cards.

"As you can see," Marcus said, "you're going to play a simple game of Providence. I'm sure each of you played this game of knights and peasants as children. This Severing is not about moving quickly or out-coding your rivals or anything other than logic. I need the three of you who can outmaneuver and out-think the others. So here we are."

"But our game, of course, has one small twist," Marcus continued. "Each time you lose a peasant to an opponent, you must draw from this pile."

He tapped the deck in his hand.

"In this deck are two types of cards—a white card," Marcus drew a white card from the deck to show them, "and a red card." He drew a red card to show them.

"There are exactly three red cards in this deck. If you draw a red card, you're out. And just like in the usual game, if you lose all of your peasants, you're out. When there are only three Coders left in the game, the Severing is over. Any questions?"

Marcus paused and took the time to look at each Coder in the eyes. Jessie could have sworn he lingered on hers longer than the others, almost willing her to fail.

"Wonderful! Play begins to my left," he motioned to Catharine. "The final Severing starts now."

Marcus stood, and immediately he and his chair disappeared. The small deck of cards sat in the middle of the table.

After a brief pause, Catharine reached for one of her knights.

Jessie had always hated Providence. There was so much long-term strategy that she'd struggle to keep track of everything in her head. Whenever she played with **Randy**, he had always let her think she was about to win, and then he'd take all of her peasants at the end.

She'd played a few times with **her friends**, but with more people, it was always more complicated. She had to make tenuous alliances with players next to her to arrange the knights optimally, who would, in turn, best protect her peasants.

But of course, if she became too dependent on an alliance, she was left very vulnerable to betrayal once the game got serious.

And it always got serious, even when it wasn't part of the Severing.

The first ninety percent of every game was slow and methodical as people vied for better positioning for their knights. And then suddenly, it would switch to combat, where every move would be an attack on another's kingdom.

The six of them quickly chewed through two hours of play and Jessie was still unsure if any of her moves had been the right ones.

From the first move, it was apparent to Jessie that Az, who sat directly across from her, had teamed up with **Ellis**, who was on her left, and **Craig**, who was in between Ellis and Az. Jessie recognized both Ellis and Craig as two of the boys who had blocked her and **Clifton** from the tower. Catharine arranged her defenses in a way that helped protect Jessie, but Jessie was wary of her motives. The final Coder at the board, **Finn**, seemed to be the only one going it alone.

The table had been quiet as each took their turns moving one of their pieces. **Ernst** had finally quieted down in Jessie's head, though Jessie knew he was still freaking out. **Alex** was probably shutting him up. Jessie was scared too but kept trying to push it out of her head.

She couldn't worry about Ernst now. She had plenty right in front of her that she needed to figure out.

"Jessie," Az barked at her, "it's your move."

"Oh, sorry," she mumbled and quickly reached out and slid one of her knights diagonally to position it better between her and Ellis.

Az sucked in a breath of air.

"Not a great move, Jessie," he said, "you're leaving your front far too exposed."

Jessie ignored him and tried to concentrate on her pieces and what her next move should be.

How's it going? Ernst couldn't help himself.

It's fine. You know how these games go. It's so slow at the beginning... that's why I always hated this game.

Stick with it. I'm sure you're doing great.

Jessie mentally rolled her eyes.

Catharine finished her move, and then the rest took their turns. Once Finn moved his piece, a smile crept across Az's face. Jessie looked closer at Finn's pieces and immediately saw his mistake.

He'd overcommitted to defending against Ellis and Craig's attack and left his flank open to Az. Finn didn't seem to know it yet, but he was just a couple of moves from losing the first peasant of the game.

The play went around the table twice more, and after Az's move, Finn finally realized his tactical error. He tried to move to defend Az's advance, but it was too late.

Two more rounds later and Finn's hand shook as he retreated his exposed peasant for the final time. Az moved his knight and took Finn's peasant. Immediately, the deck of cards Marcus had shuffled at the start of the game floated into the air a few inches and drifted toward Finn.

When the deck reached him, Finn reached for the top card, his hand shaking more than ever. He slid the top card off and held it in front of him. Fear flashed across his face, and he glanced around the table as if pleading for the other Coders to help. He showed the card to them.

It was red.

A growl came from the woods behind Finn. It was the same low rumble Jessie had heard when they first arrived. Finn's head snapped around, and he jumped up from his chair, knocking it over. A pair of yellow eyes had appeared in the flickering torchlight at the edge of the forest.

Finn backed away, circling the table and trying to put the game and the other Coders between himself and whatever was watching him.

Another, louder snarl came from the woods, and Finn turned and ran away. Just as he stepped into the darkness, he seemed to be sucked in. **A high-pitched scream** came from where he had disappeared, and then it was immediately cut off.

What the hell just happened? Ernst asked.

It's Finn. He just pulled a red card. He's gone.

Wait, hold on.

Several seconds passed. All of the other Coders were looking off into the distance as they communicated with their Comms as well. Everyone looked terrified.

All except for Az.

Az was staring directly into Jessie's eyes.

He was smiling.

CHAPTER FORTY-THREE

Analyzing the Scene

A STORY EVENT is an active change of life value for one or more characters as a result of conflict (one character's desires clash with another's).

A WORKING SCENE contains at least one Story Event. To determine a Scene's Story Event, answer the following four questions:

1. What are the characters doing?

Jessie and the other remaining Coders arrive in the final Severing. President Marcus tells them the final test is a game of Providence. They begin playing, and Finn is the first one to lose.

2. What is the essential action of what the characters are doing in this scene?

Jessie is trying to strategize to stay alive.

3. What life value has changed for one or more of the characters in the scene?

Jessie is already in a dangerous place, but this gets worse when the first player gets taken out of the game and dies.

4. Which life value should I highlight on my Story Grid Spreadsheet?

Dangerous to Life-Threatening.

HOW THE SCENE ABIDES BY THE FIVE COMMANDMENTS OF STORYTELLING

Inciting Incident: President Marcus tells them the final Severing is a game of Providence.

Progressive Complication: Finn is the first Coder to lose and is killed.

Crisis: Do the players continue playing or do they refuse?

Climax: No one makes a move to leave or object.

Resolution: The game continues.

NOTES:

This scene represents the climax of middle build two, 'absolute commitment.'

CHAPTER FORTY-FOUR

Jessie broke **Az**'s stare and tried to make eye contact with **Catherine**, but she just stared down at the board, doing her best to put out of her head what just happened to Finn.

Finn's chair and remaining playing pieces disappeared. It was down to **five Coders**. Only three would make it to the Threshing.

*Ernst, go over to **Catherine's Comms** and get him to tell her to partner with me. It's the only chance we have of surviving. See if they'll confirm.*

Okay, I'm on it.

Catherine had already made her move after Az's capture of Finn's peasant. Jessie studied the board.

After a couple of minutes, Catharine turned to look at Jessie and gave her a slight nod.

It sounds like they're in, Ernst said.

Got it.

Play continued around and around the board.

Finn's missing pieces had left an enormous gap on the board to Catharine's right, which gave her an advantage of space between her and the three boys still at the table.

Az continued to mock Jessie's movements, trying to play with her head. **Ellis** kept attacking her flank, but Catharine and Jessie made good use of the now-open space.

Craig and Az kept pressing their advance while blocking off escape paths for Catharine.

After another thirty minutes of play, Jessie could tell she and Catharine were in trouble. Even with their alliance, the three-against-two odds put them at a considerable disadvantage.

And it was apparent Az was pressing the attack on Catharine. Jessie knew he wanted to revel in wiping her out last.

Finally, Catharine had no choice but to leave one of her peasants exposed so she could arrange a defense for the other two. Az quickly took the peasant, and the deck of cards floated to Catharine. She stiffened her spine and pulled a card. She let out a sigh of relief as she turned it over to show the rest of them the white card.

More rounds went by, and finally, Ellis made the move Jessie had left open for him. She quickly closed ranks and was able to take half of his knights over her next several moves. She had also captured two of his peasants, but he drew white cards both times and remained in the game.

Down to eight knights and a single peasant, he started retreating toward Craig's pieces.

Catharine soon went on an attack of her own, surprising Az it seemed. Jessie moved her pieces to defend Catharine's peasants as she advanced. Catharine lost five of her knights but had taken four of Az's and six of Craig's. She was a very gutsy player.

Craig was now retreating and closing ranks, but he left one of his peasants exposed, which Jessie quickly took, but once again he pulled a white card.

Jessie surveyed the table.

The last round of attacks and pull-back defending had left all of their armies weak and somewhat exposed. The three boys still had the advantage in numbers, but they were spread out and much more vulnerable than hours before.

Az, Craig, and Ellis kept exchanging glances as they fought to regain control of the board. Catharine was more exposed than Jessie since she had last gone on the attack. She began retreating to a safer position, but all three of the boys pressed in on her. Jessie tried to move her pieces to defend Catherine's position, but it was too late.

This time Craig took a second of Catharine's peasants.

Jessie quickly did the math in her head.

The odds were still well in Catharine's favor to draw a white.

The deck floated in front of Catharine as she reached out and peeled the top card. She turned it over and stared at it for a few seconds, her face stony. Then she turned to look at Jessie as a screeching sound started to grow from the forest.

"I'm so sorry," she said.

"No," Jessie said. "No, they can't—"

The screeching sound grew louder. Catharine squeezed her eyes shut and clutched the edges of the chair.

A large black animal emerged from the forest. It moved like a cat but was the size of a grown man. It screeched once as it leaped toward Catharine, mouth wide open to reveal rows of sharp teeth.

She screamed as her chair toppled over, and the cat took advantage. It clamped down on her arm and yanked her to the ground. She beat at the monster's face with her other hand and kicked at it, but it made no difference. The animal paused briefly, surveying the other Coders who had all jumped back from the table and the sudden violence.

Then it turned and ran back into the woods, dragging Catharine's writhing, screaming body into the darkness.

Catharine's pieces disappeared from the board as the remaining four Coders retook their seats. Jessie held her hands in her lap, fighting to keep from shaking. Az immediately made his next move as if nothing had happened.

Jessie retreated and regrouped over the next few rounds. She kept her face still but was reeling inside, trying to put together a plan that would allow her to survive.

"You know why I have such a problem with you, Jessie?" Az began as he made another move. "You don't actually care about the Faction or the Threshing. You had to be forced to come to the Stack. Meanwhile, all the rest of us realized what an honor it is and worked like crazy to get here. Then you just kept sliding by on luck and, apparently, protection from President Marcus. You kept taking spots from Coders who had worked harder and trained longer. We all came here, giving up our family and friends and lives, to defend the Faction's honor and place as defending champion of the Threshing. Which means the Americas people don't starve to death in the next four years. And you've done nothing but mock and circumvent all of it."

As he talked, they continued to move their pieces. Az pressed in on Jessie's right side, Craig on her front, and, encouraged by their advantage, Ellis ruthlessly attacked her on her left flank.

"Which is why," Az continued, "I've been watching you. I've been waiting for you to make a mistake I could use to destroy you. Ever since you disappeared from the last Severing, I knew you were up to something. You had figured out some way to worm into the Capital's grid. I tried to tell Bishop Pierre, but he didn't believe me. So I started following you. It's much easier than you would think in the Capital. I knew you would finally show your hand."

Az took another of Jessie's knights.

"And sure enough, you did. We lost you right before you pulled that stunt with your brother, so we decided to check on what your two idiot friends were up to instead. We were able to record Ernst helping you in the process. All we had to do was wait for the right opportunity."

Craig had pressed too boldly forward, and Jessie took one of his knights but lost two of her own in the process. Jessie continued pushing her knights in Az and Craig's direction, leaving her flank more exposed to Ellis.

"Didn't you wonder why Ernst didn't react to what happened to Catharine?" Az asked.

Jessie slowly lifted her head, finally shifting her attention enough from the game to take in what Az was saying.

"See, now I have your attention."

"What did you do?" Az paused.

"You know, Craig," he said, looking to his right, "I forget. What is the punishment for hacking the Capital grid system?"

"I believe it's immediate Shaming and shipping off to the Numbered," Craig said.

"That's right," Az sighed. "I had forgotten."

"I believe the family of the criminal is also punished," Ellis said.

"Yes! That's right!" Az said. "Their monthly credit quota is slashed in half."

Dread filled Jessie as they spoke back and forth. Tears filled her eyes.

"Tsk, tsk," Az said. "It's such a shame when a trainee gets mixed up with the wrong people. They forget why they're here in the first place. You got Alex and Ernst to focus more on your treasonous behavior than on the real reason they are here. And now they're going to suffer for it."

Jessie's hand shook as she moved a piece. She dropped it, knocking over two other pieces, and quickly replaced them on the board.

Ellis had used the distraction to move his knights into position to Jessie's left between two of her peasants. Over the next few rounds, her hands still shaking, Jessie moved most of her knights to try and defend, but Ellis struck quickly. He dispatched first one peasant—Jessie drew a white card—and then a second. Jessie quickly pulled the second white card and threw it aside.

The three boys openly taunted her now. They speculated on the type and severity of punishment that both Ernst and Alex would receive. They mockingly consoled Jessie since she wouldn't be around to deal with the shame she'd brought on them.

Ellis wiped tears from his eyes as he stifled giggles.

In his next three turns, he quickly moved his knights into a position to expose Jessie's final peasant.

Then Jessie moved one of her knights diagonally to the left, and Az's laughter cut off suddenly.

"Pay attention, Ellis!" he shouted.

Ellis looked at the board, confused, and then his eyes grew wide. He hastily pulled back his knights, but it was too late.

Jessie's final peasant was still two moves away from being taken, but her knight sat within striking distance.

There was nothing the boys could do.

Jessie would take Ellis's final peasant on her next turn. It didn't matter that she had left her last peasant exposed to Az and Craig's attacks. She would still be one of the last three Coders standing.

A stunned quiet fell over the four of them.

"You idiot!" Az yelled at Ellis.

"Do something!" Ellis yelled back.

"What can I do?" Az spat at him. "We had her cornered, and you stopped paying attention."

A fresh set of tears ran from Ellis's eyes.

"No, no, no," he pleaded. "Don't let her do this to me, Az!"

Az dropped his eyes to the table as Jessie's turn came up again. She quickly took Ellis's last peasant.

Ellis's eyes flitted around the circle as the screeching sound started growing again.

Az gritted his teeth as he stared down at the table. His jaw muscles worked underneath the skin.

He looked up slowly at Jessie. When he locked eyes with her, she smiled at him. Then she winked.

A growl slowly built inside of Az's throat, but then it turned into a shrill scream as he lunged across the table. The knights and peasants scattered as he scrambled toward Jessie. She tried to push her chair back, but it was too late. He was twice her size and threw himself onto her body.

Jessie's chair tipped back, and they both hit the ground. She tried to get to her feet, but Az dropped onto her, straddling her and holding her down. He landed two quick punches to her face, stunning her, and then closed his hands around her neck and began squeezing.

She reached up and tried to pull at his hands, but he held on tightly. The screeching sound got louder all around them. Jessie's vision began to swim, but she fought to retain consciousness. She dragged her fingernails across his hands, but he didn't relent. She reached up and clawed at his face, leaving deep, bleeding gouges across his cheek.

He continued to scream and started picking up her head and slamming it into the ground.

Jessie blacked out and then came to just in time for him to slam her head back into the ground again.

Blackness swept over her again, but she could still hear the screeching sound growing. She couldn't imagine it getting any louder before she realized she heard Ellis's screams as well.

The blackness that had taken over started slowing fading to white.

<hr>

CHAPTER FORTY-FOUR

Analyzing the Scene

A STORY EVENT is an active change of life value for one or more characters as a result of conflict (one character's desires clash with another's).

A WORKING SCENE contains at least one Story Event. To determine a Scene's Story Event, answer the following four questions:

1. What are the characters doing?

The Coders continue playing Providence. Catharine loses and is killed. Eventually, Jessie outsmarts the other players them and wins. Az attacks Jessie and tries to kill her before they log out of the Severing.

2. What is the essential action of what the characters are doing in this scene?

Jessie is trying to play dumb to distract her opponents from her strategy.

3. What life value has changed for one or more of the characters in the scene?

Jessie moves from being on the brink of death and losing the Severing to winning the Severing and then to almost being killed by Az.

4. Which life value should I highlight on my Story Grid Spreadsheet?

Death to Life to Death

HOW THE SCENE ABIDES BY THE FIVE COMMANDMENTS OF STORYTELLING

Inciting Incident: The Coders start playing again after Finn's death.

Progressive Complication: Jessie winks at Az after she wins.

Crisis: Best bad choice. Does Az take the insult *or* does he attack Jessie?

Climax: Az attacks Jessie and tries to kill her.

Resolution: They log out of the Severing just in time to save Jessie.

NOTES:

This is one of two scenes that represent the resolution of middle build two, 'preparations.'

CHAPTER FORTY-FIVE

Jessie sat alone in the small room. The table and chairs were metal and bolted to the floor. There were no windows. Just a single pale-yellow light came from the low ceiling.

It felt like a place where the condemned waited before they were dragged out to the square and shot. The door creaked open, and **Harry** slipped in and sat down across from her.

Silence hung between them for several seconds. Jessie's hand stayed grasped around the domino in her pocket.

"They let me out so I could see you one last time."

He paused.

"Ready?" he asked.

Jessie shrugged.

"You know, if I had a half credit for every time you've shrugged your shoulders at me over the last few months—" He stopped and rubbed his face. "I suppose I could afford a nice meal." He paused. "You're as ready as anyone I've seen. Nobody has ever done what you've done in the Severings. You have this way of being inept, but. Not."

"Is this supposed to be encouraging?"

"Jessie, you can win this. Now listen. Every year the theme is around the Burning. It's to remind everyone watching what happened and what purpose **the Reapers** serve. And yet, even with us all knowing the theme, it's always a surprise. When I was here training, they gave everyone sickles and put them in a wheat field. One year, they were all dropped on the remains of the glaciers. The one **Randy** won was in an oil field. Whatever it is, you have to be the last one standing. There's no mercy here. **The other Factions** are desperate. **Their people** are dying of starvation, and they will be doing anything they can think of to win."

He leaned down close to her and whispered. "You have to win this. It's—it's our only way out. Me, Alex, Ernst, Randy. You're it. You know that, right? They let us go so we can support you in the Threshing, but if you don't make it out—"

Jessie kept her eyes on the table.

Harry sat back and sighed as he glanced at the light above them.

"Look, it wasn't easy, but I got you a few minutes with him."

Jessie's head snapped up.

"He's awake? He's okay?" she asked excitedly.

"I don't think I'd say he's okay, but he's awake. He wanted to see you before you started."

Harry stood and turned toward the door. Jessie sat up straighter in her chair and pawed at her short hair that was sticking up at odd angles. The door opened, and **one of the guards** wheeled Randy's chair into the room.

Harry was right. Randy wasn't okay at all. He was still pale and sickly. Tubes ran out from underneath his hospital gown and up to an IV drip attached to the chair. He was painfully thin and hunched over.

But he was awake.

His eyes were open wide, and he smiled his crooked sort of smile at her.

"Five minutes," the guard said and then stepped out of the room and shut the door behind him.

"Jessie—" Randy began, but Jessie cut him off.

She leaned forward on the table, and tears streamed down her face.

"I'm so sorry, Randy. I didn't know you were here. I didn't know you were alive. I would have come for you, but I just didn't know. And I was visiting you. Every night. But then Harry stopped me and took you, so I didn't know where you were, but I just wanted to be with you, and I was going to take you out of the city but didn't get a chance before—"

Randy finally held up his hand, cutting her off. He shook his head.

"It's okay, Jessie. It really is. You didn't know. Nobody knew. Only **Marcus.**" A flash of anger went across his face at the mention of his name.

"What am I going to do, Randy? I finally have you back, and now I have to this thing, and there's no way I'm going to win. There's no way I can win. And then, what will happen to you? And **Mom and Dad**? And—"

"No, Jessie," Randy said. "None of that is true. You're going to win."

Randy leaned in close and spoke just above a whisper.

"I've already ensured it."

"But how? How can you possibly—"

Randy put a finger to his lips and shushed her.

"You just go in there and do your work and then when you win—"

"We can be together?" Jessie asked, hopefully.

"Yes. Yes, we can," Randy paused. "But—" Randy broke in midsentence and glanced over his shoulder at the door.

"What?"

"When you win, I need you to do something."

"Okay."

"What do you think Marcus is going to do with us when you win?"

"Send us home. As victors. That's what happens. We go home or go to the Reapers. It depends on whether or not they need us there."

"Is that what he did with me?" Randy asked, an edge to his voice.

"No, but this is different. Everyone knows about us, and Marcus will have to let us go."

Randy shook his head.

"That's not how it is going to work," he said. "Marcus will kill Ernst and Alex and Harry and probably me, and then he will hook you up to the grid just like he did me."

"No, he can't."

"What's going to stop him?"

Jessie opened her mouth to answer and then fell silent.

"Exactly. Which is why I need you to do something for me."

Jessie nodded slowly.

"You have to understand. There is no going home. Remember that story I read you every night before bed?"

Jessie nodded again.

"There are no ruby slippers, Jessie. Not in the real world. There are only the choices we make and where those lead us. And as I see it, you only have one choice."

"What do you mean?"

"Directly after winning the Threshing, you will be ported over to a meeting with Marcus. The protocol is automatic, and it is completely private. In this meeting he trapped me four years ago and made up the story of my death. He'll do the same to you if you don't do something."

Randy kept his eyes locked with hers. "Jessie, when you get into that meeting. I need you to take Marcus down."

"What do you mean?"

"You need to kill him."

Jessie was confused at first. She must have misheard him. She replayed what he said over in her mind several times.

"Kill him?"

"Yes."

"I can't do that."

"Why not?"

"I don't want to kill anyone."

"What do you think you'll have to do to survive the Threshing?"

"That's different."

"How?"

"That's the only way I can survive. There's no choice."

Jessie sank back into her chair, realizing just how much effort she'd put into hoping for the best. It was true. All of the other Coders were dead. It was down to her, Craig, and Az.

"I'm sorry, Jessie," Randy got his anger under control and soothed. "But this is the only way to save us."

"But then what?" Jessie asked. "Who will be charge? Won't someone else just take over?"

"I'll be in charge," Randy said. "*We* will be."

Jessie's brow furrowed at this, confused.

Randy took in a deep breath and let it out slowly.

"Jessie, it's no accident that you're here. It's no accident that you were summoned to the training. It's no accident that Harry and Eighty-three protected you when you were Numbered. And why he's here now. And that we have Faction guards who were helping us along the way so you were able to navigate through Aeta so easily."

"So you've been—" she started but then stopped.

"Yes. Planning this. It was the only way—"

"You had me sent to the Numbered?"

Jessie ran a hand through her short hair.

"No, of course not. That was not my intention, but I had to get you here. I had no idea you would resist so much."

"And the Severings. I could have died!"

"No," he said. "No, I was watching you. I knew you'd be okay."

"But you said it was an accident that I was here."

"I know," he said. "I couldn't tell you what was go ing on yet until I knew you could get me out."

Jessie sat quietly for several seconds, staring down at the table.

"Jessie—"

She held up her hand, and Randy sat quietly, waiting.

"So, you need me to kill Marcus?"

"I do."

More silence.

"Jessie, we only have a couple more minutes.

Jessie ignored him, lost in thought.

"And then what?"

"What do you mean?"

"So, you take over—"

"*We* take over."

"Okay, we take over. And then what?"

"What do you mean?"

"What are we going to do when we are in charge?"

"We'll get to run **the Faction** the right way. We'll ensure we bring up the best recruits and leverage the grid to keep the Americas Faction on top for decades to come. Marcus is an idiot. He wants to keep his hold on power by force and will, but we will do it through results. By showing the people how capable we are."

"What about Mom and Dad?"

"What about them?"

"Would we bring them here to the Capital with us."

Randy paused, just a beat too long. "Of course."

"And what about the Numbered? Would we free them or leave them where they are?"

"Our entire Faction runs well because of the Numbered. We can't just—"

"And what about all of the **people hooked up to the grid**? Do we just leave them there?"

"Jessie, you don't understand how things work. We humans barely exist as it is. We have a delicate balance and a delicate relationship with the Reapers. We have to maintain that. This is why getting Marcus out is so important."

Jessie nodded.

"What are you thinking?" Randy asked.

"I'm just sad."

"I know."

"I just wanted to go home. I thought maybe if I could win this Threshing, you and I could go back and be with Mom and Dad, and I could see my friends and we'd finally be together. And safe. And Mom would be okay cause you were home."

Tears streamed down Jessie's face.

Randy pushed back from the table a bit.

"Come here. It'll be okay."

Jessie stood and came around the table. She knelt in front of Randy and laid her head on his lap. He gently stroked her head.

"I'm so sorry," Randy said. "I didn't want any of this."

"I know."

"This is the only way we can be together and safe."

Jessie nodded her head against his legs.

Randy put his finger under Jessie's chin and lifted it so their eyes met.

"Are you with me, Domino?"

"Of course," Jessie whispered. "You're all I have."

CHAPTER FORTY-FIVE
Analyzing the Scene

A STORY EVENT is an active change of life value for one or more characters as a result of conflict (one character's desires clash with another's).

A WORKING SCENE contains at least one Story Event. To determine a Scene's Story Event, answer the following four questions:

1. What are the characters doing?

Jessie is meeting with Harry and then Randy before the Threshing starts.

2. What is the essential action of what the characters are doing in this scene?

Randy is trying to get Jessie to agree to kill President Marcus.

3. What life value has changed for one or more of the characters in the scene?

Jessie is forced to let go of her heroic, pure image of her brother and see his motives.

4. Which life value should I highlight on my Story Grid Spreadsheet?

Motivated to Disillusioned.

HOW THE SCENE ABIDES BY THE FIVE COMMANDMENTS OF STORYTELLING

Inciting Incident: Randy comes in to meet with Jessie.

Progressive Complication: Randy asks Jessie to kill President Marcus.

Crisis: Best bad choice. Jessie can stay loyal to her brother and do something that she doesn't want to do *or* she can defy him.

Climax:

Resolution:

NOTES:

We don't see the Climax or the Resolution until after the Threshing is over.

This is the second of two scenes that represent the resolution of middle build two, 'preparations.'

THE THRESHING

CHAPTER FORTY-SIX

Jessie felt the heat before the plug-in whiteness completely faded. Her skin began to sear, and her pores opened up. She blinked hard, squinted against the intense light and put her hand up to shield her enough so she could make out her surroundings.

She could see the dark silhouettes of two figures standing alongside her.

After a week of training together, **Az** had finally spoken to her on the last day. Not that she was all that interested in interacting with him, but she knew her survival depended on it.

"You have to talk to me, Az. We have to be able to work together."

"Why?" he had snarled. "You don't even want to be here. It's up to **Craig** and me to try and win the Threshing on our own."

He turned to walk away, but Jessie snatched at his arm.

Az spun around, his face twisted in anger.

Jessie forced herself to stay calm and stand firm under the gaze of the much taller boy.

"I'm in this," she said.

Az scoffed. "Since when? All you've done is try to get out of everything the whole time."

"And yet, I still won the Severings every time!"

Az blew it off. "Luck," he said.

"Three times? Even you're not that stupid."

"The second one doesn't count! I still don't know what you pulled there."

"Exactly. You don't know what I can do. You're so used to thinking of me as a stupid little girl that you can't get it through your head I belong here. I bested everything **Marcus** threw at us. And now—" Embarrassingly, her voice broke, but she cleared her throat and pressed forward. "And now I have **Randy**." She paused. "The only way he gets out of this alive is if we win the Threshing. So, work with me. I can do this."

Az relented. Having Randy's brain available to him, even if he had to listen to him through his irritating little sister, was irresistible. He summoned Craig over, and the three of them began planning their grand strategy.

And now here they were.

How hot is it? **Ernst** said. *You're already sweating like crazy.* **Alex** *is getting fluids back in your body as quickly as he can, but you've got to find shelter fast.*

Okay, but what's that sound? Jessie realized there was a loud buzzing in her ears. It was hard to make out at first because it was a constant presence since they'd dropped in, but now she could tell it was coming from somewhere.

She turned toward the noise and squinted but couldn't make out the source.

"Come on, Jessie," Az said. "We have to find some shelter first."

Jessie nodded but didn't answer. She took a few steps forward toward the noise. She could hear the buzzing getting louder as she approached.

"Jessie! Where are you going?"

"Hang on!" she called back.

There seemed to be a shadow in the distant sky, but it wasn't a typical kind of shadow. It was swirling darkness that morphed in its approach.

Jessie kept walking forward, and the buzzing was getting louder.

If she only had something to shade her eyes against the glare, she could figure out what was going on. She kept moving toward the darkness, drawn to it for some reason, and now the buzzing was deafening. It seemed to be all around her.

She gasped. "It's **the Swarm!**" she yelled.

"What?" Az called back.

He sounded far away. Jessie turned around to look back and could barely make out their shapes. She hadn't realized how far away she had walked.

"It's the Swarm! They destroyed the last of the crops in the Burning! They—" Jessie let out a yelp and slapped the back of her neck. Something had stung her.

Then there were more stings, and suddenly, she felt bugs all over her, biting and stinging. She screamed and thrashed as she ran away from the swarm. She made it a short distance, and then her legs buckled and gave out. She pitched over into the dry, sandy dirt.

Jessie tried to continue swatting at the bugs, but her hands and arms seemed to have grown enormous and heavy. She heard Az and Craig calling for her in the distance, but when she opened her mouth to answer, she realized her tongue seemed to be taking up all of the room in her mouth. She couldn't move it.

Jessie tried to open her eyes so she could see what was happening but realized her eyes were already open. She just couldn't see anything.

Fear flooded through her. She realized Ernst was calling for her too, but she couldn't form a clear enough thought to communicate with him.

The last thing she remembered was painful hands on her body and feeling the ground move beneath her.

CHAPTER FORTY-SIX

Analyzing the Scene

A STORY EVENT is an active change of life value for one or more

characters as a result of conflict (one character's desires clash with another's).

A WORKING SCENE contains at least one Story Event. To determine a Scene's Story Event, answer the following four questions:

1. What are the characters doing?

Jessie, Craig, and Az have landed in the Threshing and are starting to get their bearings.

2. What is the essential action of what the characters are doing in this scene?

Jessie is trying to understand the environment they have landed in.

3. What life value has changed for one or more of the characters in the scene?

Jessie starts out curious about her surroundings but then gets attacked by the swarm.

4. Which life value should I highlight on my Story Grid Spreadsheet?

Safe to Near Death.

HOW THE SCENE ABIDES BY THE FIVE COMMANDMENTS OF STORYTELLING

Inciting Incident: Jessie, Craig, and Az arrive in the Threshing.

Progressive Complication: Jessie can't figure out what the approaching shadow is.

Crisis: Irreconcilable goods. Jessie can keep moving and trying to figure out what is going on **or** she can listen to Az and turn back to join him and the others.

Climax: Jessie keeps moving toward the shadow.

Resolution: She is attacked by the swarm.

NOTES:

This scene represents the inciting incident of the ending payoff, 'no holds barred.'

CHAPTER FORTY-SEVEN

Jessie languished in her sleep, and could not understand why **her dad** kept shaking her, trying to wake her up. Didn't he know it was too early for her to get up?

She was exhausted, and she felt like her body weighed a thousand pounds. Jessie slapped at the hands shaking her and mumbled to her dad to let her rest. She kept trying to turn over to get away from his nudging, but before she could, her dad's hand slapped her in the face.

Jessie sat up, screaming, and looked around frantically.

"Damn it, Jessie, we have to move," **Az** was saying. "The swarm is still coming."

Jessie looked down at her hands and legs. Everything looked normal, but they still felt like they were bulging and stretching the skin. She looked around.

They were in a dark, concrete room with no windows. It was much cooler here, but Jessie could still feel the heat pulsing through the walls and into the interior. The only source of light was a small LED lantern that **Craig** held.

"What happened?"

"That swarm," Az said, pointing outside, "got ahold of you. And apparently it's only made of bugs that shoot venom into you that will eventually kill you. I got **my Comms** to have **Alex** shoot you full of epinephrine and some anti-inflammation cocktails, and that seemed to bring you back from the edge. But if Craig and I hadn't of grabbed you, you would have died already."

Jessie looked at Az and Craig.

"I'm sorry. Thank you," Jessie mumbled.

"We're in this together. Right?" Craig said.

Jessie nodded.

"Where are we?" she asked.

"I'm not sure," Az said. "And we won't have long. The swarm seems to be advancing. It's not fast, but it's steady. We just dragged you as fast as we could away from the heart of it and found this building. If that swarm overtakes us down here, we're done. Can you get up? Can you move?"

Jessie sat up and shook her head, trying to clear the fog threatening to overtake her again.

"I'm okay. Let's go."

Craig helped Jessie up to her feet and kept his arm around her shoulders as they made their way to the stairs. Once they were up on the main level, she got her first good look at Az and Craig. Their faces were already bright red from the sunburn. She looked closer at Craig's hand on her shoulder and could already see the little bubbles of blisters starting to rise.

The ground-floor room they emerged in looked like one of the thousands of abandoned buildings that had been left behind in the Burning as **millions of people** headed north trying to escape the sun and the heat.

The space looked as if it was a former office. Desks were pushed against the walls, chairs tipped over, and random papers strewn across the floor. Jessie squinted out the windows.

"We can't go back out there," she said. "Look at us. We're already being burned alive."

Az walked to the back of the room and pointed out the window.

Jessie could see the shadow advancing their way. The swarm would be back on them in a few minutes.

"We don't have many choices," Az said.

Jessie shrugged Craig's arm off of her shoulder and stepped away from him. Her knees buckled slightly, but she managed to lean against a desk to stay upright.

Tell Alex I need more of whatever he's giving me, she said.

No response.

Ernst?

Still nothing.

"Jessie," Az said, annoyance flaring up in his voice.

"Give me a second," she said, squeezing her eyes shut.

She shivered as she felt the drugs hit her system. Her mind snapped to attention, and her eyes popped open.

"We need a way to get from building to building without being exposed to the heat."

"We're not going to find anything like that," Craig said. "Nothing can keep the heat back."

Jessie went up to the window and gazed into the apocalyptic city.

The streets were wider than she'd seen before, and most of the buildings were squat compared to the towers of New York, but there should still be the markers.

"There!" she said as she pointed out the window. Then she stepped back and ran to the door.

"What?" Az asked. "What is it?"

"Who moves through the cities during the day? At the peak of the sun?" she asked.

Az and Craig looked at her, confused.

Jessie huffed, annoyed.

"Who cleans up your trash while you're plugged in?"

"**The Numbered**?" Craig said.

"Exactly. The Numbered are the only ones who have equipment that allows them to move around during the day."

She opened the door and pointed diagonally down the street. The two boys winced against the heat that came rushing in but squinted in the direction she was pointing. A black box with a white arrow was painted on the side of a run-down building.

"That's where we'll find what we need," she said. "Stay close. We have to move fast." But she wasn't sure if she would be able to if she didn't have a consistent flow of epinephrine and anti-inflammatories.

CHAPTER FORTY-SEVEN

Analyzing the Scene

A STORY EVENT is an active change of life value for one or more characters as a result of conflict (one character's desires clash with another's).

A WORKING SCENE contains at least one Story Event. To determine a Scene's Story Event, answer the following four questions:

1. What are the characters doing?

Jessie, Craig, and Az are hiding in a building and trying to figure out what to do next.

2. What is the essential action of what the characters are doing in this scene?

Jessie is trying to work out a solution to their problem.

3. What life value has changed for one or more of the characters in the scene?

Jessie starts out confused and lost as she tries to get her wits about her and think through the problem. She comes up with a potential solution.

4. Which life value should I highlight on my Story Grid Spreadsheet?

Lost to Having a Plan.

HOW THE SCENE ABIDES BY THE FIVE COMMANDMENTS OF STORYTELLING

Inciting Incident: Az tells Jessie that they have to keep moving soon.

Progressive Complication: Jessie finds one of the Numbered's markings that point the way back to one of their hovels.

Crisis: Best bad choice. The group can stay and risk the swarm catching up to them *or* they can leave and go after Jessie's idea.

Climax: They decide to leave.

Resolution: [Next scene] They are moving through the streets, following Jessie.

NOTES:

This is an example of Jessie using what she has learned throughout her journey.

CHAPTER FORTY-EIGHT

Ernst surveyed the bay.

Up until this moment, his time in Aeta had been a nightmare.

From the moment **Jessie** arrived, he felt a growing dread. At first, he thought it was because there was no way she would make it to the Threshing. Then, as she progressed through the Severings and seemed to get stronger through each one, her capabilities didn't make him feel any better.

It didn't help that he was falling for her. Something about her presence had drawn him in. He found himself wanting to help her. Not just through the Severings for his own mission. It was something more.

When she made it through the final test, that crazy game of Providence, he should have been excited. He was going to be at ground zero to complete his mission and be a hero.

All he had to do was sabotage her once she was in the big event. He'd had the plan in his mind for weeks.

He'd wait until **Alex** was doping her up with something. His back would be turned, and Ernst could easily knock him over the head with something heavy. He'd then inject Jessie's body with something lethal, and then he'd knock himself out. It would look like they were attacked while Jessie was inside the Threshing, and there was no way **Az** and **Craig** would win it on their own. Without Jessie, they were toast.

Then, after the dust settled and suspicions fell by the wayside—maybe that would take a few months—he could start working his way back to the West Coast. Soon after that, he could be extracted back to his Europa home. He'd be a hero.

He looked around the bay again.

Unfortunately, just as Ernst was about to bring the red fire extinguisher down on the back of his head, Alex sensed something and turned. He'd gotten an arm up just in time to parry the blow.

With the weird way Alex's arm looked, Ernst was pretty sure he had broken the boy's arm. Alex's ankle had to be broken too. The extinguisher dropped on it just before it crashed on the bay's floor. When Alex tried to get on his feet, his leg had immediately buckled underneath him.

Despite his broken bones, Alex had put up quite a fight.

Now, Ernst sat opposite him with his back against the bay door. He put his hand against his ear, shuddered, and removed his hand.

Why do I keep doing that? He knew it was hanging by a thin stretch of skin, mostly torn off. Blood still flowed down his neck, soaking his grey uniform.

Ernst had never seen someone turn into such a raging lunatic, but Alex still looked like a caged animal. After their scuffle, and his practically ripping off Ernst's ear, Alex shoved Jessie's table against the opposite wall. Now he was sitting with his back against it. He had an empty syringe clutched in the fist of his working arm, the needle pointing down. The needle pointed at a weird angle, but Ernst knew it was still a lethal enough weapon.

The jagged cuts across Ernst's arms and face were proof enough that Alex would not hesitate to use it. Now they sat in a kind of stalemate. Both of the boys' breathing had calmed down a bit, but the tensions were still extraordinarily high.

Alex was protecting Jessie's inert body, and Ernst was now sure the boy would die before he let Ernst get near her. And yet, there was nothing Ernst could do otherwise. The comms terminal had crashed on its side, the screen cracked and black. But even if he could communicate with Jessie, what would he say? He couldn't leave the bay looking like he'd just been in a war either. Even if he could take out Alex and Jessie, how could he explain his injuries?

"Why?" Alex demanded after a few minutes. "Why would you do this?"

"Same reason as you," Ernst said. "I want **my Faction** to win the Threshing."

Alex's face screwed up in confusion, and then it dawned on him.

"You're **the spy**? You've been here all along?"

Ernst shrugged.

"There could be others. **The Faction leaders** don't tell us all their plans in case we get caught. I have my orders. Get to the Threshing and then take out **the Coder**."

"How could you do this to her? You've seen what she's been through. You've helped her so many times."

"Well yeah, it doesn't do me much good if my Coder dies in the Severings."

Alex shook his head in disgust, and Ernst let out a bitter laugh.

"What?" Alex spat at him.

"You think your Americas Faction is so special? Why do you deserve to win over us? We're starving in the Europa Faction while your Faction gets a double portion. I've watched friends waste away to nothing. **My uncle** jumped off a bridge so **my little cousins** could have his rations."

Ernst pointed at Jessie.

"All I have to do is take her out of the Threshing, and then I go home a hero." Ernst touched his ear again and winced. "Even if I don't make it home, at least I know I did everything I could." Ernst looked across at Alex, measuring him again.

Alex lifted the syringe a little higher.

"Stay back, Ernst," Alex warned. "You'll have to kill me to get to her."

Ernst struggled up to his feet and leaned against the door.

"I know," he said.

CHAPTER FORTY-EIGHT

Analyzing the Scene

A STORY EVENT is an active change of life value for one or more characters as a result of conflict (one character's desires clash with another's).

A WORKING SCENE contains at least one Story Event. To determine a Scene's Story Event, answer the following four questions:

1. What are the characters doing?

Ernst and Alex are in a standoff. Ernst has tried to attack Alex and kill Jessie.

2. What is the essential action of what the characters are doing in this scene?

Ernst is trying to kill Jessie so he can give his Faction a better chance of winning.

3. What life value has changed for one or more of the characters in the scene?

Ernst is waiting to decide what to do next, but he strengthens his resolve and decides this is worth dying for.

4. Which life value should I highlight on my Story Grid Spreadsheet?

Thwarted to Committed.

HOW THE SCENE ABIDES BY THE FIVE COMMANDMENTS OF STORYTELLING

Inciting Incident: Ernst attacks Alex.

Progressive Complication: Ernst realizes that he is not going to make it out alive to a hero's welcome in his Faction.

Crisis: Best bad choice. Ernst can give up and try to escape *or* he can attack Alex again to get to Jessie.

Climax: He decides to finish the job of killing Jessie.

Resolution: [We don't see it in this scene]

CHAPTER FORTY-NINE

The heat was excruciating. Thanks to the shade from the buildings surrounding them, **they** were out of the direct sunlight, but the temperature was past halfway to boiling. **Jessie** knew they could only have a minute, maybe two, left before they would start to succumb to the heat.

She hugged the building, moving in the direction the arrow pointed for **the Numbered**. Her eyes darted around, looking for the next one. If they missed it, they were almost certainly on the path to extreme dehydration, shock, and eventually death.

Jessie glanced behind her. **Az** and **Craig** were staying close to her, fear written over their faces. They worried she didn't know that she was doing. They kept glancing over their shoulders to get a visual on the steadily approaching buzzing sound.

Taking leadership was not how Jessie had thought the Threshing would go. Az was supposed to be leading the way. He was the oldest and most experienced. Not to mention his complete hatred of Jessie had seemed to fuel all of his movements for the past six months.

Or had it?

He and Craig had saved her from the swarm when they could have left her behind. Craig did whatever Az said to do, but why would Az come back for her?

Jessie paused at the corner of a building. They would have to cross the street, which would leave them exposed to the sun and to **the other Factions**. There was about a ten-foot patch of direct sunlight they would have to get through.

She looked back at Az and motioned toward the street. He looked over her shoulder. His face hardened a bit, but he nodded at Jessie to go.

She got up to her feet and sprinted across the opening. Just as she reached the edge of the sunlight, she dove into the air, hit the dirt a foot from the edge of the shade, and rolled quickly out of the direct light.

Even for that brief second, the sun felt like a blowtorch on her skin.

Jessie scrambled back close to the buildings on the other side of the street and looked back.

Az was already running.

He followed Jessie's technique and launched himself across the sunlit area, but he was able to land back in the shade without the stumbling roll Jessie had done.

Az joined her next to the building and crouched down beside her.

Craig walked up to about a foot from the edge of the shade. Jessie could see huge beads of sweat rolling down the chubby boy's face.

"I don't know about this," Az said.

Jessie glanced at him and then back to Craig.

"Get a running start!" she called to Craig.

He nodded and backed up several steps. And then backed up a few more.

"Come on!" Az yelled. "We have to keep moving!"

Craig nodded and licked his lips. He backed up a few more steps and then started running.

He pumped his arms hard and leaned forward. As he approached the patch of sunlight, Jessie could see his eyes were closed.

Craig got two steps into the sunlight when his feet couldn't keep up with his forward momentum, and he fell hard, tumbling forward. Before Jessie could react, Az was already past her running hard for

Craig. The large boy had come to a stop just inches from the shade. He was thrashing around against the heat, disoriented.

Az reached out, grabbed the large boy's wrist and dragged him to the safety of the shade. Jessie knelt beside him and put her hand on his arm.

"You okay?" she asked.

Craig rolled over onto his back, breathing hard. He nodded.

"One upside is it makes the shade feel amazing," he rasped out.

Az and Jessie met eyes and started laughing despite themselves.

Az pushed himself back to his feet.

"Come on, Craig, get up."

The large boy nodded again and started pushing himself up to his feet.

"Lead the way," Az said to Jessie.

She nodded and cut her eyes at Craig. He nodded to her, so Jessie turned and started walking fast in the direction of the arrow.

Halfway down the block, another black box had an arrow pointing down an alley. The three of them bunched up by the corner, and Jessie peeked around the edge of the building.

A narrow lane went down between the tall buildings. Large trash cans were set against the wall sporadically, and old trash covered the alley ankle deep. It looked like no one had been here in years.

No one has ever been here, she reminded herself. *This isn't real.*

Jessie motioned to the two boys to follow and made her way down the alley. They shuffled through the trash, and Jessie's eyes darted back and forth as they moved until her eyes stopped on a large, blue, metal trash can. A solid black box was painted on the front of it.

She looked all around the sides of the metal box but couldn't find anything. She dropped to her hands and knees to look underneath. The trash bin was sitting on wheels a few inches off the ground.

She reached her hand underneath to feel around. She paused. The air under here was slightly cooler than it should be. She squinted to look, and she could just make out a slightly darker patch of shadow behind the bin.

She scrambled to her feet.

"Help me move this thing," she said.

Az and Craig pushed against the bin. The rusty wheels squeaked sharply as they rolled back to reveal a small hole in the wall no more than three feet wide and four feet high. Inside the opening, a narrow wooden staircase led down into the darkness.

Cool air rushed out of the opening and into their faces.

Ernst? There?

No response.

What was going on with him? Where was he? Over the course of the training and all of the Severings, she'd gotten used to having his voice in her head. He was always there, walking her through things and calming her down. Now he was gone, and she didn't know why, but she couldn't do anything about it. With Ernst quiet, she was alone.

Jessie took a deep breath.

"Let's go," Jessie hunched over and started down the stairs. After a couple of steps, she looked back. Az and Craig's faces were silhouetted against the opening.

"Are you coming?" she asked.

"How do you know what's down there?" Craig asked.

"It's the Numbered's hovel," she said. "If we want to survive the sun, they have the equipment to do it."

"Why is the temp control still running?" Az asked. "Shouldn't it be down like everything else here?"

Jessie shrugged.

"I dunno. But it feels nice, and it's our best bet at getting a jump on **the other teams**. They'll be stuck hiding out in buildings and staying ahead of the swarm."

Az looked at Craig, who shook his head. He didn't want to go down.

Az shrugged. "Suit yourself," he then hunched over and followed Jessie as she continued down the stairs a couple more steps.

"Craig! Come on!" she shouted. "You really want to stay up there by yourself?"

There was a moment of silence.

"Fine!" Craig relented, and she heard the stairs sigh as they stepped into the darkness that led below ground.

CHAPTER FORTY-NINE

Analyzing the Scene

A STORY EVENT is an active change of life value for one or more characters as a result of conflict (one character's desires clash with another's).

A WORKING SCENE contains at least one Story Event. To determine a Scene's Story Event, answer the following four questions:

1. What are the characters doing?

Jessie, Craig, and Az are making their way through the city to the Numbered's hovel.

2. What is the essential action of what the characters are doing in this scene?

Jessie is trying to keep them alive and moving.

3. What life value has changed for one or more of the characters in the scene?

Jessie has a better chance of surviving now that she has found the Numbered's hovel.

4. Which life value should I highlight on my Story Grid Spreadsheet?

Unsheltered to Sheltered.

HOW THE SCENE ABIDES BY THE FIVE COMMANDMENTS OF STORYTELLING

Inciting Incident: Jessie leads them into the city toward the Numbered's hovel.

Progressive Complication: Craig doesn't want to follow them into the hovel.

Crisis: Best bad choice. Craig can stay up in the heat by himself *or* he can follow Jessie and Az down into the Numbered hovel.

Climax: Craig decides to follow Jessie and Az.

Resolution: All three of them enter the hovel.

CHAPTER FIFTY

They made their way slowly down the stairs, running their hands against the rough cement wall. The bit of light from outside was quickly getting filtered out.

"I don't like this," **Craig** said.

Jessie ignored him and kept moving.

It continued to get cooler as they moved downward. They had gone down almost two stories by the time Jessie's foot hit the flat earth. She stumbled in the darkness.

She ran her hands up and down the walls, slowing her movement.

"Check the other wall," she said.

Az huffed his consent, and she heard his hands moving over the wall.

"Still with us, Craig?" Jessie asked.

"Yeah," he answered. "I'm here."

"Got it!" Az yelled.

A loud snap and the lightbulbs hanging from the ceiling flickered on to reveal a long concrete hallway. They could see openings every twenty feet, or so that led into other passageways.

"Let's go," Jessie said and started moving down the hallway. "They probably kept the suits toward the front."

She glanced into the first door.

"Yep!"

Az and Craig followed her into the room.

Bright white suits hung on the hangers, plus a large crate of boots sat next to a trunk filled with gloves. The helmets were all arranged neatly on shelves running the length of one of the walls. It was a lot neater than the New York Numbered kept their gear.

"Okay, find one that's close to your size and put it on."

The boys followed Jessie's lead and started pulling down suits off hangers and shoving their hands and feet into the gloves and boots.

"This is awesome," Az said, smiling at Jessie. "I think you may have just saved us."

Jessie smiled quickly and then turned back to inspect the helmets.

"They probably won't keep out the swarm, but they'll make the heat bearable, at least."

"Right," Az said. "While everyone else is getting burned up and rushing from building to building, we'll be cutting a straight path."

"Exactly."

"Think there's anything else here we could use?" Craig asked.

"What do you mean?" Jessie said.

"Well, do they have stuff to carry water or any weapons or anything?"

Jessie's face lit up.

"I didn't even think of that. There won't be any weapons, but I bet they've got some canteens we could use."

"Alright!" Az said. "Let's get finished up. We'll do a quick scan for supplies, and then we need to head out before the swarm catches up to us."

Jessie nodded, and they hurried to finish getting dressed. They wrapped up their wrists and strapped the white pants to their ankles. They each grabbed a helmet and then moved into the hallway.

They walked quickly, glancing into the rooms as they went. Most of them were dark rooms lined with cots. Jessie thought she saw movement a couple of times, but ignored it, hurrying to keep moving forward.

After they passed several rooms, they found the kitchen, outfitted much better than her **New York Numbered**. There was a working sink and even a refrigerator.

She knew this was just a simulation, but it made her angry all the same. Someone somewhere had to code up this room that they understood none of the participants would ever find, and they still had to tell a lie about the way the Numbered lived. It was gross.

The three of them rifled through the cabinets.

"Found them!" Craig called out.

He reached high into the cabinet and grabbed two large canteens. But as he pulled them out, a ceramic cup caught on his sleeve and fell.

It hit the counter below it and shattered. The sound was like a gun shot in the quiet basement room.

"Shhh!" Az hissed.

"Why?" Jessie said. "There's no one here."

"I don't know," Az said. "Just feels like we should be quiet."

Jessie rolled her eyes.

"Grab a third," she said as she took the first of the canteens and started filling them at the sink.

She capped each one and handed them to Az and Craig, keeping the third for herself. She tucked it into the pouch on the side of her baggy white pants.

"Let's go," Az said. "I'm beginning to agree with Craig. This place is giving me the creeps."

The three of them pushed out into the hallway and froze.

A single figure was standing halfway down the hallway between them and the stairway up and out.

His head was bald. He was tall and painfully skinny. The man was rubbing his face and then stopped when he saw them. The man spoke.

Jessie could tell it was a question but couldn't understand what the man was asking. Whatever he was saying was in a language she didn't understand. He must be confused. Three people, obviously not the Numbered, dressed in their suits and coming out of their kitchen.

"He wants to know who we are," Az whispered.

"You can understand him?" Jessie asked.

"Barely. **My parents** speak Mandarin, and I can understand some of it."

Jessie held up her hands and stepped forward.

The man immediately yelled out and then kept yelling.

"Go!" Az yelled.

He pushed past Jessie and began running at the man.

Jessie hesitated for a second and then began running after him. She could hear Craig directly behind her.

Az ran directly toward the man. As he got closer, he lowered his shoulder and barreled into him. They got tangled up and hit the floor. Jessie and Craig reached them as Az was already struggling to get back to his feet, but the man grabbed onto his leg. He pulled Az's leg to him and bit down hard on his calf. Az yelped and kicked at the man, but he held fast.

Craig grabbed the man's legs and tried to drag him away from Az. Jessie dropped to her knees and started beating on the man's arms and face and peeling at his fingers.

Az's foot popped out of the man's grip, and he stumbled away. Craig fell back as the man slid across the floor. Jessie went to help Craig up, but before she could, two more figures appeared in the doorway and lunged at Craig. The man Az had run into latched on to Craig as well. This time he sank his teeth into Craig's arm.

Craig screamed. Jessie saw **one of the Numbered** grab a handful of Craig's hair, pull his head back, and then sink his teeth directly into the boy's face.

"Help him!" Az called and took a step toward Jessie, but more figures were already pouring into the hallway. Several of them turned toward Jessie and Az.

"Run!" Jessie said.

"No!" Az said. "We have to—"

But then he saw what Jessie saw. Already almost **a dozen Numbered** were pushing their way into the hallway.

Jessie cast one more glance at Craig. His screams were echoing through the hall but all she could see in the mass of the Numbered was a single leg sticking out kicking.

She and Az turned and ran down the hallway. Somewhere halfway up the stairs, she finally stopped hearing Craig's screams.

CHAPTER FIFTY

Analyzing the Scene

A STORY EVENT is an active change of life value for one or more characters as a result of conflict (one character's desires clash with another's).

A WORKING SCENE contains at least one Story Event. To determine a Scene's Story Event, answer the following four questions:

1. What are the characters doing?

Jessie, Craig, and Az go into the hovel, put on Numbered suits, and look for more supplies.

2. What is the essential action of what the characters are doing in this scene?

The three of them are looking for supplies that will give them an edge in the Threshing.

3. What life value has changed for one or more of the characters in the scene?

Jessie goes from feeling safe to almost dying at the hands of the Numbered.

4. Which life value should I highlight on my Story Grid Spreadsheet?

Safe to Death.

HOW THE SCENE ABIDES BY THE FIVE COMMANDMENTS OF STORYTELLING

Inciting Incident: The three of them enter the hovel.

Progressive Complication: A Numbered man comes out into the hallway and sees them.

Crisis: Best bad choice. Do they stay and wait to see what happens *or* do they try to rush past the man and escape?

Climax: Az leads the way, and they try to escape from the hovel.

Resolution: Craig is caught by the Numbered and killed. Az and Jessie escape.

NOTES:

This scene represents the turning point progressive complication of the ending payoff, 'someone the audience cares about dies.'

CHAPTER FIFTY-ONE

Az and **Jessie** tumbled out into the alley. They scrambled to their feet and then pushed hard against the trashcan to get it back in front of the opening.

They leaned back against it, sucking in deep breaths.

Despite witnessing the horror of seeing **Craig** eaten alive, Jessie couldn't help but be relieved to feel the suits keeping the heat at bay. She still felt a bit of the cool of the Numbered's hovel trapped inside the suit.

"Jessie," Az's muffled voice floated over to her.

Jessie cocked her head and could just make out his eyes through the shaded visor. They were large. Dilated, even against the brightness.

"We just left him," he said.

"We didn't have a choice. There was nothing we could have done."

Az leaned his head back against the trash can. He fought to slow down his breathing.

"I know," he said. "But. The screaming."

It was still ringing in Jessie's ears too. She had never heard anything quite like that. She shut her eyes but only saw the Numbered's teeth sinking into Craig's face. The blood spurting out. His eyes wide in shock.

"They're not really like that, you know."

Az looked over at Jessie.

"What do you mean?"

"**The Numbered**. They're not like that in the cities. That's just the stories **the Faction** tells to keep people scared."

"You don't know that," Az argued. "Maybe you were just with a saner bunch. I know in **my father**'s city they have insane **Scavengers**. The only thing that keeps them in check are the plugs."

"Have you ever seen them?"

"No, but—"

Jessie shook her head.

"What?" Az shot at her angrily.

"Are you really going to believe everything **Marcus** and the Faction and your dad tell you? Do you never think to question what everyone says? Even after all the lies you've already seen?"

Az shrugged his shoulders.

"What choice do we have? I know it's not all real, but it's what we have to do to keep the Faction fed and safe. Without **the Reapers** and people like Marcus and my father, it would be chaos."

Jessie opened her mouth to argue, but she realized the drone of the swarm had grown louder again. Az heard it too. They looked down the alley toward where they had come in.

The shadow was approaching.

"We have to keep moving," Az said.

He brushed past Jessie.

"Let's go."

"Slow down," Jessie called out to Az.

He glanced over his shoulder.

"What is it?"

"You don't want to get overheated. Even with the suits, the heat can come on quickly."

Az slowed to wait for her to catch up. Then he started again, but a little slower.

They had been walking away from the swarm, assuming that was the direction they were meant to go.

They continued to hug the sidewalk of one of the roads that led in the general direction they'd been going. Buildings loomed in close around them, but a broad strip of sunlight still ran down the middle of the street.

"What do you think we'll find at the center of the city?" Az shrugged.

"There's usually some artifact that we have to find. Sometimes it's hidden. Sometimes it's obvious where it is, but it's hard to get to."

"What happens if we see the **other Factions' Coders?**"

Az cut his eyes at her.

"What do you think?"

They took several steps in silence.

"I don't think I can do it, Az."

Az didn't answer at first.

"You'll be surprised what you're capable of when there are no other choices. What happens when they attack you? You're not going to fight back?"

"Of course I will. I just don't think I could kill another Coder."

Az spat out a sharp laugh. "What did we just do to Craig?"

Jessie turned and shoved Az hard. He stumbled a couple of feet but was laughing as he found his balance.

"That's different!" Jessie yelled at him.

"Oh, sure. Of course. But if I had asked you before this if you would leave Craig behind while he was being eaten alive? Would you have said yes?"

Jessie glared at him but didn't answer.

Az shrugged but then turned and kept walking. Jessie fell into step behind him.

They walked for a solid ten minutes in silence.

Jessie couldn't shake what he had said.

Should she have fought harder to save Craig?

She thought back to the third Severing and how she had won. She knew playing that last piece would mean Ellis's death, but she did it anyway.

But it wasn't just for her anymore. Right?

It was for **Randy** and **Ernst** and **Alex** and **Harry**. It was for **her mom and dad.** If she lost, Marcus would have punished all of them. Probably killed Randy.

All of that was still true, but was it worth the death of someone like Craig to protect only the people she deemed worth saving? But everything she'd done up until now wasn't her directly taking someone else's life. Wasn't there a difference?

Jessie was pulled out of her thoughts by a loud smack behind her. She turned to see several red rocks skittering across the sidewalk.

"Az!"

"What?"

"See that?"

She turned to look across the street. Her eyes ran up the side of the building. Just as her eyes landed on an open window and she saw a figure framed by it, her vision filled with a large red brick.

It smashed into her visor, and her head whipped back. She stumbled a step before landing on her back.

The world around her continued to tumble.

Az screamed something at her.

Jessie tried to sit up, but Az was on top of her pushing her down and then dragging her somewhere.

She blinked hard several times, trying to make out Az, but then she realized her visor was spider-webbed with cracks. It had absorbed most of the impact from the brick, but not enough for her to remain thoroughly conscious.

"Jessie!" Az's voice pushed through the ringing in her ears.

"Yeah?"

"You hear me?"

She nodded.

She saw another brick whip by Az's head and smash into the wall behind them.

Az dragged her behind an abandoned car that gave them barely enough cover from the barrage. The bricks still fell from above every couple of seconds. **The other Coders** were throwing them from high enough that even backed up against the car, Jessie and Az were in danger of another direct hit.

"We have to keep moving!" Jessie yelled, louder than she needed to. She realized she still heard ringing in her ears.

"Did you see them?" Jessie asked.

Az shook his head. "I just got us behind the car."

"I only saw **one of them** up there before the brick hit," she said.

As if on cue, they heard a skittering on the pavement behind them as **a figure** rolled through the sunlight and came up to his feet. He was a huge boy, standing at least six feet tall and as bulky as a refrigerator. His face and arms were red and blistered. Some of the blisters had already popped and were bleeding, and his face was locked in a snarl.

Jessie and Az instinctively started moving backward away from him, still hugging the side of the car.

A brick hit the window of the car and shattered, spraying them with little red rocks, and Jessie yelped at the noise.

Another skittering sounded behind them, and they turned to see a girl appear. She had a mess of black hair pulled back and was small but lithe like a snake.

She looked to have spent less time in the sun than the boy, but it was apparent the environment was taking a toll on her too.

"They want our suits," Jessie said.

"They want *us*," Az said.

CHAPTER FIFTY-ONE

Analyzing the Scene

A STORY EVENT is an active change of life value for one or more characters as a result of conflict (one character's desires clash with another's).

A WORKING SCENE contains at least one Story Event. To determine a Scene's Story Event, answer the following four questions:

1. What are the characters doing?

Jessie and Az are continuing to make their way through the city.

2. What is the essential action of what the characters are doing in this scene?

They both want to keep moving toward their goal.

3. What life value has changed for one or more of the characters in the scene?

They are safe with their suits in the heat, but they get attacked while they walk out in the open.

4. Which life value should I highlight on my Story Grid Spreadsheet?

Safe to Attacked.

HOW THE SCENE ABIDES BY THE FIVE COMMANDMENTS OF STORYTELLING

Inciting Incident: Az and Jessie keep moving through the city.

Progressive Complication: A brick hits Jessie in the face.

Crisis: Best bad choice. Do they stay hidden *or* do they try to escape?

Climax: Before they can make a decision, two Coders show up, ready to attack them.

Resolution: Az and Jessie realize they have to fight their way out.

CHAPTER FIFTY-TWO

Ernst was getting more and more anxious. It had been a couple of hours since his plan had fallen apart, and here he still sat across from **Alex**, both of them refusing to give up any ground.

Every few minutes, Alex would glance up at the screens monitoring **Jessie's** vitals. Nothing had changed much since he stabilized her after the swarm attack. Several times they saw her heart rate spike but no other indications that anything was critically wrong.

Ernst knew it was killing Alex not to know what was going on.

In truth, it was killing him too. What if Jessie was about to win the Threshing? Sure, it was still far too early, but who knew? After everything that had happened, Ernst wouldn't put it past her.

And what if she did win during his stand-off with Alex? Everything would come crashing down around him pretty quickly. They would enter into the bay to find him, and Alex would tell them what happened. It wouldn't take much digging into Ernst's logs for them to confirm he was communicating with people from **the Europa Faction**.

Ernst swallowed hard.

Marcus would make sure it wasn't a quick, painless death, either. The guy enjoyed watching people squirm and die in absolute terror. The last Severing surely proved that.

428 | TIM GRAHL

He reached up and touched his ear again, which gave him a severe jolt of pain, and then cursed. Alex looked up at him, disgust and worry mixed on his face.

Suddenly, the monitors attached to Jessie began beeping wildly. The lines on the screens shot up and dipped down again. Alex looked up at the screen.

Everything in Ernst screamed at him to attack, but he waited. Sure enough, Alex immediately cut his eyes at Ernst. He forced himself to stay calm, leaning against the door as he had the last two hours.

Alex's eyes remained locked on Ernst. He kept his crooked left arm close to his body and reached up behind him to the railing of Jessie's bed with the hand holding the syringe. He hooked his wrist over the railing and struggled mightily to pull himself up on his good foot.

Ernst waited until he got his foot underneath him and then made a move.

Ernst took two steps across the area between them. Alex instinctively lifted his hand, holding the syringe to protect himself, which forced him to put weight on his bad ankle.

Alex screamed at the pain as his ankle caved under his weight. He swung wildly toward Ernst as he fell, but it was too late. Ernst timed it perfectly and connected his knees to Alex's face on his descent.

There was a loud crunch as Alex collapsed to the ground. The syringe dropped out of his hand, and Ernst stood over him, breathing hard. For all the coding and technical training he'd had, power shifts still came down to this kind of sudden violence.

He watched Alex for a few seconds to make sure he wasn't moving and then turned his eyes to Jessie lying on the table. The beeping on the monitors had stopped. Ernst studied the lines running across the screen but was unsure of what they meant other than Jessie was still alive.

That's what he had to change.

CHAPTER FIFTY-TWO

Analyzing the Scene

A STORY EVENT is an active change of life value for one or more characters as a result of conflict (one character's desires clash with another's).

A WORKING SCENE contains at least one Story Event. To determine a Scene's Story Event, answer the following four questions:

1. What are the characters doing?

Ernst and Alex are still in a standoff over Jessie's inert body while she is still engaged in the simulated Threshing fight. Ernst attacks Alex when there is an opening.

2. What is the essential action of what the characters are doing in this scene?

Ernst is looking for a way to get the better of Alex.

3. What life value has changed for one or more of the characters in the scene?

Ernst starts in a bad position but ends up getting the better of Alex.

4. Which life value should I highlight on my Story Grid Spreadsheet?

Standoff to In Control.

HOW THE SCENE ABIDES BY THE FIVE COMMANDMENTS OF STORYTELLING

Inciting Incident: The monitors attached to Jessie start going off.

Progressive Complication: Alex stands up on his good leg to check on Jessie.

Crisis: Best bad choice. Does Ernst keep waiting for a better opportunity to attack *or* does he go after Alex now?

Climax: Ernst attacks Alex.

Resolution: Ernst knocks Alex out and regains control of the room.

CHAPTER FIFTY-THREE

Az and **Jessie** crouched back to back next to the car as **the other boy and girl** approached slowly.

The girl started speaking, and a split second later, the words rang into Jessie's ears, dubbed over a computerized sort of English.

"Give us the suits, and we'll let you go."

"It's a lie," Az said. "They have no reason to keep us alive. We'd just be a threat."

"But what if they're telling the truth?" Jessie asked.

"Who cares? All it'll mean is they'll have the advantage of getting to the city center ahead of us."

"Az, wait, if—"

But before she could finish, she heard Az let out a sort of roar, and she felt his weight shift behind her. She looked around to see him running for the boy. Az leaped into the air, but before Jessie could see what happened, the girl was upon her.

The girl lunged for Jessie as soon as her head turned to watch Az.

Jessie fell back, kicking wildly and trying to get the girl off of her. She was able to land a solid kick to the girl's forehead, which sent her tumbling away. Jessie jumped to her feet, but the girl had already regained her footing.

Jessie sprinted toward the nearest building, thinking maybe she could get inside and hide. But just as she reached the front door, the girl's weight collided with her again, and Jessie slammed into the wall.

Her head, still rattled from the brick, immediately began to swim again.

She felt a kick to her side and heard her dislocated rib snap. The breath immediately escaped her body, leaving her puckering for air.

The girl was now on top of her, straddling her. She felt the girl's hands close around her neck and begin to squeeze.

The mortal threat brought Jessie's senses back to her.

Her eyes popped open, and she could now see through the foggy, cracked panel of her helmet into the wild eyes of the girl trying to kill her.

The girl's eyes were dark brown. But the pupil of her left eye looked as if it was a cracked egg leaking blood instead of yolk. The girl's face was locked in a snarl.

Despite herself and her situation, Jessie couldn't help but wonder what had brought her and this girl together. This girl she didn't know was hooked into the grid somewhere else in the world, probably starving until they brought her in for her Preparing. She was desperately trying to win this Threshing just so she and her family would have enough food.

Jessie grabbed at the girl's fingers and wrists, but they were locked too tightly. Between Jessie's rattled head, the girl's dominant position, and the massive amounts of adrenaline the girl's Medic was surely pumping into her system, Jessie resigned herself to death.

Which was okay. Really. She understood, maybe for the first time.

Jessie thought about **Randy** and **her parents** and **Alex** and **Ernst** and **Harry**. She knew they would all suffer. Probably die.

Jessie looked into the eyes of the girl again. She looked past the sunburnt face and the snarl. This girl was trying to save the people she cared about too.

Jessie's vision faded, and she let her hands drop to the ground. The black that had started at the edge of her sight was quickly taking over. She could see through just a tiny, closing circle. She moved her head slightly, so the last thing she would see was the girl's eyes. That's how she wanted to end.

Suddenly her attacker's head slammed forward. Her forehead hit the visor and smashed into her nose. The pain shot through Jessie's face and pushed the blackness back.

The girl was already going to win. Why would she smash Jessie in the face?

The girl's head lifted. Something was wrong. Her right eye filled with blood, the blood now dribbling onto Jessie's visor from the girl's nose and mouth.

Jessie realized the grip on her neck had loosened just as the girl roughly fell off of her.

As Jessie's vision came back into focus, she saw Az's face through the visor. She looked down at his hands. He held a brick, matted with blood and strands of black hair.

"No—" she started to say, but Az was already grabbing her arm and picking her up roughly. She got to her feet and instinctively wrapped her hand around Az's waist as he grabbed her under the armpit and started her moving.

"One team down," he muttered.

Jessie glanced back to where Az had lunged at the boy and then immediately away. The boy lay face up in the direct sunlight. His skin was black, open, and peeling.

"What about the one in the building?"

"He came to help the first one, but I knew he was coming."

Jessie nodded as they continued onward.

She didn't need to know.

They came to a cross street.

"Which way?" he said.

"We need to take a right."

Az nodded, and they turned. Just before they disappeared around the corner, Jessie looked back one more time. She could just make out the girl's black hair. She thought she might have seen it blow slightly in the hot breeze.

CHAPTER FIFTY-THREE

Analyzing the Scene

A STORY EVENT is an active change of life value for one or more characters as a result of conflict (one character's desires clash with another's).

A WORKING SCENE contains at least one Story Event. To determine a Scene's Story Event, answer the following four questions:

1. What are the characters doing?

Jessie and Az defend themselves from a team of Coders from another faction.

2. What is the essential action of what the characters are doing in this scene?

Jessie and Az are doing what's necessary to survive.

3. What life value has changed for one or more of the characters in the scene?

The Coders die at the hands of Az.

4. Which life value should I highlight on my Story Grid Spreadsheet?

Life to Death

HOW THE SCENE ABIDES BY THE FIVE COMMANDMENTS OF STORYTELLING

Inciting Incident: The boy and girl Coders demand Jessie's and Az's protective gear.

Progressive Complication: Az attacks.

Crisis: Best bad choice. Jessie can kill the girl *or* Jessie can submit.

Climax: Jessie decides to not fight.

Resolution: Az fights for Jessie and saves her.

CHAPTER FIFTY-FOUR

Ernst had watched **Alex** before, figuring out where he pulled the particularly potent vials of meds from the cabinet. Ernst figured he would give a massive dose of one of those to **Jessie**, and that would take care of things.

But in the struggle with Alex, the cabinet knocked over, and vials had gone everywhere. Many of them had smashed. Ernst didn't know enough of the names of all the drugs to know which would do what or what combination would stop Jessie's heart.

He supposed he could just give a bunch of different ones, but he didn't have much time left. He couldn't keep dosing her and waiting for something to happen. If he wanted to get out of this alive, he needed to make quick decisions.

He glanced down at Alex. He still hadn't moved.

Ernst looked around the room. His eyes fell on the red fire extinguisher—the one he had initially swung at Alex to no avail. He stepped over the unconscious Alex, leaned down, and picked it up.

He went back to Jessie's body on the table. She was so young, and whenever she was plugged in, she looked even smaller. Ernst remembered how they had to reset and retool the entire table so she could fit on it.

438 | TIM GRAHL

He looked down at the fire extinguisher. Could he really cave in a little girl's skull? Was that who he was? Sure, sticking and plunging some stuff into an IV was still killing her. But it was less messy. Nonviolent. Jessie probably wouldn't even feel anything. She'd just pass out in the Threshing and never wake up.

But this? How many times would he have to hit her? What would her face look like when he finished? Did he really want to live with those images in his head for the rest of his life?

Resolved, he lifted the heavy extinguisher over his head. His arms wobbled. Do it! he yelled at himself. He raised it up just a bit higher—

"Ah!" he yelled and jumped back, dropping the canister. Pain arched up his leg from his calf. He looked down, confused t first. How could a syringe be sticking out of his leg?

Then he saw Alex. The boy's cheekbone was obviously shattered with the way it was swollen and had forced his left eye closed. But he had a kind of crooked smile on his face.

"Night, night," Alex croaked out.

Ernst opened his mouth to ask what he meant but realized he couldn't speak. The room seemed to tip over somehow. The blackness had already overtaken him by the time he slumped to the ground.

CHAPTER FIFTY-FOUR

Analyzing the Scene

A STORY EVENT is an active change of life value for one or more characters as a result of conflict (one character's desires clash with another's).

A WORKING SCENE contains at least one Story Event. To determine a Scene's Story Event, answer the following four questions:

1. What are the characters doing?

Ernst is trying to figure out how to kill Jessie.

2. What is the essential action of what the characters are doing in this scene?

Ernst is trying to keep his moral view of himself while killing a little girl.

3. What life value has changed for one or more of the characters in the scene?

Ernst is in the position of power and is about to kill Jessie. Alex takes Ernst out once and for all.

4. Which life value should I highlight on my Story Grid Spreadsheet?

Death to Life

HOW THE SCENE ABIDES BY THE FIVE COMMANDMENTS OF STORYTELLING

Inciting Incident: Ernst is trying to figure out the best way to kill Jessie.

Progressive Complication: Ernst retrieves the fire extinguisher.

Crisis: Best bad choice. Does Ernst use the fire extinguisher to kill Jessie and deal with the moral consequences *or* does he find some other more humane way to end Jessie's life?

Climax: Ernst lifts the fire extinguisher over his head to bring it down on Jessie.

Resolution: Alex doses Ernst with a sedative and knocks him out.

CHAPTER FIFTY-FIVE

"You think we can leave the suits behind?" **Az** asked.

Jessie shrugged.

"Depends," she said. "Think this will last through the night?"

They had trudged all day through the city, having to stop often to let Jessie rest. Her lungs weren't working quite right since **the girl** had kicked her in the ribs. The air felt frothy when she tried to take deep breaths.

The pain was the worst she'd ever felt in her life. She kept waiting for **Alex** to dull it, but it persisted.

Az hadn't complained once about having to support her as they walked. Each time they stopped, they waited until they heard the familiar buzz of the swarm approaching. This was their cue to get up, put their helmets back on, and head out into the heat again.

Az pointed out that continuing this way almost ensured nobody would be able to sneak up behind them.

"What if **the other Faction** is moving faster?" Jessie asked even though she already knew the answer.

With the first team already out of the game, it was down to just two other Factions. **The Reapers** would ensure there was a showdown between them. They wouldn't just let the other Faction waltz in and win without conflict. The whole world was watching, and the entertainment value had to pay off.

Jessie also knew she would be almost useless in whatever fight ensued. Sharp pains shot through her side continuously, which kept her hunched over and feeble. The only way she could keep any steady pace was by leaning heavily on Az.

And now, as they waited for the buzzing to catch up with them, they watched as the shadows quickly grew longer.

The night was coming.

With it came both cooler air and the ability for **their enemies** to hide in the shadows.

"I doubt they're doing any better than we are," Az said. "And twenty-four hours is usually the limit for Threshings. Most are over before that. Though one did last a day and a half."

"If we don't find and confront them, we can move easier to the city center. And hear and see better without the swarm on us."

"Think you could find another **Numbered** hovel?"

Jessie shrugged.

"Maybe. But do you think the Reapers would let us use one this late in the game?"

Az looked out into the dusk, chewing on the inside of his cheek. Jessie's ears caught the low drone of the approaching swarm.

Az swore.

"Let's leave them. We're going to end this tonight one way or another."

He came over to Jessie and helped her gingerly pull the protective jacket over her shoulders. Then he pulled off the pants. Afterward, he pulled off his gear too. He removed the comms from her suit and stuffed it in her pants pocket and then did the same with his.

"Take this too," he said, producing a knife.

"Where'd you get that?"

"Off **the boy** throwing bricks at us. You almost died as I was searching him, so I figure you should have it."

Jessie shivered as the warm air hit her clothes, drenched in a day's worth of sweat.

"You've smelled better," she said, smiling at Az.

"Back at you," he answered, a smirk playing at the edges of his mouth. "Let's take a look at that."

Jessie slowly lifted the back of her shirt, and he rolled it up.

His face stiffened.

"That bad huh?" She strained over to see it.

The area was one gigantic bruise the size of a dinner plate and almost black in the middle. Jessie took a deep breath, but the bubbling caught in her throat, and she coughed against her hand. When she pulled it back, it was wet with her blood.

She showed it to Az.

"What do you think?"

"I think we better end this tonight. Come on."

He stood and reached to help her up.

"No, I mean, do you think we should stay together? You're moving a lot slower because of me."

Az shook his head. "Like I said, you know they'll make sure we confront each other. And two bodies are better than one, even if one of them is pretty busted up."

Jessie nodded.

She reached out to **Ernst** again but only received silence.

"Still nothing from your Comms?" Az asked.

Jessie shook her head.

They had been relying on **Az's Comms** as they made their way through the city. That's how they knew **the Far East Faction** had been taken out by **the Europa Faction**.

It was down to two teams.

He cocked his head at her.

"You're not?"

Jessie shook her head again.

"Not since the beginning. Ever since I got caught in the swarm, I haven't heard anything. And something's wrong with the pain. **Alex** should have given me something by now. Right?"

Az didn't answer, but his face showed the worry.

"Let's keep moving," he said.

He helped her slowly to her feet and put his arm around her to keep her steady.

"Besides," Az said, "you know if it comes down to it, I'll leave you to win the Threshing."

"I know."

"And you'll do the same to me."

Jessie nodded, and then they stepped out onto the street, heading deeper into the city center.

CHAPTER FIFTY-FIVE

Analyzing the Scene

A STORY EVENT is an active change of life value for one or more characters as a result of conflict (one character's desires clash with another's).

A WORKING SCENE contains at least one Story Event. To determine a Scene's Story Event, answer the following four questions:

1. What are the characters doing?

Jessie and Az take a break from walking all day to remove their suits.

2. What is the essential action of what the characters are doing in this scene?

They are trying to figure out the best way to end the Threshing.

3. What life value has changed for one or more of the characters in the scene?

Jessie has realized that Az is with her until the end on this. This realization makes her feel safe – not from physical danger but from being alone in this struggle.

4. Which life value should I highlight on my Story Grid Spreadsheet?

Immobile to Mobile

HOW THE SCENE ABIDES BY THE FIVE COMMANDMENTS OF STORYTELLING

Inciting Incident: Az and Jessie stop for a break.

Progressive Complication: Jessie still hasn't heard from Ernst or had Alex give her drugs for the pain.

Crisis: Best bad choice. Do they keep the suits and prolong the Threshing *or* do they leave the suits behind and try to end this quickly?

Climax: They leave the suits behind.

Resolution: They start walking toward the city center as the sun fully sets.

CHAPTER FIFTY-SIX

"Of course it's a tower," Az said. "It had to be."

They stood on the top of a two-story warehouse. They had come up the stairs to get a better vantage point.

A tall metal tower stood at the center of the city with a slowly blinking red light at the top. It was a tall and skinny metal pyramid scaffolding. A single elevator shaft ran from the ground to the top of the pyramid, where a single, small room sat at the top.

"I say we burn it down," Jessie said, smirking.

Az shot her a look of disbelief and then smiled when he realized she was joking.

"Let's go," he said.

Ten minutes later, they were both crouched down at the corner of a squat, bombed-out building.

"Where are they?" Jessie asked.

Az shrugged.

"No way to know. Maybe they haven't made it yet. Maybe they're waiting for dawn. Maybe they're keeping watch. I think it's better we make our play, though, to force their hand."

"Ready?" Az said.

Jessie nodded and stood slowly. Then she turned and crouched back down, looking into Az's eyes.

"What is it?" he asked.

Tears ran down Jessie's cheeks as Az blinked at her. She reached out and hugged him. After a couple of seconds, he returned the hug loosely.

"Thank you," she said.

"For what?"

Jessie smiled at him and then stood and realized her pain had decreased some. Alex must be giving her everything he had. Or everything she could handle.

She started walking slowly into the opening between her and the tower. It looked enormous from her perspective. She craned her neck back and stared up at the blinking light against the black sky. She only made it about halfway before Az cursed loudly behind her. She turned in time to see **a boy** sprinting at her at full speed. Jessie tried to backpedal, but the pain in her side immediately forced her to slow down. Az ran at full speed to intercept the boy.

When the boy saw Az, he immediately changed course and took off back toward the buildings. Az kept after him and disappeared around the corner.

"Keep going!" he shouted at Jessie.

Jessie nodded, turned back to the tower and started hobbling as fast as she could go. She only took a few steps before she sensed something off and glanced behind her.

Two more figures had stepped into the clearing.

She realized their strategy.

The first boy was the fast, small, decoy.

The two figures starting to run toward her were the muscle and brains.

Jessie screamed for Az and kept trying to move backward.

As they approached, she could see it was a boy and a girl. Both were lean and strong. Their bright blond hair stood out in the little bit of light illuminating the clearing. They looked like siblings with identical long, pointy noses and deep sunken eyes.

Jessie dug into the back of her pants for her knife. She pried the blade open and held it out in front of her. Its four-inch length wasn't all that intimidating, but it was enough to have them pull back.

"Stay back," she screamed at them, her eyes wild.

She swung the knife around in front of her and kept walking back toward the elevator.

The girl ordered the boy.

"Go get her."

The boy snarled something back, but Jessie missed it.

They started walking toward her slowly but faster than she could navigate backward.

Jessie pushed against her rapidly returning pain. She'd never been in a knife fight before. She'd barely ever been in a fight. The odds of her being able to slash them both were pretty slim.

The gap between them closed.

Jessie's eyes caught movement over the shoulder of the boy.

Az was sneaking up on them. He moved deliberately, trying to stay quiet.

Jessie started screaming at them louder to stay back and waved the knife around even wilder, trying to keep their attention.

She glanced behind her.

She was so close now. Maybe another thirty feet, and she'd be there. She fought the urge to turn and run for it, knowing they'd catch her long before she made it.

Az was close to the boy now.

Jessie shrieked at them again, doing her best to mask Az's approach.

Az crouched, paused for a second, and then lunged at the back of the boy. He connected with him hard, and they both hit the ground. The girl turned and immediately dove on Az. She began clawing and punching at him as Az struggled to maintain control of the boy.

Jessie froze for a second and then turned and started hobbling as fast as she could to the elevator.

She heard the boy yell out, "Stop her!"

Jessie pushed herself forward, refusing to turn back. She felt like the entire right side of her body was on fire, but she continued. She reached the elevator and slapped the large green button. The doors began to open.

Jessie glanced over her shoulder and looked right into the face of the girl. The girl slammed into Jessie, and they both tumbled into the elevator. She heard the girl gasp as they hit the ground. Pain exploded inside of her as Jessie landed on her damaged side.

Stars burst into her vision, and she fought against the darkness that befell her before she lost consciousness. She curled into the fetal position waiting for the girl to attack her again, but nothing came. She thought for a moment that maybe she'd passed out, but she opened her eyes to find herself staring at the rusted metal wall of the elevator car.

She heard a cough and a grunt and pushed herself up so she could see.

The girl was sitting against the wall, her legs crumpled underneath her. The knife Jessie had been holding was sticking out of the girl's chest. Blood poured out of her wound. The girl coughed again, and a little bit of blood dribbled over her lip. She was looking down at the knife as if she was confused.

Jessie got up to her knees and crawled over to the girl. She put her hands around the wound and pressed, trying to staunch the bleeding.

"Jessie!"

She snapped her head around to Az's voice.

Az was lying on the ground, desperately clinging to the bigger boy's foot, as the boy tried to free himself. Az's face was a mangled mess. He'd taken a horrific beating.

"Go!" Az screamed at her.

The boy pivoted around and kicked Az directly beneath his armpit. Jessie heard the crunch as Az's grip on the boy's foot slipped, and he started charging straight for the elevator.

Jessie looked up at the panel.

There was only one button.

She slammed it instinctively, and the doors started to close. The boy was only a few feet away as he jumped forward.

A single hand shot through the opening and gripped at the door's edge.

Jessie had fallen away from the door when he lunged and sat staring blankly at his hand, caught in the doorway, unsure of what to do.

The elevator began moving up quickly. There were no windows, but she felt a tremendous force as they lifted.

The boy screamed in terror. The tips of his fingers grew white, and they began to slip. The scream started to fade away as his fingers disappeared, and the doors slid shut completely.

The elevator gained momentum.

Jessie sat for several seconds. She looked from the closed elevator door to the girl bleeding out next to her. She was still breathing, but Jessie could tell it wouldn't take much time.

"Jessie," a voice crackled from inside her pants pocket. "Jessie, can you hear me?"

Jessie snapped back to reality and dug the comms unit out of her pocket.

"Az! Az, are you okay?"

"Yeah," Az chuckled, "I'm pretty sure he's not getting up again."

Jessie looked desperately at the control panel and then all around the other walls.

"There's no down button Az. I don't know how to stop the elevator and come get you."

"Yeah," Az coughed, and she heard him spit something. "Yeah, it's a one-way trip, I guess. Once you get to the top, you'll win it for us."

"So, you'll make it out too?"

"No, just **the Faction members** who make it into the room."

"What about this girl?"

"She's on there with you?"

"Yeah, but she's not in good shape."

"Well, it won't end until there's just one Faction in the room."

Jessie stared down at the girl. The amount of blood that had pooled up around her indicated it wouldn't be much longer.

"What about you?" Jessie asked.

"It's okay, Jessie. We both knew you'd be the one to make it."

Several seconds passed.

"I'm sorry, Az."

"Why? We're going to win the Threshing. It's what we came here to do. I don't matter. Only the Faction matters."

Az coughed again.

"Just," he paused. "Just tell **my dad** how hard I fought okay? Can you do that? Make sure he knows you couldn't have done it without me."

"I will. I promise. I'll tell the whole Faction that you were the hero, not me."

Silence followed.

There wasn't anything else to say.

Jessie sat down next to the girl. She moved close and wrapped her arms around her. The girl leaned into her and laid her head on Jessie's lap. Jessie trailed her fingers through the girl's hair.

"It'll be over soon," she whispered. "I'm so sorry."

She listened to the whirring of the gears as the elevator kept moving up.

Tears streamed down Jessie's face. She felt the girl shudder as she let out her last breath. Jessie kissed her forehead as everything went white.

CHAPTER FIFTY-SIX

Analyzing the Scene

A STORY EVENT is an active change of life value for one or more characters as a result of conflict (one character's desires clash with another's).

A WORKING SCENE contains at least one Story Event. To determine a Scene's Story Event, answer the following four questions:

1. What are the characters doing?

Az and Jessie make a final run for the tower at the center of the city.

2. What is the essential action of what the characters are doing in this scene?

Jessie just wants this to end, one way or another.

3. What life value has changed for one or more of the characters in the scene?

Jessie moves from almost dying at the hands of her attackers to being the sole survivor of the Threshing.

4. Which life value should I highlight on my Story Grid Spreadsheet?

Death to Life.

HOW THE SCENE ABIDES BY THE FIVE COMMANDMENTS OF STORYTELLING

Inciting Incident: Az and Jessie start moving toward the tower.

Progressive Complication: Az jumps the remaining boy Coder.

Crisis: Best bad choice. Jessie can stay and help Az *or* she can try to make it to the tower first.

Climax: Jessie starts heading for the tower.

Resolution: She is the last one to make it to the top of the tower and win the Threshing.

NOTES:

This scene represents the crisis of the ending payoff, 'do the ends justify the means?'

CHAPTER FIFTY-SEVEN

As the white faded back into black, **Jessie** could hear someone clapping.

Marcus appeared before her. She was upright, floating in the darkness. **Three Faction guards** made a circle around her.

"I'm still not sure if I'm surprised or not. On the one hand, there was no reason you should have made it out of the Threshing. And yet, you should have never made it to the Threshing in the first place."

"It wasn't me," Jessie said, staring down. "**Az.** He did it."

Marcus laughed. "And yet, here you are. The sole survivor. You still don't understand."

"You've gotten what you wanted. We won the Threshing. Are you going to hold up your end of the deal?"

Marcus tugged on his ear, thinking.

"You despise me. Don't you?"

Jessie lifted her head and stared at him.

"Is it because of **Randy**? Or was it before that?"

"Before."

"I don't know. I remember a wide-eyed girl in my office begging to go home. You didn't mind me then."

"That was before I realized you are a liar."

"Yes, I'm a liar. But when you're in my position, that's usually the best bad choice. You have no idea what hangs in the balance. You see me as this evil dictator keeping everyone in control. When, in fact, if it weren't for me, there would be nothing."

Marcus continued, "We are, at all times, less than thirty days from starvation and chaos. You don't remember the brief famine that hit a decade ago. One tiny hiccup in the system was all it took to wipe out millions of lives. One little piece of the machinery was out of place and ten percent of **our Faction's population**—"

Marcus snapped his fingers.

"I'm the reason we all don't starve. Is it good for everyone? Of course not. But they're alive. They get to eat today. And tomorrow. And that's because of me. You can hate me. That's fine. You can think I could do things differently. That's fine too. The truth is, I'm just a cog in the machine myself. If I stopped or changed, people would die, and then **the Reapers** would find someone just like me to replace me.

"So here I am. Faced with a decision."

Marcus reached up to stroke his ear again and then pulled his hand down and shoved it in his pocket.

"Four years ago, your brother tried to use his status as Threshing conqueror to overthrow me. He hacked into my system and set my work back for a year. Even installed some backdoors I've yet to find. Thus the reason I had to imprison him.

"And now, here you are before me. Another Threshing conqueror. You only add to his power. Whether you know it or not, his one aim is to take over my place as Faction president. And, trust me dear, he would be quite the evil replacement."

Jessie opened her mouth to respond, but he cut her off with a wave of his hand and took a step toward her.

"I know what you're going to say, and I'm not interested. The truth is, with the popularity you now wield as the Threshing conqueror, combined with brother's disgusting, fake martyrdom and the conniving nature of **your little crew**, I don't have much choice. I can let you live. Even send you back to New York. But then I'd constantly be having to watch my back. Wondering, wondering, wondering. What is your brother going to do next? What kind of seeds of discontent will he be sowing? What kind of hacking will the two of you be able to accomplish together?"

Marcus took another step toward Jessie. He was now within arm's reach of her. Jessie instinctively took a step back but immediately met the muzzle of one of the guards' weapons and froze in place.

"So when faced with two bad choices, I must once again choose to lie. The **Americas Faction** will, of course, be in an uproar when they find out that the **Europa Faction** was able to sneak an **assassin Coder** into our system, which resulted in the deaths of our two living Threshing conquerors."

Jessie's body went rigid at this. She felt suddenly cold.

"But, alas, what could I do to stop them? It's too bad those closest to her gave the assassin the access he needed. So, of course, her team and **her mentor** had to be publicly executed for this serious act of treason."

Marcus took another step toward her as he finished. He now towered over her, just inches away.

"No!" Jessie screamed.

She swung her fist at Marcus's face, but he caught her wrist easily. She swung at him with her other fist, and he simply let it connect. How much damage could she really do at her size?

Marcus reached out with his other hand. He moved his index finger slowly toward her face.

Jessie yanked and screamed and kicked at Marcus, but his grip held fast. She finally stopped struggling, breathing heavily.

Marcus stopped his finger an inch from her forehead.

"I really will miss our talks," he said.

"You'll never—"

Marcus's finger touched her head, and her voice cut off. She collapsed to the floor.

He knelt slowly beside her and placed his fingers on her neck. He waited a few seconds and then nodded.

"Let's go," he said to the guards.

CHAPTER FIFTY-SEVEN

Analyzing the Scene

A STORY EVENT is an active change of life value for one or more characters as a result of conflict (one character's desires clash with another's).

A WORKING SCENE contains at least one Story Event. To determine a Scene's Story Event, answer the following four questions:

1. What are the characters doing?

President Marcus has a final meeting with Jessie inside the grid.

2. What is the essential action of what the characters are doing in this scene?

Marcus is trying to get Jessie to understand why she must die.

3. What life value has changed for one or more of the characters in the scene?

Jessie goes from surviving the Threshing to being killed by President Marcus.

4. Which life value should I highlight on my Story Grid Spreadsheet?

Life to Death.

HOW THE SCENE ABIDES BY THE FIVE COMMANDMENTS OF STORYTELLING

Inciting Incident: Jessie wins the Threshing.

Progressive Complication: President Marcus makes it clear to Jessie that he is going to kill both her and Randy.

Crisis: Best bad choice. Jessie can fight back against Marcus *or* she can give in to the inevitable.

Climax: She tries to fight.

Resolution: She makes no real progress, and President Marcus kills her.

NOTES:

This scene represents the first of two scenes that climax the ending payoff, 'the protagonist at the mercy of the antagonist.'

CHAPTER FIFTY-EIGHT

Marcus really did hate this room. **His predecessor** had used it extensively. Which, in Marcus's opinion, was one of the reasons he lost control after such a short term.

The chair he sat in was ridiculous and ornate. It had clean, harsh lines and, somehow, was enormous without making the person sitting in it look small.

It also sat on a small stage that was a couple of feet above the main floor.

He much preferred his basement office.

This was too much like a king's chambers. And as much as his job was to rule over the people in his Faction, reminding them of that fact in such a visual way was something he felt should be used sparingly. And only in the right circumstances.

Like this one when he needed to be seen as the vindicator and safeguard for their Faction. It was true that an opposing Faction had begun to infect the fabric of their society, and he had stepped in to save the people from the threat. Which was nice, but he did need to misdirect the population's eyes a bit.

The room was long and narrow, stretching out in front of him. A large contingent of Faction guards stood in the shadows along the walls.

They were there if needed, but it was best to seem as if Marcus was not afraid of being alone with the criminals that had posed such a threat.

The door at the far end of the room slid open to reveal three figures, one of them seated in a wheelchair.

The muscles along the back of Marcus's neck tensed when he saw **Randy**. That tension had tormented him for four years. He should have executed him at the very beginning when he uncovered his plot, but his engineers had convinced him there was something to be learned by studying his actions inside the grid.

They'd had plenty of time for their studies.

The three prisoners moved slowly down the path to stand before Marcus. **Harry** stood behind Randy, pushing his wheelchair while **Alex** hobbled alongside, his arm in a sling.

The three looked solemn and broken, but Marcus noticed something in Randy's face as the pathetic trio worked its way down the aisle.

Why did he look so calm? If pressed, Marcus would have said there was a confidence about him. How? His sister was dead. He'd already seen to that. And these pathetic leftovers were all completely under his control. He could order them all shot right this moment if he so chose. And everything would be over. The only reason he hadn't was because he needed them for just a few more minutes to spin up the right sort of narrative.

But why the confidence?

They came to a stop in front of the stage, directly in front of Marcus's dramatic chair.

Marcus let the silence hang. There wasn't a lot to say. They were beaten down. Their hero was dead. They knew he had no reason to keep them alive. All was lost.

Alex mumbled something.

"What was that, boy?" Marcus asked.

Alex lifted his head and spoke louder this time.

"Why? I said why? I don't get it. She won the Threshing for you. She almost died so many times to get here and then you just killed her. Why? Why would you do that?"

Marcus breathed deeply as if to control himself.

"You don't know enough to ask that question. This game we play is bigger than your schoolboy crush."

Alex's face turned red as he opened his mouth, but Harry reached out and gripped his arm. When Alex cut his eyes to the older man, he shook his head. Alex closed his mouth and returned to staring at his feet.

"And you," Marcus said, fixing his eyes on Randy. "I think our story has finally come to an end. I'm going to do what I should have done four years ago."

He started to raise his hand to the guards but stopped himself.

Randy sat in his chair, still hunched and weak from the four years inside the grid. They had shaved off his wisps of hair, which somehow made him look even older.

This weak, little man held Marcus's eyes and simply smiled at him. He knew something. But what could it be? Marcus's confidence wavered.

I should have him interrogated, Marcus thought. *He knows something important.* **Other conspirators.** *Other code in the works. Forget connecting him to the grid. They could use the old techniques. Peel him open from top to bottom until he shares what he knows.*

Marcus stared at Randy, thinking, considering.

No! This was over. He had found the conspirators. Randy was only messing with him again. Randy knew the end was here, and this was his desperate game to buy a bit more time.

Marcus waved the guards over.

Three appeared out of the shadows and approached. The first guard roughly pushed Harry back from the chair, and then they escorted Randy from the room.

Marcus had already given his orders. Randy would be dead inside of ten minutes. They were instructed to notify Marcus as soon as Randy flatlined.

Marcus tried to force the tension out of his neck. This would all be over soon. Control would be back. **The Reapers** would stay happy. The food would keep coming.

Marcus tapped a button on the side of the chair, and the floor in front of the two remaining prisoners opened up. Two chairs rose up.

"Have a seat," Marcus said.

Alex looked at Harry, and he nodded. They took their seats, but Harry stopped and stood back up.

"I get it," he said. "You think you've won this. And you probably have. But we won't be the last ones to rise up. You can't enslave or put down or corrupt everyone. It's not how it works with people."

Marcus nodded his assent and then motioned to the chair.

Harry nodded back before taking his seat.

As the chairs leaned back, and the plugs inserted into Alex and Harry's heads, Marcus's chair rotated back as well. He closed his eyes as his plug inserted.

As Marcus's eyes opened, two screens appeared before him.

The first was a reflection of his face. The second had the first few words of his speech printed across it. He knew the feed was being pushed out to **the entire Faction**. All mining paused, and all Americas' citizens were summoned for this announcement. Even the screens **in the Numbered** hovels across the Faction had lit up with this announcement. What Marcus had to say would be broadcast in every town square in every Faction city.

"I come to you today with both joy and sadness. As you have no doubt already seen, we have once again retained our rightful place as the winning, conquering Faction of the Threshing. Our victory ensures the benefaction of the Reapers remaining on the Americas' ledger. Your food shipments will continue, and with continued faith and hard work inside of our grid cooperatives, our resources will increase to even greater numbers.

"That is our joy.

"But, with sadness, I must say that our joy comes at a great cost too.

"We've discovered that **Europa trolls** have been plotting to infiltrate our great Faction with the goal of undermining our success in this Threshing. Through the prodigious efforts of **our enforcers**, we were able to thwart their plot to destroy our Threshing team before the play began.

However, we were only able to delay their plot, not completely stop it. Before we could destroy the infiltrators, it gives me great sorrow to report that they took the life of both **Jessie Marston**, our new Threshing conqueror, and Randy Teller, the previous conqueror who was just so recently returned to us from their Faction's evil grips.

"And, while we were unable to save them, we were able to capture their assailants. These are the men recruited and turned for the Europa Faction."

The screen filled with Marcus's face and then substituted for the images of Alex and Harry.

"All it took was a small number of credits for these men to turn against their Faction, sow discord, and commit these treasonous acts. If it weren't for the work of our own Faction enforcers, these men would have had us lose the Threshing and put us in the ire of the Reapers and all on the brink of starvation!

"While just and true, it is with great reluctance that I must now enact the ultimate punishment against these men. The Europa Faction must learn that they will never be able to overcome our rightful place as Threshing conquerors, and those in our own Faction who might be led astray must know we deal harshly and immediately with anyone who stands against us."

Marcus paused, considering the next words that would end the life of the two people plugged in just a few feet from his throne.

CHAPTER FIFTY-EIGHT

Analyzing the Scene

A STORY EVENT is an active change of life value for one or more characters as a result of conflict (one character's desires clash with another's).

A WORKING SCENE contains at least one Story Event. To determine a Scene's Story Event, answer the following four questions:

1. What are the characters doing?

Marcus is in his throne room, ready to address the Faction. He brings in Randy, Harry, and Alex so he can sentence them.

2. What is the essential action of what the characters are doing in this scene?

Marcus is reestablishing his control over the Faction.

3. What life value has changed for one or more of the characters in the scene?

Marcus is scared and unsure, based on what happened with the Threshing. He is still scared of Randy, but he strengthens his resolve.

4. Which life value should I highlight on my Story Grid Spreadsheet?

Scared to Resolved.

HOW THE SCENE ABIDES BY THE FIVE COMMANDMENTS OF STORYTELLING

Inciting Incident: President Marcus brings everyone into his throne room.

Progressive Complication: Randy alludes to the likelihood that there is still more to his conspiracy.

Crisis: Best bad choice. Does President Marcus keep Randy alive *or* does he end his torment it by executing him?

Climax: He sends Randy to be executed.

Resolution: He readies to address the Faction.

CHAPTER FIFTY-NINE

"Jessie."

The voice filtered slowly into existence. Muffled and disorienting at first, Jessie fought against listening. Being asleep felt so good. She was so very tired.

"It's time to wake up, Jessie. You've got some work left to do."

That voice...

Jessie moaned a little and then forced her eyes open.

Her eyes darted around the room. The low concrete ceiling. The hanging lightbulbs. The cots. She was lying on a cot too. She rolled over toward the voice.

"**Eighty-three**?" she asked.

The woman smiled. She sat on the cot across from Jessie, cross-legged. Her long, blond hair fell over her shoulders.

"Hi, Jessie," she said. "Welcome back."

Jessie sat up slowly, looking around.

"I'm still plugged in?"

"Of course."

"What did **Marcus** do to me?"

Eighty-three smiled.

"What?" Jessie asked.

"Still pretending like you don't know what's going on?"

They sat quietly for a few moments.

"But it doesn't make any sense," Jessie said.

"And yet, here we are."

"How is that possible? If you die in the grid, you're dead in real life."

Eighty-three shrugged. "I guess we're not so sure about that. Are we?"

"We?"

"Yes. We. All of us who brought you to Aeta to win the Threshing."

"What are you talking about?"

"Jessie, the reason you're here is for this moment. **Harry**, me, **Mayor Charles**, **Randy**, and many others have been working on this for a very long time."

"Randy? What do you mean?"

"Well, the original plan was to have Randy win and then leverage that power to bring down Marcus. But you were always the backup plan in case something went wrong. So when Randy didn't return from the last Threshing, we began planning on how to get you in place."

"Randy didn't know about any of this," Jessie said.

"Of course he did. He was the one leading the plans. He hates Marcus more than any of us."

"No, no way. There were so many times I could have died in this process."

"And yet, you didn't. Every single time, you found a way out."

"No, I screwed something up every time. Or Randy bailed me out."

"Randy didn't bail you out. There's no way he could have."

"What about in the second Severing when the hole appeared in the wall? What about all of the stairs and trap doors that kept the guards from finding me after we met? What about burning down the tower and screwing up the first Severing?"

Eighty-three sighed and re-crossed her legs.

"You know, I heard someone say once that your greatest gift to the world is the thing you do so naturally that you don't even know it's special."

"What's that supposed to mean?"

"Why do you think **the Rats** wanted you to join them so badly? Why did they send you alone on all of their missions? You were the only one who could hack into **the Elite**'s systems and come away unharmed to talk about it. Every time they tried, they got fried. Until you came along, they were running small-time scams stealing a handful of credits at a time.

"And yet, somehow, with you, they were able to bankrupt an Elite in a few minutes while you walked away unscathed.

"Marcus hacked your sim to send that monster after you, and you coded your way into a safe room that didn't exist in the code.

"Randy didn't open that portal. Randy didn't help you escape. He couldn't have. He was locked up tightly inside the grid. He hadn't heard from any of us or communicated out to any of us in almost four years. I'm sure he was as surprised as you were when you showed up."

"But when I met with him, we were in our parents' apartment. I didn't code that up. There's no way..."

Eighty-three held up her hands and motioned around.

"Look at where we are now! Back in the **Numbered hovel** of New York City. In the handful of seconds between your unconscious recognizing my voice and you opening your eyes, you completely coded this room from nothing.

"Impossible?" Eighty-three continued. "Of course, it is. And yet, here we are."

Jessie sat in silence for a few moments, trying to take in all of this remarkable information.

"So what does this mean?" she finally asked.

"It means you have a choice. At this moment, Marcus is on an all-Faction live feed announcing yours and Randy's deaths at the hands of **assassins**. He's moments away from publicly executing Harry and your friend **Alex** for treason. What are you going to do?"

Jessie's last meeting with her brother floated back into her head.

"Randy wants me to kill Marcus."

Eighty-three nodded.

"Is that what you want to do?"

Jessie shook her head.

"I haven't wanted to kill anybody."

"And yet you did."

"It was an accident!" Jessie yelled.

Eighty-three nodded.

"I know. Just like it was an accident to build this room."

Jessie sat for a moment.

"Ask the question," Eighty-three said.

"What question?"

"The one you are most afraid to ask."

Jessie shifted on her cot and then met Eighty-three's eyes.

"Will Randy be any different than Marcus?"

Eighty-three smiled. "I've been wondering that myself for a long time. When we first started planning together to overthrow Marcus and **the Faction**, it was exciting. It was dangerous, and your brother was so passionate. He constantly talked about the atrocities that bore down on us. The manufactured slavery of the grid.

"But as we grew closer to his chance to go to Aeta, things started to shift. His anger grew more pointed. He was scared, I think, but he started talking about how lazy all the people hooked to the grid were. He wondered if maybe they deserved it for not rising up to fight."

Eighty-three shrugged, "What do you think?"

"I don't think a new president of the Faction will actually change anything," Jessie answered.

"What will?"

"You know what I see when I look at this grid? At all the simulations?" Jessie asked.

"What?"

"The cracks. Always the cracks. I know a lot of people say the grid feels so real they have a hard time telling the difference from reality. But I always know. I always see."

"What's behind the cracks?" Eighty-three asked, something like a smile playing at the edge of her lips.

"I've always been scared to look."

"Of course you have. Anybody who walks behind the simulation never comes back."

Jessie took a deep breath and stood up.

"I think it's time for me to take a look."

Eighty-three stood as well. "I agree."

CHAPTER FIFTY-NINE

Analyzing the Scene

A STORY EVENT is an active change of life value for one or more characters as a result of conflict (one character's desires clash with another's).

A WORKING SCENE contains at least one Story Event. To determine a Scene's Story Event, answer the following four questions:

1. What are the characters doing?

Eighty-three wakes Jessie up and has a talk with her about what is next.

2. What is the essential action of what the characters are doing in this scene?

Eighty-three is trying to get Jessie to see her true power.

3. What life value has changed for one or more of the characters in the scene?

Jessie accepts that it is her responsibility to actually change things.

4. Which life value should I highlight on my Story Grid Spreadsheet?

Denial to Acceptance.

HOW THE SCENE ABIDES BY THE FIVE COMMANDMENTS OF STORYTELLING

Inciting Incident: Eighty-three wakes Jessie up.

Progressive Complication: Eighty-three helps Jessie see the truth about Randy.

Crisis: Best bad choice. Jessie can do what Randy asked her to do *or* she can find a better path.

Climax: Jessie decides to step behind the grid.

Resolution: [Next scene] The grid is shut down.

NOTES:

This scene represents the second of two scenes that climax the ending payoff, 'the protagonist at the mercy of the antagonist.'

CHAPTER SIXTY

"What is happening?" **Marcus** yelled. "What's going on?" He had been just about to give the execution order when everything went black, and they were logged out. He had to unplug himself in the darkness of the room manually. It had been decades since he had to do that.

Something had gone horribly wrong.

Only a few red emergency lights in the corners of the room were lit.

Marcus now stood next to his chair, clutching the railing. **The guards** had **Harry** and **Alex** surrounded. They had unplugged and sat up in their chairs too.

"What is happening?" Marcus yelled into the darkness.

No one answered. No one knew.

Marcus mashed at the buttons on the chair again, knowing they would still do nothing. Everything was out.

One of the guards approached him.

"What should we do, sir?" he asked. The metallic twinge to the voice was gone.

Marcus opened his mouth to answer, but nothing came out. He realized he had no idea what to do. He had no idea what was going on. Even in power failures, the grid remained intact. There were backups and redundancies. There were assurances for every disaster. Marcus knew this. He had lived through many of them.

A scraping sound emanated from the far end of the room, and the flat end of a crowbar came through the doors. A crack pried open, and then several hands reached through the doorway. As they opened, Marcus breathed out a sigh of relief.

A dozen Faction guards stood in the opening as it slowing expanded, but the guards didn't immediately enter. Instead, they all stepped back to create an aisle.

Marcus squinted against the darkness.

A small figure approached.

He visibly shuddered when **Jessie** stepped into the room.

Jessie walked down the center aisle, her back straight. She kept her eyes locked on Marcus. As she walked, the guards fell in beside and behind her, weapons at the ready.

"Guards!" Marcus yelled. "Stop her! Stop her!"

As he yelled, he stepped back and hid behind the chair, just his head poking out. The guards in the center of the room weren't sure what to do. They waited, guns lowered, looking between Jessie, her guards and Marcus.

"I'm the conqueror of the Threshing," Jessie addressed Marcus's inner circle of guards. "And the new president of the Americas Faction. You can resist, and we'll fight, and you'll die. Or you can understand that things have changed, and you can go arrest Marcus and put him in a holding cell."

The guards hesitated only a second before turning to obey her command.

Marcus screamed as they approached, and Jessie watched as they dragged him out of the room.

CHAPTER SIXTY

Analyzing the Scene

A STORY EVENT is an active change of life value for one or more characters as a result of conflict (one character's desires clash with another's).

A WORKING SCENE contains at least one Story Event. To determine a Scene's Story Event, answer the following four questions:

1. What are the characters doing?

Marcus is stuck in the throne room trying to figure out why the grid has shut down. Jessie comes in with Faction guards and has him arrested.

2. What is the essential action of what the characters are doing in this scene?

Jessie is establishing her rule of the Faction.

3. What life value has changed for one or more of the characters in the scene?

Jessie has taken over as Faction president.

4. Which life value should I highlight on my Story Grid Spreadsheet?

Dead to Resurrected.

HOW THE SCENE ABIDES BY THE FIVE COMMANDMENTS OF STORYTELLING

Inciting Incident: The grid completely loses power.

Progressive Complication: Jessie enters with her own detail of guards.

Crisis: Irreconcilable goods. Do the guards obey Jessie and risk the anger of the existing president *or* do they accept her as the new ruler?

Climax: They accept Jessie as the new president.

Resolution: They arrest Marcus.

CHAPTER SIXTY-ONE

Dust flew and swirled in the darkness as the transport hovered and slowly descended to the ground. Jessie peered through the window, watching the skyscrapers move past them.

"Still no sustained electricity?"

Alex shook his head.

"It's coming intermittently," he said, "but still pretty unreliable in the cities."

Jessie stayed quiet as she looked out into the darkness.

She stood as the transport touched down.

Her hair was pulled back into a very short ponytail, and she wore a black suit she'd had custom made to fit tightly and crisply against her small frame.

The door to the transport lowered onto a ramp as the engines of the transport died down. When Jessie stepped out, she was immediately greeted by a dozen people, all with shaved heads. She scanned the mostly familiar faces, nodding in particular to Eighty-three.

Harry and Alex and six Faction guards followed closely behind her as she descended the ramp.

Eighty-three approached as she stepped onto the dirt.

"Good evening, madam," she said.

Jessie nodded in response.

She walked to the center of the square, knelt, and ran her hands along the circle of bricks. She turned over the loose brick at its base.

"Can I get an update?" she said.

"Things have mostly calmed down," Eighty-three said. "We created some makeshift cells and padded them up for those worse off. Mostly, though, people are just lethargic. No energy. Depressed. But between the heat of the day and the electricity being out most nights, most people stay indoors and docile."

"How many didn't make it?"

Eighty-three hesitated and looked to Alex, who nodded at her.

"A few thousand."

"How?"

"Different ways," he said. "Many died when they were logged off. Their hearts just couldn't take the transition. More died in the panic of the crazy days after the grid went offline. The rest just... they lay down and never got back up."

Alex stepped forward.

"I'd like to get you indoors, madam," he said.

Jessie nodded and turned to follow the guards into the nearest theater. Several more **Numbered** were inside with a lot of controlled energy in the room. Salvaged chalk boards had lists and diagrams drawn on them. Large stacks of boxes and crates along the walls were all labeled and numbered.

"What's the state of supplies?"

"We immediately put everyone on rations, so the reserves are lasting longer than other cities, I think," Eighty-three said. "But we have about three weeks left before a crisis really hits."

Eighty-three hesitated and then asked, "Still no word from **the Reapers**?"

Jessie shook her head. "Nothing. Nothing since... everything went offline."

Eighty-three nodded. "So, no word on any supply runs?"

Jessie shook her head.

Eighty-three rubbed the stubble along her head, a worried look on her face.

"Permission to tell you my worries?"

"Of course."

"We have no supplies from the Reapers. We're struggling to get power to the city without the grid. I'm assuming all of the other cities are in the same shape. Water is fine since we've always supplied that ourselves, but things are going to get rough pretty quickly."

Silence hung between them.

"What are we going to do, madam," Eighty-three finally asked.

Jessie stared across the room, her eyes focusing on nothing.

"I have no idea."

CHAPTER SIXTY-ONE

Analyzing the Scene

A STORY EVENT is an active change of life value for one or more characters as a result of conflict (one character's desires clash with another's).

A WORKING SCENE contains at least one Story Event. To determine a Scene's Story Event, answer the following four questions:

1. What are the characters doing?

Jessie arrives back in New York City with her contingent and meets with Eighty-three.

2. What is the essential action of what the characters are doing in this scene?

Jessie is assessing the impact of having destroyed the grid.

3. What life value has changed for one or more of the characters in the scene?

Jessie has become completely overwhelmed by her new position.

4. Which life value should I highlight on my Story Grid Spreadsheet?

Control to Overwhelmed.

HOW THE SCENE ABIDES BY THE FIVE COMMANDMENTS OF STORYTELLING

Inciting Incident: Jessie lands in New York City.

Progressive Complication: Eighty-three outlines all the problems currently facing the Faction.

Crisis: What is Jessie going to do next? Fight for flee?

Climax: She doesn't know.

Resolution: As this book is the first novel in a trilogy of novels, it ends with a cliffhanger.

NOTES:

This scene represents the resolution of the ending payoff, 'the reward.'

ACKNOWLEDGMENTS

I'm eternally grateful to my love and soulmate, Candace. We have been together for 20 years, and she has always encouraged and supported me running down my dreams, which included fighting with this book for the last four years. I love you, baby.

This book would 100% have never happened without my editor and friend, Shawn Coyne, who allowed me to mine his brain for free on the Story Grid Podcast. He is a storytelling master, and if you enjoyed this book at all, it was his influence that made it happen.

Thanks to the Story Grid Publishing crew and others who helped get this book across the finish line. Spring Hoteling, Amanda Brown, K.C. Procter, Dan Portnoy, and Derick Tsai are all masters of their crafts.

I am so thankful for the fans and listeners of the Story Grid Podcast. Somehow they suffered along for years as I flailed and floundered my way to writing this book. I received so many notes of encouragement along the way, and I know they are the first ones reading this book. Knowing they were out there listening and cheering me on gave me the courage to keep going.

I started trying to list all of the writers who have in- spired me and the list was getting way too long and I knew I was leaving important people off. Here's the thing... if you write, keep going. You will inspire someone one day. If you've already published, thank you. I couldn't have written this story without standing on the shoulders of all the storytellers that have come before me.

ABOUT THE AUTHOR

TIM GRAHL is the author of four books — *Your First 1000 Copies, Book Launch Blueprint, Running Down a Dream,* and the one you're holding in your hands.

He spends most of his time helping authors achieve their dreams. He is the founder of BookLaunch.com and partners with Shawn Coyne in Story Grid Universe and Story Grid Publishing.

He lives in Nashville, TN with his amazing and beautiful wife, Candace, and two handsome and talented sons. Keep up with what he's doing at runningdownadream.com.